The Ever-Changing Past

The Ever-Changing Past

Why All History Is Revisionist History

JAMES M. BANNER, JR.

Yale UNIVERSITY PRESS/NEW HAVEN & LONDON

Published with assistance from the Kingsley Trust Association
Publication Fund established by the Scroll and
Key Society of Yale College.
Published with assistance from the foundation established in
memory of Philip Hamilton McMillan of the Class of 1894,
Yale College.

Yale University Press books may be purchased in quantity for
educational, business, or promotional use. For information,
please e-mail sales.press@yale.edu (U.S. office) or
sales@yaleup.co.uk (U.K. office).

Designed by Mary Valencia.
Set in Minion type by Integrated Publishing Solutions.
Printed in the United States of America.

Library of Congress Control Number: 2020944298

ISBN 978-0-300-23845-7 (hardcover : alk. paper)

A catalogue record for this book is available from the British
Library.

This paper meets the requirements of ANSI/NISO Z39.48-1992
(Permanence of Paper).

10 9 8 7 6 5 4 3 2 1

For my wife, Phyllis Kramer, the center of my life,
and for my beloved children,
Olivia P. Banner and Gideon B. Banner

Everything changes, nothing is lost.
—*Ovid*

Contents

Acknowledgments

One of the many satisfactions of membership in the confraternity of historians is its collegiality and the willingness of its participants, far-flung and diverse as they may be, to assist others, even those with whom they may disagree, who ply them with questions and requests for assistance of all kinds. Often, especially in our era of electronic communication, one can solicit and receive help from colleagues never met in person. And in a work like this one, which covers so many more centuries and subjects than those that have been my specialty, reliance on others has been as necessary as their assistance has been bountiful and ungrudging.

The first person I salute is the late Roger H. Brown, a superb historian of the early years of the American republic, who was with me when this book germinated in the chambers of Justice Clarence Thomas. Were he still alive, he would doubtlessly smile, and I like to think that he would also approve of what has resulted from that conversation at the Supreme Court. Those of whose assistance, through conversation and correspondence, I have more recently been the fortunate beneficiary in the course of writing this book (some of whom may not even recall our exchanges) have been John E. Bodnar, Angus Burgin, Andrew Burstein, Bruce Cumings, Don H. Doyle, Marc Egnal, John R. Gillis, John F. Haldon, John Earl Haynes, George C. Herring, David A. Hollinger, Nancy G. Isenberg, Linda K. Kerber, Alice Kessler-Harris, Peter Kuznick, Melvyn P. Leffler, Edward T. Linenthal, Gerald W. McFarland, Charles E. Neu, the late Howard P. Segal, Martin J. Sherwin, Marjorie J. Spruill, Jack B. Tannous, Frank Towers, Samuel R. Williamson, Jr., and the late Marilyn B. Young. If I could not, and in some cases did not, take all the advice they offered or cover the subjects about which we were in communication, I remain hugely grateful for their enthusiasm for this project and for the advice they so willingly and characteristically offered. My longtime friend and Princeton colleague James M. McPherson eased my worries about invading the territory of his deep knowledge by giving a close reading to Chapter 1, a reading that saved me from errors and omissions. Norman S. Fiering, friend and colleague since graduate school, provided reassurances about Chapters 2 and 3 while provoking my thinking with characteristically sharp questions and setting me right on numerous matters. David A. Bell, Richard H. Kohn, and Carol Lasser provided me acute, indispensable reviews of sections of Chapters 4 and 5. And Norman M. Bradburn gave me the benefit of his knowledge for part of the final chapter.

Two people have gone beyond the normal calls of professional collegiality to read the entire manuscript. One is Sarah Maza, author of a kindred work, *Thinking About History,* a book that reveals her knowledge of and sympathy for what I have endeavored here, who responded gracefully to my request that she read a draft of the book's early manuscript. The astuteness of her observations as well as her suggestions for improvement have been of immense assistance to me. The second is Eric Arnesen, a reviewer for Yale University Press and as engaged, sympathetic, and deep-probing a critic as any historian can hope for. His critical acuteness and attention to detail are rarely encountered in the community of historians, and his influence is to be found on every page of this book. As always, what the reader encounters here also shows the influence of Olivia P. Banner—of editorial pen, as well as of mind, unsurpassed.

A book is more than its contents; it is an artifact, whose publication and production are the end product of many hands. In thanks for this dimension of the work, I start with my agent Peter W. Bernstein, who shepherded the manuscript to Yale University Press, which, the publisher of two of my previous books, is a kind of home to me and just where this book ought to have ended up. My editor in New Haven, Adina Popescu Berk, has guided the book from submission to publication with emollient skill, sharp intelligence, and unstinting support. Her assistants, Eva Skewes and Ash Lago, have been of immense help in watching over the progress of the book's manuscript after its submission. As always, and not without my gently stern insistence to the Press that I would allow the book to go into print only after his editing, Dan Heaton, for this third of my books to pass under his indispensable scrutiny, has once again put his keen eye, command of our common tongue, and affable suggestions on many fronts into play in ways that, though unseen by readers, help give the book whatever value it may possess. To Mary Valencia goes credit for the crisp elegance of the book's design, to Jenny Volvovski for its dust jacket, which brilliantly reflects one of my major arguments. Erica Hanson's superb, sharp-eyed proofreading saved the book from errors too numerous to count. Margaret Otzel has skillfully and with unbroken good humor carried the book through its entire production process from submission to bound copies.

In expressing my deep appreciation here for the assistance of all of these colleagues, I also happily accept the scholarly convention, so often expressed and long honored, of absolving them of responsibility for what I have written and for any errors that I may have committed.

November 2020

The Ever-Changing Past

Introduction

This book has its origin in a conversation with Justice Clarence Thomas some years ago in his Supreme Court chambers. At his invitation, a colleague and I were preparing Justice Thomas to meet with a group of teachers who were studying the origins of American constitutional government with us. In the course of a lively conversation, Justice Thomas reported that he was spending the summer reading the history of slavery and the American South. Of course pleased, we asked him whose works he was reading. He named a number of historians, among them John W. Blassingame, John Hope Franklin, and Kenneth M. Stampp, but, he quickly added in so many words, not the "revisionists." That statement alerted us, as it would all historians, to the justice's readiness, while seeking authoritative knowledge of the subjects he sought to learn about, to dismiss works of history—works that he had somewhere learned challenged what he thought should constitute and be written about the past—as not worth his attention. It also suggested his misapprehension about the ways historians have approached the past and disputed with each other over two and a half millennia of historical thought, as well as his misunderstanding about the changing nature throughout those centuries of historical inquiry and argumentation. For in fact the works of all the authors Justice Thomas named were "revisionist histories," books widely known among professional historians for having deeply altered historical understanding of American slavery, slave society, and the South. From that conversation grew my determination to try to make sense of the realities of what is known as "revisionist history." This book is the result.

It ought to be bracing that many people understand enough of the origins, uses, and satisfactions of historical knowledge that they engage with continuing curiosity and pleasure in the play of reasoning that is part of all historical thought and accept with ease the provisionality of historical interpretations that are available to them. Yet it is also troubling to encounter people who dismiss substantiated historical evidence, plausible historical perspectives, and strongly argued, evidence-based interpretations of the past simply because those versions of the past differ from their own, from what they think is proven and safe from challenge, or from what they dream the past ought to have been even if it never was as they imagine it. Consequently, in these pages I attempt to achieve two goals. The first is to strengthen the convictions of aspiring historians in graduate school; their academic teachers, advisers, and mentors; and historians employed outside academic precincts—all of whom may benefit from considering some of the often-overlooked intellectual and theoretical realities of the history of which they are the legatees—while arming them to explain those realities to others. My second goal is to explain to those in another group—the legions of general readers who take pleasure in learning about the past—the grounds on which I invite them to feel more comfortable about the surprises and complexities of the past, about what historical knowledge and arguments consist of, and about how and why professional historians go about creating and evaluating works of history in the way they do. In seeking to do both, I acknowledge the difficulties people everywhere face when asked to accept new understanding of the past and incorporate fresh interpretations into the received ways, to which they are accustomed, of thinking about earlier times. Yet I hope that this book will make clear to them that, as citizens of nations and members of society, they themselves, like millions of others before them, help to shape the way in which the past is conceived and taught. The interpretive changes and contests that I consider are not mere academic realities. Forces and developments outside scholarly circles—what social scientists call "externalities"—exert potent influence on what professional historians conclude about the past at all times. Historians are no more exempt from the realities of their own times than anyone else.

In the modern era, historians' understanding of major subjects has almost never stood still; new views have rarely gone long without objection and challenge; and even professional historians seldom escape the struggle to keep up with new knowledge and readjust their understanding of what they think they know. If at the time of our conversation Justice Thomas was troubled by what he considered "revisionist" history, today he would be even more disturbed by the newly challenging and disruptive scholarship about slavery and the South that has appeared since we spoke, scholarship that places slavery and racism squarely at the center of the larger history of American capitalism, the nation's government, and some of its most illustrious institutions—North as well as South, twentieth- and twenty-first-century as well as earlier. Similarly, since the 1970s a large cohort of scholars—female, African and Latin American, and gay and lesbian as well as white, male, and straight—have helped transform how historians think and write about most dimensions of the past. My purpose in these pages is not to defend or criticize any particular ones of these new ways of understanding historical reality but rather to explain why such interpretations have emerged, why historians consider it normal that they do so, and why public life is never free of the very kinds of disputes and reinterpretive efforts that historians in the contemporary world consider the normal condition of their professional endeavors.

But it is critically important to understand that the mission to revise understanding of the past is not and never has been located exclusively on either side of the political spectrum—not always on the Left, as many believe, nor the Right, either in the United States or elsewhere. As the following pages reveal, both liberals and conservatives have often set out to establish and protect their orthodox readings of the past and have often at least temporarily won interpretive contests about it. During the mid-1990s in the United States, for example, bitter controversies caused headline-creating news about the effectiveness of Soviet espionage against the United States, national history standards, and the display of the fuselage of the iconic *Enola Gay* bomber in the Smithsonian Institution's National Air and Space Museum. In at least provisionally winning those battles, the Right revealed that what are sometimes termed "projects" about the past do not originate only among left-leaning scholars. The truth is that purposeful intellectual, ideological, and political endeavors concerning the past take root across the political landscape.

They also transcend the boundaries of the world of scholarship. As recent events surrounding the display of monuments celebrating the southern Confederacy and military installations bearing Confederate generals' names attest, debates about how a society should commemorate elements of its past can evoke strong emotions and reopen deep political and cultural fissures. In an era less tolerant of white southern defenders of slavery than in the reconciliationist years of the early twentieth century, statues of Confederate generals Robert E. Lee and Thomas J. "Stonewall" Jackson are now under widespread attack, and pressure has built to remove the names of leaders of the southern armies from military bases throughout the United States. Neither a new nor an exclusively American phenomenon, such contests over memorialization—public contests that involve debates about the meaning of the past—have spanned time and space. Take, as one non-American instance, the Iraqis' toppling of the likeness of Saddam Hussein from its pedestal in Baghdad in 2003. Moreover, destruction is not the only fate of monuments to fallen heroes. After the dissolution of the Soviet Union, Muscovites removed statues of Lenin, Stalin, and other Bolshevik and Communist figures from their pedestals around the city and left them lying jumbled ignominiously together in a field until post-Soviet officials decided to integrate them into a new Park of Arts devoted to public sculpture. Hungarians founded their own analogous Memento Park in Budapest to preserve some of the statuary from Hungary's Communist past. Yet even the removal and destruction of memorials sometimes fail to put an end to their history or to the controversies surrounding them. Should memorials to Lee and Jackson simply be replaced in southern city squares by those to W. E. B. Du Bois, Sojourner Truth, and Martin Luther King, Jr., whose historical stature has grown with time, or should formerly honored figures cohabit the same space with sculpted likenesses of these more recently celebrated people? Is it preferable to preserve and display sculptures of now disdained figures out of sight in museums for future educational purposes or, alternatively, to consign them to the trash heap?

To complicate matters still further, it has sometimes proved the case that growth in understanding of long forgotten or dishonored past relationships, people, and events can open the door to a softening of earlier bitterness toward them and an acknowledgment of their historical significance. For instance, the halting voyage from two wars to gradual reconciliation and finally to firm alliance between the United States and Great Britain has allowed a replica of Jean-Antoine Houdon's sculpture of George Washington to grace London's Trafalgar Square outside the National Gallery since 1924, while a reconstructed version of the statue of King George III that stood on New York City's Bowling Green until destroyed by the Sons of Liberty in 1776 has more recently been installed in no less a venue than Philadelphia's Museum of the American Revolution. Yet although the passage of time and alteration of circumstances sometimes open the door to revisions of views that underlie such developments, they cannot be taken for granted. Bitter controversies over the past are unlikely ever to be stilled. In an open society, they should not be expected to be.

Political, social, and cultural developments also often intrude on periods of interpretive tranquility to roil scholarly consensus. This was the case after the 1960s in the United States and most Western democracies when demographic, social, and cultural changes brought on a reconsideration of a wide variety of previously conventional historical interpretations. In following decades, scarcely a single subject of American and European history, long encased in a kind of comfortable orthodoxy, remained unaffected by interpretive storms originating within and outside the West. What had previously been taught as the accurate and complete history of each Western nation came under sharp attack. One has only to cite the popularity and influence of Howard Zinn's *A People's History of the United States* and James W. Loewen's *Lies My Teacher Told Me: Everything Your American History Textbook Got Wrong* to secure the point. That the books' authors were intentional, adversarial, and altogether successful provocateurs in their attacks on interpretive uniformity made clear that no single way of presenting the history of the United States could any longer hold the field to itself whether in schools and colleges or among the general public. The basic history of the nation was now to be the subject of extended dispute. It remains so today.

Yet if, as some believe, Zinn's and Loewen's books show that interpretive zeal resides on the Left alone, it is often also found on the Right. As I write, the government of Viktor Orbán in Hungary is busy trying to rehabilitate the reputation of Miklós Horthy's autocratic, Nazi-supporting government of the 1930s and 1940s to justify his own "illiberal democracy." The Polish government is attempting to criminalize all references to Poles' complicity in Nazi war crimes. Vladimir Putin's regime is scrubbing Russian history textbooks of criticism of the Soviet Union and its Bolshevik foundations as a way of protesting the dissolution of the USSR. And India's ruling Hindu nationalist Bharatiya Janata Party is promoting the adoption of triumphalist and Islamophobic textbooks. Moreover, such attempts to invoke historical claims rejected by reputable historians to buttress political positions are not unique to autocratic or ethnoreligious regimes. The refusal of the Japanese and of many Japanese textbook authors to accept Japan's complicity in the barbarities of the Second World War in Asia is not unlike the morally reprehensible efforts of the Hungarian and Russian governments. Closer to home, in 2010 the Texas Board of Education removed the name of Thomas Jefferson from the list of people who inspired the American Revolution on the grounds that, offensively to board members, he had originated the concept of a "wall of separation" between church and state. Ignoring evidence, condemning it as spurious, or placing excessive interpretive weight on it for purposes of ideological warfare is not limited to any single sector of the political spectrum.

Governments of all sorts, fearing the established facts of empirical history, promote and sometimes force acceptance of tub-thumping views of their nations' pasts even when such sweeping claims have been shown by historians to be invalid, and they engage in attacks on their history-invoking critics and in the suppression of authoritative historical knowledge whenever it suits their political needs. Historians themselves have sometimes proved complicit in providing support for popular happy talk. For instance, unnuanced narratives of Euro-Americans' victorious sweep into the American interior until recent decades kept from history textbooks written by historians the known record of the destruction of Native American cultures. The debates that arise when such silences are challenged are rarely tranquil, nor do all of them take place in some out-of-sight intellectual enclosure. They remain hotly contested, and their outcomes are sometimes considered important enough for governments to cite—or, as the case may be, to condemn.

Yet if such controversies are inevitable in most human communities and surely in open ones, it is unfair to criticize only those who dismiss them as outrageous assaults on known truths for misunderstanding such debates. Yes, those people could work harder, by reading more widely, to overcome their misconceptions. They could keep up with the news, which sometimes carries reports of historians' disputes. They could apply to the past more effectively, honestly, and without political prejudice than they do the methods of reasoning and the evaluation of evidence that they learned in school and college and like to think they apply when at work. And they could acknowledge others' greater professional knowledge as they would like everyone to acknowledge their own. But it turns out that historians have not been of much assistance in helping them do so. Not a single book about revisionist history as a distinct subject worthy of systematic consideration has been written since 1929. Lucy Maynard Salmon's admirable *Why Is History Rewritten?*, appearing that year, never called into being another book-length work on its topic. Many justly esteemed works about the pursuit of historical knowledge and the nature of historical thought—I think here of such classics as R. G. Collingwood's 1946 *The Idea of History* and Edward Hallett Carr's 1961 *What Is History?*, as well as more recent works like Joyce Appleby, Lynn Hunt, and Margaret Jacob's 1994 *Telling the Truth About History,* Hunt's 2018 *History: Why It Matters,* and Sarah Maza's 2017 *Thinking About History* — do not deal extensively and comprehensively with revisionist history per se. They do not focus on the phenomenon of changing historical interpretations as a discrete subject of inquiry, nor are they meant, as this book is, to pull together from centuries of well-known arguments among historians all the major strands of thought, including the most recent ones, that converge on the subject in the wake of major changes in the way historical inquiry is practiced and historical thought and memory understood.

In this book—the only successor to Salmon's directly focused on revisionist history—I seek to answer her question for our time with arguments more in keeping with today's historians' understanding of their craft and its possibilities. I also seek to explain what historians do and why we do it. In this way, the book provides arguments against the attacks of those who feel at liberty to disregard historical knowledge and argument at will. But more important, it may also promote recognition of historical understanding as a fluid body of knowledge open to many readings and carrying many varied meanings despite the normal human desire for stable, unchanging knowledge that can be relied on as indisputable. History is not and has never been inert, certain, merely factual, and beyond reinterpretation.

Yet some people's rejection of challenging accounts of the past does not stem only from ignorance about the nature of historical thought. Some dismissals of historical interpretation are ideological, willful, and obtuse. No one expects every new account of some aspect of the past to be met with universal acceptance and acclaim; it never has been and never will be. No one expects historians themselves to be of one mind about any specific subject; they never have been and never will be. But to dismiss serious historians' efforts to better and more fully understand the past, to dismiss them solely on the grounds that historians can be motivated (as some are) by political and other inclinations rather than by the desire to come to terms with the evidence they possess and to get right the conclusions they draw from that evidence, is deeply to misapprehend how historical knowledge is accumulated and made part of human understanding.

It does not help that so honorable and useful an adjective as "revisionist" and its sibling nouns "revision" and "revisionism" have in some popular usage become words of opprobrium, sometimes attached to the most odious ways of thought and thus made doubly pejorative. People the world over have witnessed the rise of crackpot "Holocaust revisionism"—Holocaust denial under another name. Americans have heard a president of the United States condemn as "revisionist history" views of the past opposed to his own—as if application of the adjective "revisionist" to a particular view of the past takes care of the matter. One has read in newspapers the vulgar dismissal of "the revisionist history crew" by those who hold views with which they disagree. "History is real simple," a radio commentator has asseverated. "It's what happened. It's no more." And a cynic can be found writing that revisionism is "the itch of historians to say something new about something already known." Some professional historians themselves, those of both the Left and Right, are known to reject as "revisionist" works of history with which they take issue. Even if they agree with particular interpretations, some historians are given to easy characterizations of them as "revisionist," as in a reviewer's comment that a biography was "an admiring and engaging work of presidential revisionism"—that is, one that differed from previous examinations of its subject, which, as I argue throughout this book, is not saying much. And we are now treated to literary scholars who have come up with the notion that interpretations can be "post-revisionist"—whatever that may mean. From being descriptive nouns, "revisionism" and its kin terms have been turned into curse words and denotatives that have lost all concrete meaning.[1] And they have become curse words often tossed about by people of widely differing partisan and ideological stripes for the sole purpose of getting the political upper hand on someone else. The resulting negative connotations of the term—connotations that I refer to throughout this book—have consequently misled many people who otherwise might have been open to considering the arguments that were at stake had the term "revisionist" not been affixed to them. What suffer in such cases are not only historical understanding but political debate and civic comity.

In this book, therefore, I want to try to bring some intellectual clarity to the subject of revisions in interpretations of the past so as to help readers understand what leads to alterations in our understanding of what has gone before us. I want also to explain why historians have for so long disagreed with one another; why historical knowledge is unlikely ever to be unchanging; why, as a branch of knowledge, history is always a search for meaning and a constant source and subject of argument;

1. It is only slightly less unhelpful that historians and others sometimes distinguish between "old" and "new" history, as in the "old" and "new" Cold War history, even the "old" and "new" revisionist history. Such distinctions can help differentiate changing interpretive emphases or interpretive schools of thought from one another and indicate which ones have preceded and succeeded the others. But terminological tags like these, while sometimes useful, should not be taken to suggest that any "new" history, because it is more recent, is necessarily superior in quality to an "old" one.

and therefore why history—whether asserted, debated, challenged, or memorialized—is essential to individuals' awareness of their location in the world and to every group's and nation's sense of its identity and destiny. Historical subjects are important because they are always alive—always argued about, always objects of fascination, never dead. They constitute, as the great Dutch historian Pieter Geyl once remarked, "an argument without end."

All historians are revisionists—at least in some respects. They are always trying to get a grasp on the past—not only for their simple need and desire to understand that past and for the pleasures and satisfactions such understanding may bring them, but also for their visions and hopes. Thus all works of history should be approached as presumptively revisionist. Yet calling a history "revisionist" (or, more recently, "neorevisionist") is like calling water wet; the use of the term speaks to what is inherent in historical writing, not what is distinctive about any example of it. Since historians always have some purpose in writing their histories, written history is always intentional—an effort to understand and present a rendering of a subject more complete than previous historians' understandings of it and thus different from what was previously understood. That is, since every historian, by virtue of possessing a distinct mind, disposition, perspective, and purpose offers a particular "take" on a subject or issue that, by the very fact of existing, is a unique expression of that historian, all historians come to their work with the aim of bringing their own selves and no one else's to bear on the subject at hand. Even a history that is a mere chronicle of facts can offer a fresh look at the past by its selection of those facts. Accordingly, each history shares in two characteristics that have existed since ancient Greece: from Herodotus, history as a portrayal of a specific subject; from Thucydides, history as an argument, often with other historians. Each work of history is a unique element in a continuing, open-ended search for meaning. It is in the spirit of trying to clarify what constitutes revisionist history that I want to capture in this book some of what is at stake in thinking and writing about the past and why historical investigation, knowledge, and writing cannot be separated from historians' political and personal commitments and predispositions.

But how is the term "revisionist history" to be given due specific-ity? During the first two millennia of written history, as Chapters 2 and 3 should make clear, histories that can now be seen as revisionist were rare, and those few that qualify for the designation were strongly heterodox, occasionally truly revolutionary. They challenged the dominance of, and occasionally replaced, previously unassailed historical worldviews. They attacked what had come to be orthodox ideas about the past. They dissented from conventional interpretation. They brought to bear evidence that strategically and powerfully claimed to undermine what had been earlier believed to be complete and valid knowledge. Deemed to be heretical, they often scandalized the public and were savagely attacked, sometimes outlawed. There was little denying their impact, their threat to constituted authority, and their challenge to convention. Among such alternatives to previous, accepted views of the past were Eusebius's Christian substitute for Classical, pagan histories and Karl Marx's variant interpretation of the Western past. Little remained the same, either within historical literature, general culture, or public debate, after their works appeared.

But to qualify as a revisionist history—a term not known before the twentieth century—a work is not required to turn conventional or accepted interpretations of a subject on their head, as did the writings of Eusebius and Marx. If that were the test, then most pre-nineteenth-century historical works, even those of greatest impact for their break with previous approaches to the past (such as the protosecularist assumptions of the Florentine historians Niccolò Machiavelli and Francesco Guicciardini) might fail to qualify. Accordingly, any examination of revisionist history must be capacious and encompass within its reach any and all histories that, in relation to their subjects, constitute a shift in, or addition to, previous ways of understanding those subjects.

Furthermore, if we accept as revisionist histories only revolutionary replacements of previously settled views of the past, we have not advanced far in understanding changes in historical knowledge over time nor have we adapted to current intellectual realities. The day when single reinterpretations of large subjects could sweep all before them and exist effectively unchallenged by other interpretations within a single culture has passed. Given the proliferation of sources, the expansion of subjects considered open to historical evaluation, the sheer increase in the number of professional historians around the globe, the spread

of scholarly specialization, and the revolution in travel and communication, revisions to formerly conventional views are vastly greater
in number than in the past, and they challenge one another in rapid
succession. Moreover, although they often gain traction in more limited
circles than did, say, the reevaluations of history that Eusebius and Marx
proposed, they are no less significant in challenging and altering previous understanding of discrete subjects. It therefore becomes necessary
to distinguish different varieties, scales, and significance of revisionist
history so that we can fully understand the advance of historical understanding and clashes over historical interpretations both in the past and
in our own time. The subject of revisionist history's varieties is the focus
of Chapter 4.

Another matter relating to revisionist history is that of historical scale. For more than two centuries, for example, one of the most
contentious debates among historians has concerned the origins of the
French Revolution, a subject I take up in Chapter 5. Did it arise from
the immiseration of the French working class, from rising bourgeois
aspirations, from the appearance on the historical stage of "the people,"
from the collapse of the French economy, or from some other cause or
causes? No one would dispute the claim that the challenge of getting this
interpretation right ought to be of major interest to those trying to understand the foundations of modern Europe, especially its nation-state
system, politics, and society. Therefore, any challenge to a previously
widely held interpretation of the seismic revolutionary events that shook
France and the Continent after 1789 constitutes, almost by definition,
an instance of revisionist history. If, however, we reduce the scale and
boundaries of any subject—if we look at events that took place in more
limited circumstances, not those of the French Revolution, but, say, of
a single Civil War battle—do we thereby take ourselves out of the realm
of revisionist history? Such a proposition would be difficult to maintain.
Revisionism is relative to the subject it concerns. An alteration in understanding of a relatively minor battle ought not to be excluded from
the category of revisionist history simply because it concerns an event of
lesser significance to the history of the United States than the larger Civil
War itself. Within its specific context, it is revisionist.

Similarly, the designation "revisionist" cannot depend on the claimed

significance or insignificance of any particular alteration in the interpretation of past events. Whether or not an interpretation is revisionist
derives from the degree to which it alters a specific, previously ventured
explanation of a segment of the past, not whether that segment is or is
not deemed to be important to any individual historian or member of
the public. Thus the reevaluation of known manuscripts, the unearthing
and interpretation of new evidence, and advances in genomic science—
all over roughly thirty years—have recently provided authoritative
weight, lacking before, to the view that Thomas Jefferson had fathered
children with his enslaved concubine Sally Hemings. This evidence not
only changed the view that Jefferson had avoided sexual contact with
African Americans; it also made sharply clearer how entangled white and
black people had been at the dawn of American nationhood. From then
on, the conclusion was no longer tenable that the slaveholding author of
the ringing claim that all men are created equal had somehow avoided
the kind of contact that we already knew many planters, overseers, and
other whites had had with their slaves. The written history of race relations in the United States gained new depth.

But we also need to be precise about what falls within the general
category of "revisionist history." It does not include views about the past
unconnected to known fact, nor is it mere opinion—the kind offered by
politicians, pundits, and ideologues whose use of claimed knowledge of
the past is often polemical. Nor does it include the opposite—history
charged with being "revisionist" simply because it offends some person
or political group.[2] Like all historical understanding, revisions must
be able to pass the test of authoritative knowledge—of understand-

2. An example of a change in the presentation of the past because one political party finds
another party's interpretation contrary to its chief office holders' convictions is the alteration
ordered in 2017 by the incoming administrators of the U.S. Environmental Protection Agency
to the EPA's in-house exhibit on the agency's history. Those officials removed references to the
agency's past efforts to slow global warming and halt climate change—as if removing these
references would change reality itself. With limited space to present the past, institutions
must always ration what they place on exhibit and choose among interpretations; and no one
can prevent adherents of one particular view from substituting their convictions for differing
ones. But whether from the Right or the Left, this is revisionism still. The only difference
between Right revisionism, which this clearly was, and Left revisionism is the direction from
which a reinterpretation comes.

ing gained through extended reading, research, study, reflection, and criticism. This does not mean that arguments about the past must be confined to academic circles, for many nonacademics have proved themselves deeply versed in various subjects of the past. It does, however, mean that what may be measured against each other as "standard" or "revisionist" histories can legitimately be considered one or the other only when they result either from archival research or from deep, knowledgeable consideration and reconsideration of what historians have earlier written.

Yet such attempts at definitions of revisionist history still do not provide conclusive guidance to its meaning or to ways to identify it. There are solid grounds for the conviction, which is mine, that as long as we keep in mind the considerations that I note here and in Chapter 4, we need not expect conclusive guidance about the meaning of revisionist history or about ways to identify it to make itself known. There can be no question that a change in interpretation that is contrary to what has generally been believed to be the case in the culture at large and among most historians must be considered revisionist; histories that cause controversy are, in that respect alone, probably entitled to the term. But should the routine revision-making all historians engage in whenever they sit down to work be banished from the definition? While others will disagree with me, I think not. And what about alternative ways of viewing the past that simply put forward a fresh approach to it without taking issue with other ones? Because they do not present themselves as revisions of what has been argued before, should they not, too, be dismissed as not being revisionist? Here again, I think not. Implicitly, and in the full record of historical thought and writing, such nonargumentative histories are likely to set their course to a different compass reading than previous ones; they use the same facts but present a narrative differently or give greater emphasis to particular figures and events than previous works on the subject. Accordingly, even if they do not contain sharply new approaches to or arguments about their subject, they are revisionist histories. Consequently, because such issues will always remain a matter of argument, some of it severe, the safest, and I think therefore the most justifiable and defensible, course is to consider every work of history as revisionist until proven, through convincing argument, otherwise. And that is probably not worth the effort.

If we are all revisionists now and if all history is potentially revisionist, then we find ourselves facing the inherent uncertainty and
enduring provisionality of all historical knowledge as well as unending
conflicts over the meaning of the past. If such conflicts are not always
to the good and occasionally cause harm, they are deeply human. Were
we to arrive at an imagined Eden where historical debate had ended,
it would mean that we had arrived at the end of human culture and
human thought. History's vitality, and the vitality of argument and conversation about it, sustains the public life of a representative democracy
and open society like our own. In such a society, an unchallenged interpretation of the past stands out as an oddity. That we can argue passionately about the meaning of the past reveals how a free society offers and
protects the possibilities of multiple views and enduring searches for
meaning. Only closed and totalitarian societies forbid arguments about
their historical pasts. And well they should, for challenges to orthodox
and official histories always threaten autocratic efforts to govern and
repress behavior and thought. In George Orwell's words, "Who controls
the past controls the future; who controls the present controls the past."
And because conflicting ways of understanding the past suggest that
knowledge itself, and interpretations of it, may be provisional, alterations to existing, deeply held portrayals of the past make those who fear
change deeply anxious. Nevertheless, such revisions are the lifeblood of
free thought and free expression; they constitute part of the enduring
contest of ideas and convictions that shapes modern open societies; and
they characterize much of the play of thought that makes up intellectual
and public life everywhere that people are free to think, write, and talk
as they wish. Better that historians and others be at liberty to fight over
the past than that knowledge and discussion of it be suppressed.

If all historical knowledge is to some degree uncertain, partial, and
open to debate and alteration, especially in a democratic society where
reason is free to combat error, how are we to have any confidence in
what is taught to us as history? How do we avoid slipping into the cynical error of concluding that historical knowledge is not worth much
because it is never fully certain? How do we avoid the equally serious rel-
ativist error of thinking that because people differ about the past, all interpretations of it are equally valid? How, that is, should we think about

both the provisionality of historical knowledge and its always changing richness and utility? How should we look on the never-ending debates among historians as they go about creating new knowledge and refining, revising, and challenging existing knowledge (which means disagreeing with each other) in their search for dependable understanding of the past?

These questions are at the heart of this book. To get at them, I define historical revisionism not simply as alterations in historical interpretations but more specifically as any challenge to existing interpretations of any aspect of the past brought about by new evidence, new arguments, new perspectives, or new methods. This definition removes from consideration mere additions to historical knowledge unless those additions result in changes to previous ways of understanding a segment of the past—a distinction, I concede, that is difficult to maintain. My definition allows entrance to some examples of argumentative history while excluding others, thus granting the existence of interpretive freedom while leaving unresolved the question of how far arguments validly can extend and when further argument yields nothing.

I open the book with a survey of the varied approaches historians have taken to a subject that has long seemed immediate to Americans: the causes of the American Civil War. I thus commence in an unorthodox chronological manner—putting consideration of arguments about a nineteenth-century phenomenon in front of developments in historical writing dating to the half millennium before the onset of the Christian era. I do so solely for the purpose of introducing readers to major dimensions of revisionist history via a review of arguments about a subject central to Americans' sense of their nationhood and moral commitments. Writing for another audience, I would have chosen to start with an illustrative topic equally close to its members' historical consciousness. I then turn in Chapters 2 and 3 to a brief survey of history's own history—what historians know as historiography, a term that, because I use it often, requires explanation and clarification here. It can have two meanings. In one sense, historiography—from the Latin terms *historia* (narrative, inquiry about the past) and *graphia* (writing)—is simply all writing about the past, the accumulated literature about any historical subject. Thus we can refer to the historiography of the American Revolution and the historiography of modern Africa. When we do so, the term means the body of interpretive historical works about a subject—published books and articles, as well as productions in such more recent media for the dissemination of ideas as radio and film. In its second sense, historiography means the formal study of historical thought and writing—that is, scholarship into changes in thinking about the past. In this sense, historiography is the repository of history's criticism of itself. Someone who practices this kind of scholarship is thus a historiographer, a person who studies historical literature the same way that another one studies British literature or writings about psychology—for the ever-changing contents, meaning, style, and significance of works in those fields. In both senses, historiography is a genealogy of changing historical argument and meaning.

The genealogical metaphor also suggests the inevitable embodiment within the most recent interpretation of any part of the past of previous interpretations of it. No work of history is history-less. While each work is the result of a particular historian's examination of part of the past, that historian's ideas about the past have been formed by the existing historical literature of the subject. In turn, that work is open to examination by every succeeding historian who takes up the subject anew. This means that no work of history, any more than its author, can maintain a disguise. All works of history are open to review, their texts revealed to be constituted, like a genome, of distinct, identifiable elements of past historical thought as well as of a unique human mind at work on a subject of the past. In this sense, historiography is also like geology: it studies the layers of sediment—the accumulated works of history—that have piled up over millennia, now standing exposed by the application of human thought into what was once taken for granted because it was buried out of sight. Each new work of history is but the surface that appears to us while covering up what lies underneath it from earlier deposit. Seen from the perspective of historiography, it turns out that history commenced millennia ago in an argument that still shapes the ways we think about the past and the subjects historians contend over. That is, revisionist history was with us from the start, and even the term "revisionist history" has a history of its own.

In Chapter 4, I propose a typology of the many varieties of revisions to the historical record, following which, in Chapter 5, I offer examples of the immediacy of historical arguments in the past, the uses to which they have been put, and the sometimes surprising resting places of understanding. In conclusion, in Chapter 6, I take up the vexed issue— one that underlies all the rest—of historians' objectivity and how we can retain faith in the strength, credibility, and usefulness of historical knowledge in the face of advances in neuroscience and substantial philosophical doubts about the objectivity of historical claims. Throughout, I try to make clear how and why historians go about their work—how they use evidence, why their arguments take the forms they do, and what their differing intentions are. By the end of the book, I hope that readers can understand better what the pursuit of historical knowledge always has been and always will be and that the teachers among them can better transmit that understanding to their students. I hope, too, that readers will come to see that historians, in their own partial knowledge, are engaged in a never-ending discussion among themselves and with their students, readers, auditors, and viewers about the meaning of the past and the uses of historical knowledge.

The book has limitations that I must acknowledge here. It is confined to historical subjects and to the historical literature of the Western world. Those subjects and that body of works are so vast in providing examples for my purposes that I need not turn elsewhere. Nevertheless, the historiography of other cultures and traditions, like that of Islam and the Middle East and of China, are rich beyond reckoning in variety and disputation. Any book like this one that, because of limits on my knowledge, omits consideration of such histories as those of the great fourteenth-century Muslim historian Ibn Khaldun (see his *Muqaddimah*) or of China's Sima Qian, who wrote in the first century BCE (his masterpiece being *Records of the Grand Historian*), is only a partial history. But since so much of what I write concerns general principles of historical scholarship, thought, understanding, and argument, by extension this book has applicability to the history and historians of all parts and cultures of the world.

In addition, since this is a book whose subject possesses no long shelves of studies devoted to it, I have had to rely, more than in a work of research scholarship in the archives, on my own reflections about the whole compass of Western historiography drawn from my career as a professional historian, one that commenced when I entered undergraduate studies in history in the 1950s. Consequently, much of the book is essay-like and very much my endeavor to outline how I believe more attention to an ignored subject might proceed. In addition to the works of history taken up in the body of each chapter, in place of citation footnotes I have supplied readers with some suggestions for further reading at the end of each chapter (Chapters 2 and 3 sharing a single set of suggestions).

Finally, the book does not, because it cannot, take up every controversy among Western historians, every differing interpretation about every subject, even every major subject of long concern to those who study the past. My choice of subjects is selective so as to be illustrative, not exhaustive. I hope that, after considering what I have written, readers will be better able to approach all works of history with an increased ability to understand those works' strengths while accepting and evaluating their limitations and partiality. If they can do so, they will join the honorable company of those people who devote their lives and careers to figuring out what happened in the past.

Revisions Without End

The Origins of the American Civil War

There exists a no more classic example of the provisionality of interpretations of the past than the long history of arguments about the causes of the American Civil War. I offer the following review of those interpretations to exemplify and stand in for the scale, complexity, and significance of all the other interpretive conflicts that have existed since the origin of written history in ancient Greece. I also introduce here some of the inherent realities of all historical argument.

Because the dispute over the Civil War's causes has never lost its immediacy to Americans and because the issues raised by it continue to infuse American public life, the battle over the war's origins can sometimes seem as heated as the war itself. While professional historians' debates over the war's origins have abated and reached a tentative consensus in recent years as other issues related to the war have taken center stage, the historiographic battle over the war's beginnings, now more than 150 years old and one of the most politically, intellectually, and morally fraught of all debates about the war, illustrates many of the challenges that historians face as they try to understand any dimension of the past. For while it may be possible to calm the passions of warfare and narrow the issues concerning historical events and figures, it is often impossible, as it is in this case, to end them or eliminate their

implications for current history. An endless stream of differing, sometimes clashing, historical interpretations—an endless stream, that is, of
challenges to, and revisions of, previous histories—is the result.

The long struggle—among academic historians as well as members of the general public—to understand the war's causes also reveals
the difficulties entailed in trying to reach a consensus, even a rough
one, about the origins of any great historical episode. Even the best and
most deeply knowledgeable scholars remain at odds about portions of
the problem and grant that no interpretation of the causes of the Civil
War is without its difficulties. They puzzle over specific questions, are
sometimes stumped by the seeming impossibility of closing off certain
avenues of speculation, or remain at odds over the comparative value
and strength of different approaches to the war's causes.

If this is so a century and a half after the war ended, imagine how
much more seemed at stake at the outset of this interpretive battle—
immediately after the war's end in 1865. In the years close to any event,
especially a large and deeply divisive civil conflict, passions are raw,
interpretive distance is almost impossible to come by, and the event's
living survivors exert a kind of tyranny over interpretations of what
occurred. After Appomattox, those conditions existed for decades, and
rarely during those years could be found the American, North or South,
who sought or achieved a balanced, calm, and dispassionate view of the
war's origins. All tried to justify their own side and blame the other for
precipitating the conflict. For well over a third of a century after the last
bullet was spent, the explanations Americans advanced differed little
from those that combatants themselves had put forth in the heat of
battle.

The North-South division over the war's causes in the years immediately following the war should not surprise us, nor should the fact
that what survivors of an event write often forms the basic template for
interpretations of it, even if their claims later prove to be untenable.
That contemporaries exert such lasting influence over what the general
populace thinks as well as what historians afterward write may frustrate
professional historians, many of whom like to believe that arguments
about the past should remain with them. Yet in fact the battles over
history's meanings typically start with contemporaries and participants,

and rarely do their arguments stay within the bounds of professional discourse. Everyone has much at stake in these interpretive set-to's.

And so it was with the Civil War. The soil in which the earliest efforts to understand the coming of that great conflict germinated was not the terrain of specially trained professional historians (of whom, in fact, few existed at the time). Instead, committed nonhistorian partisans of the North and South made the first attempts to understand the war's causes and justify their claims. These partisans were journalists, military figures, and politicians, and, like almost all published commentators and interpreters of the war until our own day, they were uniformly male, almost all of them white. Their interpretations were along lines that we might expect of such people—about politics, policies, and warfare; about elites rather than common people and soldiers; about white male Americans, not African Americans, whether slave or free, and not about women. Also not surprisingly, their views reflected the sides, Unionist and Secessionist, they had supported and fought for. Those views tended to be monocausal: slavery, so northerners argued, explained the South's intransigent stance; the abolition of slavery, maintained southerners, was the North's motivation for war. And all of this in the face of the fact that historical events are rarely caused by a single development or condition.

Contemporaries' interpretations of those causes, which at the time were hardwired into each section's consciousness of itself, also had about them the aspect of images in a camera lens: what was up to northern writers about the war was down to their southern opposites, and vice versa. These commentators typified hundreds of thousands of other people in their respective sections in their views and resentments, often with the tremendous certainty and ideological fervor that winners and losers bring to the aftermath of any awful contest. Most important, since their interpretations were the first to see print and had the power of confirming views already widespread and strongly held, they were the interpretations compared to which all subsequent ones proved to be variations. From then on, when even skilled historians ventured explanations for the war's causes based on the strongest available evidence and most searching scholarship and thought, they were always looking over their shoulders at what had been written in the three decades after

1865. Ever since then, that body of sectional, committed history has remained alive in the subsoil of popular opinion, never without its partisans and always to some degree immune from the influence of more recent, evidence-based works of history.

∞

The core of the northern, largely Republican Party, view of the war's causes was the conviction that the conflict was an unconstitutional rebellion precipitated by southern "rebels" and "traitors" against the integrity of the Union, a rebellion growing out of a slave society fundamentally different from the democratic society of the North. At first, as northerners put it, it was a war to "maintain the best government on earth," a struggle "for the Union, the Constitution, and law." But eventually they came to agreement that, in Abraham Lincoln's words, slavery "was, somehow, the cause of the war." The South's treasonous acts of aggression against the North and the grip of the "Slave Power Conspiracy" on the nation's law and politics in the 1850s, they argued, had nothing to do, as the South claimed, with northern attacks on the rights of individual states. It was settled northern conviction that in 1787 the entire people of the United States, "we the people" and not the states, had formed the "more perfect union." That union could not constitutionally be rent asunder unless a majority of citizens of the Union, north and south together, agreed to its dissolution—just as they had accepted its creation in 1787 and 1788, when they ratified the Constitution in representative conventions in each state. No majority of citizens had so agreed in 1861. The South's claim that the Union was a compact of states severable by them was, in Lincoln's words, nothing but an "ingenious sophism" used to justify a conflict that the South had begun. Arising from a sense of Christian moral conviction in victory and grief over Lincoln's assassination, post-1865 northern opinion was implacable in the view that the slave South bore responsibility and guilt for what northerners then termed the War of the Rebellion, an uprising against legitimate constitutional government. It was an unavoidable conflict that, pitting slavery against freedom, had also been a righteous cause.

As was to be expected in the aftermath of a war that had rent the nation in two, an opposing set of convictions took hold in the defeated South, even if not immediately. At first, Democratic southerners followed the cue of Confederate president Jefferson Davis in arguing that northern initiative—the War of Northern Aggression was a widely popular southern name for the conflict—and attempts to prevent the further spread of slavery threatened to wipe out southern equity in their slaves. Davis's vice president, Alexander H. Stephens, unblushingly maintained that bond servitude was "the cornerstone of southern civilization." But by 1865, realizing that they had surrendered moral ground by defending slavery, southerners jettisoned that argument in favor of more clearly constitutional ones. Those arguments gained force for their grounding in most southerners' conviction, even in defeat, that the South had been justified in defending states' rights and slavery even if vanquished in their defense. To southern veterans, the war had started as a conflict among sovereign states, not between the people of those states, and the southern states had been constitutionally justified—by virtue of the theory of government that defined the United States as a compact between individual state units—in seeking their independence from the rest of the Union. Secession, to their way of thinking, did not constitute a revolution against the United States. Instead, it was undertaken to preserve original American constitutional principles. Northern aggression had violated the Constitution and provoked the South to rise in self-defense. Southerners believed that they were defending constitutional federalism against centralization and consolidation.

In addition, despite the emancipation of the slaves, or perhaps because of the shock of their emancipation, postwar white southerners insisted that threats to the institution of slavery—what they termed a "positive good"—and an instinct to preserve it had had nothing to do with their secession. Accordingly, most survivors among the South's leading opinion makers and historians failed to take the Confederacy's defeat as a spur to reconsider the justness of the southern cause or the morality of slavery. In addition to their states' rights position, they argued that the South had left the Union because of coercive northern initiatives that sought to favor commerce and manufacturing over southern agriculture. The war, former Confederates claimed, had originated in a conspiracy among northern states, led by radical abolitionists, to rule over the South. The South's stance had all along been conservative and defensive. The "Lost Cause" was innocent of charges that the South had started the war. If a sign of the future was needed, southern firmness in defeat ensured that the historiographic debate to come would be a bitter one.

The search for understanding summons us to acknowledge the psychological needs that these opposite interpretations satisfied for both victors and vanquished about a war whose prosecution had cost hundreds of thousands of lives on both sides. Yet such interpretive opposites are not equivalent any more than they are fertile ground for prudent, considered, authoritative history. While one view has come to command intellectual authority in the twenty-first century, in the post–Civil War years they both reflected hot conviction, not cool knowledge. Their weaknesses arose from their foundations in passion, the territory of contemporaries, not evidence and deliberation, the terrain of historians. Such popular, psychologically salving beliefs often prove long resistant to alteration either by the passage of time, the findings and arguments of professional historians, or even the mature views of some of the conflict's veterans. Historical convictions that have taken root in a people, convictions that remain in the air of a culture and are inculcated in children's schooling, remain long impervious to change. In the defeated states of the Confederacy, only slightly less so in the North, this proved particularly so.

Interpretive chasms like this one, created in the heat of a bloody contest, also never fail to have some effect on historians. While sometimes forcing them to stand firm in defense of their positions, diametric interpretations often point them to consider issues and evidence that the other side summons in argument. When historians put such interpretations under the lens, the passionately held views they examine may provide clues to new avenues of thought and investigation. But these passionate views may also, and usually do, have another effect: they may end up permeating informed, professional interpretation of the war's causes. Only slowly, with the passage of time and the rise of fresh circumstances, do attempts to capture the historical narrative for each section's interests begin to weaken and allow the emergence of less committed, more considered views.

When does that happen and why? Only when passions have begun to cool and—it amounts to roughly the same thing—when participants begin to pass from the scene. In fact, it should be inscribed as a kind of rule of historical interpretation that gains in interpretive distance on major historical events face heavy winds as long as those who took part in them survive to maintain a fierce hold on interpretation and as long as other people try to exploit the nostalgia of the living. Lived experience and memory of it has to cede psychological space to evidence-based research before perspective can even begin to be gained on what had earlier been part of individual lives. This is especially so with an event as great as the Civil War, whose realities burned their way into the con-sciousness of those who lived through it. (As I point out in Chapter 5, the same rule was at work during later, bitter debates over the dropping of atomic bombs on Japan.) Only when participants have begun to fade away can a clearing for less committed views open up and something like detachment on both sides be gained.

Such an interpretive opportunity came into being sometime in the late 1880s and early 1890s, roughly a quarter century after Appomattox. Those who stepped into this interpretive opening were the earliest revi-sionists of Civil War history. They were the first to raise questions about the contents of the bitterly opposed views that had taken root during and immediately after the war and the first to subject those views to evaluation and to propose alternatives to them. Sometimes basing their arguments on newly available evidence, sometimes simply changing their angle of vision, they inaugurated the enduring struggle to under-stand, rather than assert, why the Civil War had occurred.

Many factors having little to do with the war, sectionalism, or con-stitutional theory contributed to this new dispassion. As a consequence of the election of Rutherford B. Hayes to the presidency in 1876, the federal government had withdrawn the last of its troops from the South (ending the period of so-called Reconstruction) and thus returned the governance of the former Confederate states to their unrepentant white citizens. Comity between whites in the two sections had begun to re-turn in the form of restored commerce and a growing determination to ignore the status of African Americans, north and south, in preference to attending to the needs, attitudes, and desires of the white majority. The emergence of Social Darwinism—the application of evolutionary thought to social problems—and the attendant strengthening of ethnocentrism and racism, north and south, also pushed concerns for the rights of the freed slaves into the background. As we have seen in our own time with the romance of the "Greatest Generation,"[1] the aging and slow passing of the war's veterans turned the horrors and agonies of battle into a field day for nostalgia and allowed the emergence in their place of a gauzy haze of reconciliation, memorialization, and tribute. Also, fatigue with partisan and sectional passions and demagoguery, fatigue that eventually yielded to outright distaste for political bitterness, mounted among Americans wherever they lived. In such circumstances, historians no longer had to keep their eyes peeled for bitter rivals in the other section. Into a re-knit nation could be sewn new stories, new perspectives.

The first of those who took up the revisionist challenge was James Schouler, a figure now largely forgotten but one well known in his day. This New England veteran of Union forces could have been expected to adopt thoroughly northern views of the war's origins, and in many respects he did. He condemned slavery not only as immoral but also because it "obstructed the destiny and growth of the American people in homogeneous grandeur." That is, attentive readers of his multi-volume *History of the United States of America Under the Constitution* (whose first volume appeared in 1880) found that underneath his treatment of two sections at war was a firm nationalism, a conviction that contrasted with the stance that viewed the United States, as did so many survivors of the Civil War, as a kind of federation of two formerly warring sections forced back together by arms under a single constitution. It was Schouler who abandoned the theory that southern radicals had plotted secession. Instead he wrote of the Confederacy as having been united within itself and engaged in a "civil war" with the North and not in a mere "rebellion" led by a few traitors conspiring against federal authority, as so many northerners still argued.

Schouler's meliorist views found parallels in those of John W. Burgess, a Tennessee Unionist who yielded nothing of his anti-Confederacy sentiments to southern opinion. He excoriated the South for slavery and

---

1. As if the generation that secured American independence from Great Britain or the generation, especially in the North, that is the subject of consideration here somehow played second fiddle to the men and women who fought the Second World War. The notion of any "greatest" generation is a concept best consigned to the landfill of ill-considered concepts.

its misbegotten states' rights position and had no doubts that the North was the warranted victor in a just war. Yet Burgess, who would eventually end up on the Columbia University faculty as a founder of the discipline of political science, also freed himself from earlier opinion in three influential works, published between 1897 and 1902, that focused on the nation from 1817 through Reconstruction. He did so by distinguishing between the war and its aftermath. For Burgess, the North was free of culpability for the conflict, the South alone being responsible for causing it. He saw "secession as an abomination, and its chief cause, slavery, as a great evil." But in a sharp break with previous northern opinion that reflected contemporary northern as well as southern views about the freed slaves' inferiority and the wisdom of keeping them in their place via "the white man's mission," Burgess argued that Reconstruction— the effort under federal auspices to transform southern governance and race relations through federal military occupation of the South after 1865—had been a failure for which the North was responsible. Here was an interpretation that apportioned blame to both sections and did so by distinguishing the war and its causes from its succeeding era. In these two respects, Burgess broke ground by offering fresh interpretive opportunities and suggesting new questions that other historians might pursue. Had the Civil War been a failure because it did not adequately protect the freed slaves in the South afterward? Was the North to be blamed for the failures of Reconstruction or did the South share equal responsibility for forcing the freed people to fall into poverty and peonage not long after the war? These were heavily freighted moral issues, ones with which politicians and members of the public still grapple.

Such shifts in interpretive emphases, like those of Schouler and Burgess, deserve to be termed revisions even if they did not cause seismic changes in ways of looking at the causes of the Civil War—and even if the term "revisionist history" did not yet exist. They may have been subtle shifts, but they were significant ones, a result of the loosening of earlier political, social, and intellectual chains that had bound northerners and southerners to the only views publicly allowable and acknowledgeable amid the passions of war and its immediate aftermath. Those views' emergence was itself the result of the widening of cultural "permission" to war veterans and others to think matters through

afresh and to begin to free themselves from the intellectual and emotional shackles that had bound members of the war generation in both
sections, witnessed by the fact that both Schouler's and Burgess's works
were well received in the South as well as the North at the time of their
publication. As is often the case, revised views of the past became possible only when the general climate of opinion began to shift. While it
is impossible to say which came first—new interpretations of the war's
causes or an altered cultural setting—it is clear that they coincided, each
affecting, interacting with, and responding to the other. Revisionist histories do not spring up in intellectual, political, or cultural vacuums.

∾

Not surprisingly, the first sharp break with original views of the Civil
War's causes originated with the first generation of historians who were
too young to have fought in the war even if old enough to have absorbed views about it in their youth. The exemplary historian of the Civil
War among them was James Ford Rhodes. An Ohioan, Rhodes struggled
during his early years to reconcile the strong Unionist views of his native
Cleveland with his family's sympathies for the South. Afterward, the politically independent Rhodes—like many other historians in the late
nineteenth century a man of independent means—would shift between
supporting Republican and Democratic presidential candidates, and
he opposed giving the vote to African Americans. This kind of political
balancing act revealed itself in at least part of his approach to the past,
for he did his best to tally the rights and wrongs of both North and South
in his multivolume *History of the United States from the Compromise
of 1850* (the first volume of which appeared in 1893), and he weighed
such evidence as was available to him even as he unblushingly judged
the contesting sections. On the matter of the causes of the Civil War,
Rhodes believed firmly that because the South insisted on defending "an
unrighteous cause," the North had had no moral choice but to attack it
and free the slaves. Thus the Civil War had been, in the enduring earlier
words of William H. Seward, Lincoln's secretary of state from whom
Rhodes borrowed the term, an "irrepressible conflict." This assertion by
a historian immediately reopened a long argument about whether the
war had been justified or not—whether it should have been fought in
the first place.

Such firm convictions could not, however, shield Rhodes, the northern gentleman writer, from the atmosphere of his times. The unmistakable signs of the onrushing reconciliation of North and South were everywhere in his work. Rhodes thought that southern popular will (that is, a kind of democracy)—not, as many northerners thought, a conspiracy among the governing slaveholder elite—had propelled the South to secession. While slavery was an evil, he argued, few slaveholders were evil. The North, through its trading and commercial practices, as well as the cotton gin invented by northerner Eli Whitney, had been as involved in sustaining southern slavery as the Confederate masters themselves. An admirer of Robert E. Lee, Rhodes believed that, though having thrown in his lot with his native Virginia and fought for the slave South, Lee had the character of George Washington. And (perhaps the most telltale sign of the drift of this new interpretive scheme) while he held slavery to be an evil, Rhodes argued that the freed slaves, as a group, had not earned the right to vote. Here was history answering to white Americans' desire to put the Civil War behind them—or at least to put the divisions of that war out of their minds at the expense of black Americans. Here, too, was a history, written by a conservative-minded scholar who had his doubts about popular rule, that opened wide the issue of to what extent democracy had been responsible for the war—whether or not there had been, in the later historian David H. Donald's memorable words, "an excess of democracy." Not surprisingly, Rhodes's history gained wide praise in both North and South.

Does Rhodes's example mean that, as justices of the Supreme Court are said to do, historians follow the election returns? Does Rhodes's time-bound interpretation of the Civil War's causes suggest that historians exercise no freedom of conviction and judgment from the intellectual currents of their upbringing, community, and time? Answering both questions in the negative does not mean to imply that historians can ever fully escape the cultural and intellectual forces that bear in on them in their own days. Historians are as influenced by the realities of their eras as are most people. But professional historians, especially in the decades since Rhodes wrote (when standards of research and presentation had not yet been firmly established), have become increasingly subject to professional, critical, and ethical canons that

constrain their subjectivity and hold them to certain responsibilities and
more fully considered principles. Moreover, they are subjected to more
stringent criticism, and a wider variety of it, than were their predecessors. In their professional capacities and in their responsibility—ethical as
well as historical—to be as true to the past as they can be, historians are
now expected to labor hard to break free of their own times and places.

Nevertheless, in this struggle—and a struggle it is—to be as faithful
to evidence and as objective as they can be, historians come up against
two human limitations, both nearly impossible to surmount. The first
is the ways of thought of their own times. But the second—the boundaries of thought itself, the limits of intellectual insight and understanding, to which every human is subject—is inarguably the greater of the
two. Human consciousness is always circumscribed by the bounds that
nature places on the mind and by the intellectual, cultural, and social
casing that structures thinking and ideas at all times everywhere. In addition, all historians bring to their work their distinct dispositions and
ways of looking at the world; they differ among each other as all humans
differ from others in the ways they apprehend life. Also, no historian can
be expected to know everything about a subject—either to know all that
is already known about it or to know all that may eventually be known
through, say, the discovery of new sources—or to be able to think all
possible thoughts. What may seem to one historian or to one era to be
a great leap forward in knowledge and understanding may appear in
retrospect to be a mere baby step, possibly a misstep. A historian who
seems to have gained widespread respect and authority at one time may
appear limited and retrograde to those who follow. And so it has seemed
to successive generations of historians who have tried to make sense of
the causes of the Civil War. Members of each of these generations find
defects, telltale silences, and limitations in the work of its predecessors,
new questions to ask, new perspectives to develop.

That became the fate of Rhodes's histories. They met with widespread acceptance in their day. They appealed to white men and women
weary of sectional strife, tired of facing up to the enduring plight of African Americans, gripped by Gilded Age moneymaking, fearful of immigrants and of labor unrest, and desirous of finding some middle ground
on which people of calm and prudent understanding could meet. But

by the 1890s, Rhodes's historical works began to seem insufficient—especially for being out of touch with emerging intellectual currents. They seemed inadequate even though his histories had greatly advanced understanding by their subtle revisions in perspective—above all their impartiality and, embodied in such a stance, their implied empathy for at least all white participants in the war. Rhodes in effect had opened routes to his fellow historians to consider all aspects of the conflict without sectional blinders firmly fixed. It is that shift in perspective that exposed previously closed-off terrain for new historical investigation and thought—one that, ironically, would soon cast Rhodes's histories into the shadows and arouse new arguments about the causes of the Civil War.

After Rhodes, the question was what those arguments would be about. Rhodes had cleared the ground of the baldest sectional approaches. Balance was now expected of historians who wished to be taken seriously, even if "balance" would leave some issues, like the fate of African Americans, out of consideration. Most historians, from the South as well as the North, now agreed that slavery had been a curse and that Lincoln's North had carried the nation into a new phase of modern nationhood and freedom even if African Americans enjoyed little of that freedom. But agreement did not answer the central questions about the war's causes. If individual members of the Confederacy had been honorable men fighting in a dishonorable cause, then who or what was in fact responsible for the coming of the war? If individual northerners and southerners had played no role in causing the war, then what had done so? It was over these troubling questions that the next generation of historians was to argue and from which alternatives to Rhodes's way of viewing the war's causes emerged.

∾

As often happens, the departures taken by this next generation of historians originated not in any direct attacks on weaknesses in its predecessors' approaches. Instead, they sprang from new angles of vision and new sensibilities on the part of this younger generation of historians. It is not without significance that its members were the earliest to receive their training as historians from members of academic faculties. They did so, moreover, when the influence of the natural and physical sciences—especially their ethos of the rigorous use of evidence, clear statements of testable hypotheses, and the importance placed on the building up of many studies to test and then either confirm or invalidate particular empirical findings—was for the first time being widely felt in most areas of intellectual endeavor. Theirs was also an era when the influence of new intellectual currents, especially Social Darwinism, were being sharply felt; when the intellectual influences of history's sister disciplines, especially those in the social sciences like economics and sociology, were increasing; and when the United States as a reunited nation was emerging as a world power. Equally significant, they had come of intellectual age after the nation had been restabilized after civil war and after its continental boundaries had been both permanently established and increasingly filled in. Americans were now spread from Atlantic to Pacific oceans, and no longer would it prove possible for historians from one or two geographic sections to speak with united interpretive voices or gain the unimpeded and uncriticized intellectual authority that some of their predecessors had enjoyed. Compared with those predecessors, moreover, these younger historians tended to seek overarching explanations for the Civil War's origins, to be critical of previously less "scientific" interpretations of the Civil War, and to ask fresh questions about its causes.

The outstanding figure of this generation of historians was Frederick Jackson Turner, one of the most influential historians the United States has ever produced. A son of Wisconsin educated as a historian at Johns Hopkins University, then the leading American center of academic history, Turner was not only one of the earliest university-trained historians but also one of the first whose native terrain was not the East—either the Northeast or the Southeast. Moreover, Turner came of age when western farmers were mounting concerted political challenges to their felt exploitation by centers of finance and industry, especially by railroads. Their Granger and Populist protests announced the emerging force of a distinctively western kind of politics whose standard would be carried by Williams Jennings Bryan into the presidential election of 1896 against William McKinley. But politics were only one manifestation of a new western self-consciousness and particularism. So were the historical studies that were produced by westerners.

Western cultural and political self-consciousness owed much to the fact that, while the Civil War had been fought in part over the expansion of slavery into trans-Mississippi territories, that part of the West had itself escaped much, although by no means all, of the awful battlefield carnage of the East. Yes, it could be argued, as it often is today, that while most of the major battles of the Civil War were fought in the East, the war was in fact won in the trans-Appalachian West along the Mississippi and other rivers, as the North gained a strategic stranglehold on southern supplies, railroads, populations, and geography there. But that argument was yet to come. Instead, early histories of the war and its causes, histories written usually by easterners, had often downplayed the war's western theater. By comparison, even if many western young men, fighting for both North and South, had sacrificed their lives in the battles of the 1860s (many of those battles fought bitterly in western Confederate territory), many westerners—even upper midwesterners like Turner, whose Wisconsin had been solidly Unionist—had an easier time than others in taking a national view of American history, including the history of the Civil War. Their national view was comparatively free of the deeply bitter arguments that still roiled historical thinking among easterners in the North and South.

Turner was the one to sound the fanfare for a new western interpretation of American history and, by implication, of the Civil War. His "frontier thesis," which he announced in Chicago in 1893, was the prospectus for a western way of thinking about the nation's past—and thus, of course, thoroughly revisionist. Based on 1890 census figures, the frontier thesis—endlessly debated and never fully accepted even if enormously fruitful in generating thought and understanding—proclaimed the closing of the nation's fabled frontier and, by implication, the opening of a new era in American history. In addition, it was meant to explain the development of American society, politics, and character as based on the traits—democratic individualism, egalitarianism, and nationalism above all—that the exploration and settlement of an ever-moving leading edge of population was said to have instilled in the American people. While Turner never wrote more than brief remarks about the Civil War and its causes, his emphasis on the geophysical bases of society—and thus on the qualitative differences between sections that resulted from different climates, soils, land forms, settlement patterns, economic systems, and labor needs—gave to others' study of the Civil War's origins new interpretive options. The causes of the war could now be attributed to the many other differences between each warring section rather than to different worldviews and labor systems, free and slave, alone.

In addition, Turner's interpretive approach reflected a more encompassing turn to a fresh nationalistic perspective on the Civil War. As the bitterness of warfare faded with the aging of combat veterans, as the nation's continental expanse was at last consolidated by railroads, as the nation's industrial might grew, and as the United States, especially after its victory in the 1898 Spanish-American War, gained a new position on the world stage, the older battles over sectional responsibility for the Civil War seemed increasingly outdated. While Turner emphasized the role of sections in American history, other widely read late-nineteenth-century historians like Edward P. Channing and John Bach McMaster more avowedly emphasized the larger nation's shared past and wrote their multivolume national histories in the spirit of sectional reconciliation—reconciliation that their histories served to promote as well as to explain.

In this interpretive development inhered an implicit moral shift of major proportions. Blame-casting gave way to attempts to be more balanced in understanding, while the search to establish responsibility for the war—whether individual or sectional—faded in significance. It was a shift that reveals how revisions in previous ways of seeing the past can carry far-reaching, even if unintended, consequences and why people often battle so ferociously over alternatives to existing, conventional interpretations of earlier times. Even though Turner scarcely dealt with the Civil War and went so far as to term slavery "an incident" in the development of the United States rather than the epicentral reality of its entire history, his new approaches to interpreting wide swaths of the American past gradually contributed to a shift in other historians' attention away from slavery as the source of southern sectionalism. Instead, they began to explore the two eastern sections' struggle to control the trans-Mississippi West and their disputes over tariffs, land settlement, and transportation development as well as slavery's westward spread.

The North and the Cotton Kingdom could now be seen as regions brought to battle over large, inanimate, fundamental, arguably irreconcilable differences of which slavery was but a single one.

Consequently, while Turner's multivariate approach to historical interpretation had the beneficial effect of raising the sophistication of historical interpretation generally and broadening American historiography away from its disproportionate focus on political and constitutional subjects and toward social and economic ones, it inadvertently began to leech from the following half century of historical thinking about the Civil War its previously strong moral elements. This should not have been surprising. In an era when the reconciliation between the two former warring sections was gathering pace, when Jim Crow laws were spreading in the South, and when widespread and intensifying racial prejudice was causing white Americans to turn away from concern about the plight of the freed slaves and their children, the subject of war guilt gradually gave way to the kind of neutral interpretive schemes introduced by the Turnerians. Thus when the next American generation of historians emerged on the scene around the time of the First World War and the intellectual air was being filled by fresh, principally reformist ideas, new approaches to the Civil War's origins influenced by those ideas fit snugly beside interpretive approaches from the turn of the century that had avoided apportioning war guilt while trying still to explain what had caused the Civil War. Under this new dispensation, slavery became something of an abstract historical reality. The plight of the slaves and the moral blight of slavery were now little heard of as, seeking fresh ways of getting at the tangled roots of the war, historians found intellectual sustenance elsewhere. As has happened repeatedly in the long history of written history, revisions to earlier ways of seeing the past carried deep moral implications. And vice versa.

Two other intersecting features set off this new historiographic era from the previous one. The first was democratic socialist thought making its way from Europe into American intellectual and cultural circles, which found much to criticize in the excesses of Gilded Age capitalism and the antiunion corporate trusts that were pulling the American economy out of shape. The second, emerging from the first, was the strong domestic Progressive reform movement, which was attempting to correct the widespread economic harms of industrial and finance capitalism and whose emblematic political figures were Theodore Roosevelt and Woodrow Wilson. While informed by a general acquaintance with the writings of Karl Marx, Friedrich Engels, and other continental thinkers busy with their debates over socialist and communist theory, American criticisms of the Robber Barons and the often vulgar trappings of their wealth owed little to Marx and Engels and more to a kind of native, populist outrage over vast differentials in wealth. Historians could no more be immune from such currents of politics and thought than could anyone else. And this was notably true of the generation of historians that succeeded Frederick Jackson Turner and his contemporaries.

The natural process by which one generation succeeds another should never be seen as sweeping up every younger person and every older idea and transforming both. Many aspiring historians in the years just preceding the First World War, when political Progressivism was at its flood and Theodore Roosevelt, William Howard Taft, and Woodrow Wilson occupied the White House, could and did remain anchored intellectually in previous modes of interpretation, while many seasoned historians adapted to the newer interpretive dispensations. The result, as is always the case, was that new historical interpretations were added to old ways of thinking without fully erasing or supplanting the earlier ones. Consequently, older interpretations were always available to excite historians to new thinking or to be summoned, in old or altered form, to enjoy life again. Interpretations thus pile up just as geological strata do, sometimes hardened and clearly distinguishable from others, often intermixed and tossed together as seismic and other natural forces make themselves felt over a landscape. When we speak of new interpretive eras, schemes, schools of thought, and ideas, we speak of additions and replacements, rarely of obliteration, the revisions themselves, as we shall see, by their very existence being open to revision. Coexistence of interpretation is the rule, not the exception.

Previously, historians of the Civil War had battled, as had most historians until then, over what they could define without difficulty as the past of the past, the present being an offstage, unacknowledged presence in interpretive strategies. North and South hoped to capture

the day's historical high ground in debates about responsibility for the
war, but their focus was squarely on the past. By contrast, the generation
of historians who came of age in the second decade of the twentieth
century brought a new impulse to historical study: they were presentists,
and they were reformers. Their histories were much more directed to
influencing their contemporaries' thinking about their own day than at
settling scores about the past. That impulse showed up clearly in their
writings.

It was James Harvey Robinson who took the lead in making a
case for presentist history and for what he called "a history for the
common man." A Columbia University historian of Europe, Robinson
announced the birth of this new approach with his aptly titled *The
New History*, published in 1912, the year of Woodrow Wilson's election to the presidency. All social progress, Robinson believed, rested
on a clear-eyed understanding of contemporary conditions. That, in
turn, required historical knowledge of how those conditions arose. But
"historical-mindedness," as he called it with easy optimism, was not
good in and of itself. Instead, "It will promote rational progress as nothing else can do." Progress—social, cultural, intellectual, and political—
was Robinson's leitmotif (this before two horror-strewn world wars).
And he exhorted historians to explore how human society had bettered
itself through time so that it could continue to do so. History was to be
the history of progress.

Despite Robinson's claim, present-minded history was not in itself
"new" history. After all, monarchs, dictators, and democrats had long
painted the past, as they still do, in hues that might help their regimes
and their politics survive, no matter how far they had to pull the actual
historical record out of shape to do so. And the Italian philosopher and
statesman Benedetto Croce had preceded Robinson in arguing that
"all history is contemporary history" and that "history is the story of
liberty." Accordingly, although Robinson's was a young strain of acknowledged presentism in Western historiography, it was not altogether
a novel one. What was new in Robinson's approach to history—an
intention that allied him with the likes of economist Thorstein Veblen
and jurist Oliver Wendell Holmes, Jr.—was his desire to free historical
thought of all aesthetic and moral considerations when accounting for

past phenomena. Moreover, he mounted a stout defense of social, cultural, and intellectual factors as legitimate subjects of historical interest. "The present has hitherto been the willing victim of the past," he wrote. "The time has now come when it should turn on the past and exploit it in the interests of advance." His was a scholar's conviction that history could be used for social change. In that conviction, the study of history was about as far from the intellectual impulses of James Ford Rhodes as it could get.

As a reformer who sought to have history used for progressive purposes, Robinson was principally an essayist. The historian who took the lead in trying to show, through the deep probing of documents, how detailed, empirical, extended scholarship could contribute to what he considered reform was Robinson's Columbia colleague Charles A. Beard. Like Turner a son of the Midwest, Beard became the leading figure and the most publicly known of the new generation of historians, those usually termed "progressive historians" after the Progressive political era in which they arrived on the scene. The Beardians, as Beard's intellectual followers came to be called, emphasized people's and groups' distinct material interests. Although often tarred for being Marxist, Beard's kind of materialism was rather a domestic, softer "Marxian" variety of socialist thought than found among more rigidly ideological continental thinkers and reformers; it was democratic socialism in the mode of American socialist Eugene V. Debs and the English artist and reformer John Ruskin rather than the harder socialism of Karl Marx and Friedrich Engels. Like many soft- and anti-Marxists since the nineteenth century, Beard admired the intellectual ambitions of the German theorists—their determination to plot the causes and consequences of class relations—even while disdaining Marxist politics. Like so many others, the Columbia historian—whose great 1913 work of revisionist history *An Economic Interpretation of the Constitution of the United States* I take up in Chapter 3—was deeply troubled by the maldistribution of American wealth, the economic power of the Robber Barons, and the excesses of industry and capitalism. He was also a backer of such Progressive aims as an income tax, women's suffrage, the prohibition of child labor, the breakup of the great corporate monopolies, legal protection for labor unions, federal controls of banks, and a social insurance system. He came by his emphasis on people's material interests by temperament, not ideology, by close-up experiences with the ills of industrialism and the burdens of laboring people. Thus not surprisingly, as both engaged reformer and historian, he broke with earlier generations of scholars in his criticism of Rhodes's acceptance of big business and Turner's emphasis on the strength and importance of individualism. Beard's history also diverged sharply from Turner's focus on the agricultural frontier and geopolitical, sectional forces. It announced the arrival of urban-oriented, politically consequential, avowedly critical, and iconoclastic academic history.

Beard's kind of historical interpretation achieved its maturity in his two-volume *The Rise of American Civilization*. Published in 1927 and written with his wife, Mary Ritter Beard, this widely read, influential work announced yet another way to interpret the Civil War's origins. The war, the Beards wrote, had been "the Second American Revolution," which rearranged the relations of classes and the ownership of wealth in the United States.[2] "A social cataclysm in which the capitalists, laborers, and farmers of the North and West drove from power in the national government the planting aristocracy of the South," the Civil War was the result of the struggle between two different economies for political power, each characterized by different interest groups and social classes, one section founded on plantation agriculture and chattel slavery, the other on industrial capitalism and what the Beards, borrowing from earlier labor conflict usage, called "wage slavery," both economic systems defective to the core. In this interpretation, slavery disappeared as both the cause of war and as an independent moral issue, its existence instead but a single element in the South's multidimensional economy rather than basic to an entire regional culture.

2. The Beards deplored the results of this revolution. More orthodox Marxists (of whom there was but a handful in American historians' circles) were more likely to welcome it. While, in the view of the latter, the Civil War represented a mere bourgeois revolution, such a revolution nevertheless paved the way for the next revolution, one that would usher in the dictatorship of the proletariat. In the long sweep of the history of history in the United States, the comparative popularity of the Beardian democratic socialist approach, contrasted to the cool reception of the more orthodox Marxian interpretation, says much about the traction of radical historical interpretations on American soil.

Secession, in the Beards' view, resulted from the desperation of one class, the southern planters, faced with the growing power of another class in the North that was pushing for such gains as a protective tariff on industrial and agricultural products, subsidies to nonplantation agriculture, slave-free national territories, the opening of these territories to homesteading, and federal backing for railroads. The Civil War, the Beards wrote, resulted from irreconcilable differences between different economic systems lodged in different sections. For that reason, it was, as James Ford Rhodes had earlier argued on different grounds, an "irrepressible conflict."

By picturing the North as a section determined to gain the protection of its material advantages—industry, transportation, and shipping—rather than as the locus of strong moral concerns and by focusing as relentlessly as it did on economic issues in general, the Beards' presentation of Civil War–causing factors had the ironic effect of making the two historians seem sympathetic to the South. Their early-twentieth-century antipathy to northern capitalism because of its excesses led them to read the results of the Civil War—the unleashing of those northern forces—back into its origins. Irrepressible it may have been in their eyes, but the war, they implied, even with its destruction of slavery, had entailed costs—industrial capitalism, extremes of wealth, financial corruption, and the like—that were too high to have run. Had not Jefferson Davis and other southerners argued that it was northern capitalists who were fueling the sectional conflict? Had they not scoffed at the notion that slavery was the real engine behind northern opposition to southern aims? Had they not in fact predicted precisely the outcome of a war that the Beards now so bitingly assailed? Here seemed to be progressive socialism coming to the rescue of the reactionary Confederacy.

In one of the countless ironies that litter the terrain of historical interpretation as much as that of historical events themselves, the Beards' criticism of industrial capitalism, if not of plantation slavery, found an echo, shorn of their soft Marxism, south of the Mason-Dixon Line among their ideological opposites—a group of literary figures and historians centered at Vanderbilt University known since then as both the Nashville Fugitives and the Southern Agrarians. Like the Beards but from the other end of the political spectrum, these modern-day intellectuals deplored the results of capitalistic and urban civilization and sought the revival of what they thought of as an age of stable subsistence agriculture and genteel ways in the old slave South. In the Fugitives' celebrated 1930 manifesto, *I'll Take My Stand,* historian Frank L. Owsley dismissed slavery as a primary cause of civil war and, like the Beards, attributed the conflict to ruthless northern pressure on the South.

To an observer of this melding of otherwise antagonistic interpretive schemes, it might seem that a reconciliation of historians had grown from the early-twentieth-century reconciliation of North and South into a kind of comfortable racism, typified by the segregation of the federal government under southerner president Woodrow Wilson. But more was as stake, even if at this point readers can be forgiven for scratching their heads. Was it really the case that, sixty-two years after Appomattox, historians had done nothing but revert to a proto-Confederate position? Could it be that American democratic socialism was now dressed up in John C. Calhoun drag? What were historians up to, one might be forgiven for asking, that they had not advanced much farther than the antagonists of the 1860s? And—this a question fundamental to an understanding of interpretive revisions of the historical record—are we to expect historical thought to give us nothing but an endless succession of irreconcilable, presentist views of the past? Is no progress in historical understanding possible? Do historians simply go around in wearying circles?[3]

These are legitimate questions, ones with which historians themselves grapple. What is most important to recognize is that interpretive schemes originating in strikingly different impulses and aims—the Beards' forward-looking intention of taming the consequences of industrial capitalism through fresh reform, the Fugitives' backward-looking aim of restoring a measure of the South's supposed agrarian gentility—can sometimes end up in an apparently identical place. Revisions can therefore seem sometimes to bring us to an intellectual coincidence of views. But when looked at closely, each of these distinct interpretations differed in its essence. The Beards' history was out-and-

---

3. This question brings to mind the old cynical saying that history doesn't repeat itself; only historians do.

out modernist, an embrace of government intervention in the economy to correct the excesses of industrial and banking Robber Barons run amok. By contrast, the Fugitives' history was a nostalgic effort to re-capture a southern civilization that existed, to the degree it did, in the gracious ways of plantation owners who had kept government at arm's length and controlled the lives of their black slaves. Which version of the past one chose determined which version of the present one adopted, and vice versa. And those pasts and presents were starkly different.

Thus what Robinson's "new history" had heralded was really no more than a public acknowledgment of a basic reality of all historical thought—that all progress in historical understanding owes something to historians' own circumstances: to the courses of their lives, their positions in society, and the bents of their individual minds. To some extent therefore, we have to give in to the fact that all history serves the present. But that proposition, however valid, is of only modest help in understanding particular revisions to the historical record. Because history is read and understood in the present does not mean that there is no progress in historical understanding. Nor does it mean that his-torians owe no responsibility to the realities of the past as best they can unearth and analyze them. The Beards' way of looking at the origins of the Civil War may appear to be nothing but the closing of a circle, in this case the return in different words to Confederate justifications of the conflict. But it was far more than that. To those who looked deeply into their arguments, Charles and Mary Beard had opened an entirely new field of inquiry—that of the political economy of North and South, of industry and slavery, on the eve of the Civil War. Never again would understanding of the causes of the war be the same. Never again could historians seek to explain the origins of the Civil War without recourse to knowledge of the role of capital, industry, transportation, agriculture, and labor systems in bringing on the conflict—an approach that has risen to new prominence in the twenty-first century. The Beards' way of looking at the war, tucked into their larger history of the United States, could never be ignored.

That must be seen as an interpretive gain. But the same could not be said of what the Beards' approach meant for an understanding of the moral elements of the Civil War. Starting with Turner's frontier thesis, the battle over the moral grounds of the war had begun to take a back seat to newer emphases of academic scholarship. Into that seat had also settled the old chestnut questions of which section had been responsible for the war and whether war between the sections had been irrepressible. Ironically, the fairness and balance that James Ford Rhodes and others had introduced into postwar historiography had, by the outbreak of World War I in 1914, come at a cost to moral consideration. That reality, unfortunate as it may have been, illustrates another dimension of historical inquiry—one critical to understanding the nature of alterations in interpretive approaches to the past. A division among historians as to whether their role is to be "objective" or to advance moral understanding, if those two emphases can ever be distinguished, makes a profound difference.

It is here that Turner's kind of multidimensional history, itself the product of the maturation of this first American generation of academic historians, intersected with another academic development that had analogous consequences. This was the gradual displacement of narrative history by specialized monographic history. The seeds of this development arose first in the early nineteenth century and most assertively in the German universities that were pioneering what became professional academic historical studies. Until then, almost all historians—whether in Europe or in the United States—had been men and a few women of letters who wrote to edify and to promote specific political or national ideals while narrating what had occurred in the past. But the emergence to prominence of university faculty members brought that literary, storytelling approach under sharp review. These early academic historians sought to determine, under the spur of scientific inquiry and on the basis of the critical use of written sources, what had happened and why it had done so without regard (or so they thought) to political or national convictions in contrast to the narrative historians, heirs to a long tradition of historical belles lettres. The emblematic figure in this development was the German historian Leopold von Ranke, who tried, and who taught his students at the University of Berlin to try, to establish how the past had "essentially" happened. This aim quickly became one of the most enduringly charged and debated goals of historians who followed Ranke.[4]

In a typical instance of the kind of creative misunderstandings between European and American thinkers and artists that have marked the centuries, American historians misread Ranke's idealistic, Romantic aspiration for history in a way that comported with their Anglo-American, empirical approach to most things. Since then, Ranke's admonition has conventionally been translated into English as prodding historians to discover the past "as it actually happened" rather than "as it essentially happened." For this reason, historians in the United States and many elsewhere followed Ranke's focus on the evidence stored in archives—"on the reports of eyewitnesses, and on the most authentic, most immediate sources"—with the hope of approaching a kind of objective science-like history of political, institutional, and diplomatic affairs. These historians' dominant purpose became to determine what had actually occurred—as if both the search and the thinking that necessarily goes into that determination can be free of cultural, social, individual, and other influences. Their dominant method was the use of original sources, especially written ones (whether in manuscript or print), to figure out what had taken place in earlier times—as if written sources accurately reflect occurrences, are factually correct, and tell the whole story. And their dominant form was the monograph, a deeply researched, detailed, footnoted examination of a limited segment of past reality that could serve as a building block of later broader coverage of major developments.

Monographic history soon became the defining characteristic of academic history, one from which decisive gains in historical knowledge have followed. Contrasted to a multivolume history of a large event like the Civil War often written by a wealthy man, a monograph was a manageable project that a researcher, whether graduate student or experienced scholar, could complete in a reasonable amount of time. It was

4. Ranke must serve as a stand-in for a disparate group of figures, many of them German, who contributed to the "science" of history in the eighteenth and nineteenth centuries. Perhaps the greatest of these was Barthold Georg Niebuhr, a historian of Rome deeply admired by Ranke and a pioneer of Western historiography who greatly advanced the critical evaluation of historical sources for accuracy and authenticity.

also a means appropriate to acculturate aspiring historians into scholarly methods and into the presentation of new historical knowledge in what became conventional scholarly form—direct, unvarnished prose and assertions supported by footnoted citations to original sources that could be checked and their contents confirmed by other historians. In such monographs one could see historians adopting the format and other features of the published results of scientific experiments, those that offer up the methods and findings of research to replication or falsification by other scientists. A major consequence of the monograph was that in the confined borders of their subject matter and in their aim of digging as deeply as possible into a subject, historians (at least those early in their careers) increasingly put behind themselves the effort to portray larger, sweeping events. More historical writing now became what its critics, not always accurately, have charged it with being—bland, denatured, and without the moral depth and taught lessons that it had once possessed. That did not mean that monographs were necessarily devoid of moral content, argument, or implication. But historians trained under this new dispensation in the early twentieth century did not think of themselves as moralists or storytellers; they thought of themselves as truth seekers—as those who unearthed the realities of the past, in Rankean terms, "as it actually happened." In that new spirit yet another generation of historians approached the origins of the Civil War.

∾

This new generation's members came from every part of the United States. But the group that made the most significant contribution to this newer history of the Civil War's causes was composed of men born south of the Mason-Dixon Line, educated in the North (where most history graduate instruction was still centered), and most of them subsequently resident in the South, where they spent their academic careers. The largest subset of them was prepared by William A. Dunning, like James Harvey Robinson and Charles Beard a Columbia University historian. Not surprisingly, as with the works, first, of northerners Schouler and Rhodes, then of midwesterner Turner, these Dunning-schooled southerners' histories reflected much of the traditional historical views of the section of which their authors were natives. But unlike historians of the pre–Civil War South from other regions, this new generation of historians bore the burden of dealing with their section's historical attitude toward slavery and African Americans, as well as its always distinctive positions—political, economic, and cultural—in relation to the rest of the nation. Accordingly, following the lead taken by Turner and Beard, they sought explanations of the Civil War's origins that discounted the existence of deep-rooted sectional differences over the morality of slavery. In addition, they were members of a generation of Americans who accepted a reconciliationist version of the nation's Civil War history in which northerners and southerners were taken to have been equally valiant in defense of their cherished beliefs. This version of the past partook of a national mood that saluted the Klan-glorifying film *The Birth of a Nation;* sighed over *Gone With the Wind* and its movie adaptation, in which northerners were portrayed as carpetbaggers, rapists, and beasts unfit to introduce new norms into southern society; and went so far as to blame African Americans for causing the Civil War.

Yet even if this group of southern historians of the South shared in a general North-South downplaying of slavery as an important, to say nothing of the single most important, cause of the Civil War, their scholarly contributions were offered in particularly southern terms. Whether, as many did, they produced histories of individual southern states in the prewar South or wrote about slavery itself, their southern apologetics were unmistakable. The best known of these historians, Ulrich B. Phillips, was a son of Georgia who, unusual among them, spent his professional career at northern universities—first Wisconsin, then Michigan, finally Yale. In his most influential works, *American Negro Slavery* (1918) and *Life and Labor in the Old South* (1929), Phillips constructed a history of the plantation South whose axiomatic proposition was the physical differences between whites and blacks and all that resulted from those differences. Phillips depicted African Americans as members of a "savage," dependent "race" for whom slavery was a school that transformed their "ignorant and slothful labor" into "a certain fitness for life in the Anglo-Saxon community." Even while conceding that the South's economic system and climatic conditions helped explain its distinctiveness, he returned again and again to the conviction that at the core of the antebellum (and, by extension, the postbellum) South was white residents' determination to preserve it as a "white man's country."

Moreover, argued Phillips in a reprise of Confederate justifications for the Civil War, it was the aggressive North, especially its fanatical anti-slavery elements, not the South of the "fire-eaters," that had caused the conflict. But for the abolitionists' efforts to end the peculiar institution, whose slaves had been civilized by the South, chattel slavery would no doubt have ended sometime in the future without the staggering costs of armed conflict.

By focusing their attention on the war itself rather than on slavery and the slaves, many southern historians who followed Phillips's neo-Confederate lead took his arguments about responsibility for the war even further. Being unnecessary (as, for instance, the journalist and amateur historian George Fort Milton argued), the war's responsibility fell on the North's and Lincoln's shoulders, the president having maneuvered both sections into an avoidable confrontation at Fort Sumter. The preservation of the Union had not been worth the bloodshed and the social chaos of the slave manumissions that had ensued. In this view, in an inversion of earlier Unionist historiography, the extremist North bore guilt for the war, the financial corruption and plutocratic boodling that followed it, and the triumph of harsh industrial capitalism over gracious agrarian civilization. It was no accident that, after the gruesome massacres on the western European front during the First World War, many Americans would see the peaceful solution of any conflict, even at the sacrifice of the welfare of an entire segment of the American population, as preferable to war. In this view, the Civil War was increasingly seen as "needless," "a repressible conflict," those who led the nation into it viewed, in the words of the foremost champion of this view, James G. Randall, as a "blundering generation." "Lincoln's generation stumbled into a ghastly war," Randall wrote in 1940. "If one word or phrase were selected to account for the war, that word would not be slavery, or state-rights, or diverse civilizations. It would have to be such a word as fanaticism (on both sides), or misunderstanding, or perhaps politics." A more thorough repudiation of the nationalist approach of Rhodes and others is hard to imagine.

Yet it would be a major error, as it always is regarding serious efforts at historical interpretation—especially if, as in the works of these historians of the South, these efforts are now seen by historians as un-

balanced and prejudiced—to dismiss such revisions of understanding of
the past simply because they are repugnant. By many measures, Dunning's and Phillips's students and those influenced by them produced
pathbreaking histories of many dimensions of southern history. By
using sources never before examined, establishing unparalleled collections of southern manuscripts and records, and turning their attention
to a core subject of American history—the South—too little examined
previously, they laid the foundations of all subsequent histories of their
section and its slaveholding and racist past. And while their arguments
may have been less nuanced and more direct than the work of northern
historians of the same set of subjects, it was not as if their arguments
were met with quick and universal condemnation. Quite the contrary:
even if northerners reflexively rejected these historians' argument of
northern war guilt, many shared the genteel conservatism and racism
of the southern scholars. If some northerners disdained the argument
that the Civil War had made the South nothing but an economic colony
of northern business interests, they, no less than southern historians,
disliked the crass individualism, labor unrest, foreign immigration, and
African American restiveness that characterized the nation after the
First World War. Neo-Confederate historiography was nicely congruent with the yearning for a reconciliation of the sections, for social stability, and for an accord between "races" and ethnic groups that many
historians mistakenly thought had characterized earlier times. That is,
the revisionist histories of the causes of the Civil War that came from the
pens of pre-1950 southern historians were by no means out of keeping
with the general conservative intellectual mood of much of the country.

But more than this, and equally important to bear in mind, these
southerners' interpretations opened the door to the pursuit of new research and the posing of new questions by historians to whom their interpretations were anathema. Was slavery an economically fragile institution
destined to wither away without a war? Had not the slaves themselves fash-
ioned their own lives and culture under slavery? As was to become gradually clear after the close of World War II, the answers to such questions
became newly urgent precisely because of the appearance of southern
revisionism in the 1930s. It may be that advances in the understanding
of slavery and the origins of the Civil War that emerged starting in the

1950s would have come about without the challenge of southern historians' arguments. Surely the reemergence into white Americans' view
during the Depression of the plight of African Americans, north and
south, as well as blacks' growing assertiveness in consequence of their
contributions to the Second World War at home and on the battlefields,
would eventually have raised many questions about neo-Confederate
historiography. But there can be little doubt that the pursuit of answers
to the questions their studies evoked and the creation of a new, national,
authoritative consensus around the causes of the great conflict were
greatly accelerated by the confrontational views of members of the Dunning School.

    We should thus see all historical thought, revisionist and oth-
erwise, as potentially provocative. By their very nature, new written
histories incite historians to further thought and new scholarship, to
oppositional argument, and to the kind of debates that often, if not
always, end up as new understanding widely agreed on. So while individual historians may take offense at one or another interpretive
scheme, and while those who offer new and distinctive interpretations
of the past sometimes overstate their cases in order to bring their arguments to the fore, it is one of the strengths of an open society that all
historians remain free to combat others' arguments and offer alternative
perspectives that may stand the test of time under the rigors of professional evaluation. Such is now the size and diversity of the community
of historians and such the variety of outlets for the assessment of their
work that evaluation of every historian's scholarship is likely to prompt
further historical thought and research. It is this dimension of fresh
approaches to the past—their capacity to provoke historians and others
to additional thought and to generate additional knowledge—that is
the principal grounds for celebrating the role of revisionist thinking in
historians' work. That is surely the case regarding what followed World
War II when scholars continued their quest to understand the origins of
the Civil War.

                                  ∾

Ulrich Phillips and the members of the Dunning School of southern
historians could not have known when they wrote their histories of the
Civil War of the fresh horrors that would ensue after the outbreak of

renewed European conflict in 1939. The formation of their views about
the Civil War's origins, developed in the 1920s and 1930s after the massive losses of the Great War, owed nothing to the future world conflict.
But their younger colleagues, such as James G. Randall and Avery O. Craven
and two still younger northerners Roy F. Nichols and Kenneth M. Stampp,
could not ignore the Second World War's enveloping mood when they
came on the professional scene.[5] In the years immediately after 1945,
their views closely mirrored those of their older colleagues like Phillips.
These younger scholars were above all professional historians—people
driven by imperatives internal to their discipline as much as by sectional
or other associations. Because since Turner's day professional historians had slowly been reading slavery out of the story of the Civil War's
causation in favor of other factors—sectional tensions, industrial capitalism's growth, hyperemotional war fever in the North and South—it
would be too much to expect many of them to break out of this interpretive confinement without the spur of new circumstances, professional
as well as cultural.[6] While it is wise, as historian E. H. Carr urged, "to
study the historian before you begin to study the facts," that ought never
be all that someone interested in the past should do. Those inclined to
dismiss historical interpretations simply because they can be attributed
to certain biographical realities—that one historian is a southerner,
another a child of the Midwest, one old, another younger—fail to acknowledge that the discipline of history is an independent intellectual
domain most of whose practitioners' scholarly works are directed at
testing and refining existing interpretations of a distinct subject and not
mere reflections of biographical, historical, cultural, or social circumstances. Consequently, historians working within usually stable research
paradigms rarely take giant steps away from reigning interpretations—
in this case those of Phillips and the Dunning School—and surely not
when exhaustion with war is as widespread as it was after 1945. At the

5. Curiously, in this debate Randall and Craven were termed "the revisionists," as if they
were the first historians to take issue with their predecessors' interpretations and as if earlier
revisions in Civil War historiography had never before taken place. In the long history of
revisionist history, such terminology often obscures reality rather than clarifying it.

6. Although some managed to do so in the footsteps of African American historians Carter G. Woodson and W. E. B. Du Bois.

time, it was hard to imagine anyone favoring any war, even one in which the profound moral issue of slavery had been at stake. Despair about the horrors of modern battlefields and civilian casualties fit nicely with Phillips's and his contemporaries' convictions that the Civil War had been a needless war, its principal gain, the eradication of slavery, not worth the cost in lives and treasure. Or perhaps it was the other way around—that having been sensitized earlier to the "useless war" views of their fellow historians of the Civil War and having lived to learn the costs of modern conflict, many historians after 1945 were inclined to condemn all war. Accordingly, their conviction that the Civil War had been a "repressible conflict" (the title of one of Craven's books) comported well with a general disillusionment with the horrors of the recent worldwide disaster—the Holocaust, the bombing of German and Japanese civilians, and the destruction of Japanese cities by nuclear weaponry. A general suspicion of all fanaticism—including that of the abolitionists, of the fire-eating emotionalism of southern demagogues, of John Brown, who welcomed the shedding of blood for the eradication of slavery—was in the air.

Furthermore, an emphasis on the psychopathology of radicals on both sides of the Mason-Dixon Line was congruent with a widening public interest in human psychology generally. Historians like David H. Donald, Don E. Fehrenbacher, and David M. Potter reflected this interest in their focus on the mental states and psychodynamics of individuals and whole populations in the antebellum North and South. In their view, had the radical passions aroused on the eve of the Civil War been banked, negotiations leading to compromise over slavery and states' rights would have won out and a tragic conflict have been avoided. The problem with this view, of course, was that it embodied an acceptance of slavery, at least until it somehow withered away. It left the slaves to bear the continuation of their bondage—much as the Jews and millions of others in eastern Europe had been left to their fates after 1933 under Nazism and Soviet totalitarianism.

But this time, historians like Randall, Craven, Nichols, and Stampp, who had been disposed to exile slavery, antislavery, and the slaves from pre–Civil War historiography, were to be confronted by three realities not contemplated by their interpretive schemes. The first was the postwar reckoning with Nazism. The second was the enrollment in academic careers, largely through support of the G.I. Bill of Rights, of a generation of returning servicemen and women who were not likely to accept the view that they had been fighting a needless war. The third reality, not unrelated to the other two, was the coming of age of a generation of African Americans who, beneficiaries both of the pre-1941 reawakening of black culture in northern cities and of their own wartime experiences, would no longer accept the omission of African Americans from the history of the Civil War or, for that matter, from American history and life generally.

In addition, as we look back on the post–World War II years, we can see a number of historiographic forces combining to create the foundation of a new era in Civil War interpretation, one that left the older one in tatters and constituted a major conceptual revision in Civil War historiography. In the first place, monographic history—detailed research into specific, comparatively limited subjects of inquiry—had reached a level of incontestable maturity. When applied to such matters as pre–Civil War politics, abolitionism, the economic viability of slavery, and the decision for war, the consequences of monographic history, much of it written by younger historians, many of them returning war veterans not easily taken in by conventional ways of thinking, were transformative.

Second, and in large part a result of the monographic histories produced by a younger generation of historians, the historiography of the antebellum South was itself transformed. A young and more diverse cohort of scholars, now including women, African Americans, Catholics, and Jews as well as white Protestant males, once and for all cast off the magnolia and peach blossom pieties about the old South to excavate the history of a more complex, vital, and unstable society below the Mason-Dixon Line. The greatest of this new generation of black historians was John Hope Franklin. Franklin built on the earlier researches of African Americans like Carter G. Woodson (in the 1920s) and W. E. B. Du Bois (in the 1930s), as well as of white scholars, to depict the races in the South as thoroughly intertwined, the slaves as active shapers of their own lives despite the chains that bound them, and tobacco and cotton culture as economically unstable. Franklin's classic *From Slavery to Freedom,* first published in 1947 and frequently revised until the author's death in 2009, gave a signal of sorts to countless historians to feel free to pursue their own inquiries into southern history. Consequently, the history of the South, the black as well as white South, would never be the same.

The history of slavery also underwent a profound transformation. With the expansion of American higher education, an increasing number of historians who were not white males joined academic faculties and began to pursue a set of issues already embodied in the historical literature but never previously the focus of careful and deep inquiry. In addition, influenced by the agitation for civil rights and against the Cold War and the Vietnam War in the 1960s and 1970s, historians took a new look at the actual lives of African Americans under slavery and at the antislavery and abolitionist forces previously viewed as excessively emotional and irrationally radical. Yet although Woodson, Du Bois, and Franklin had led the way in bringing fresh scholarly attention to these subjects through their pathbreaking histories of African Americans, it was Kenneth M. Stampp, an earlier doubter of the utility and value of warfare, who broke most decisively and effectively with the older Phillips mold and ushered in a new history of slavery. His classic 1956 work, *The Peculiar Institution: Slavery in the Ante-Bellum South,* to wide agreement put an end to southern apologists' interpretations of slavery as benign and beneficial to the enslaved. Yet to illustrate how favoritism and prejudice can play a role in the fate of historical interpretations, it is necessary to note here that into the 1950s, because the works of Woodson, Du Bois, and Franklin had largely been dismissed in professional historical circles due to the racism and segregation of academic faculties, it required a white scholar to lead historians' break in ranks with hidebound thinking before the historiography of slavery and of African Americans generally made a decisive shift onto new ground earlier tilled by African American scholars. Even though Woodson, Du Bois, and Franklin had insisted on the enduring, scarring costs that slaves, free blacks, and post–Civil War freed people had paid for centuries of bound servitude, historians had failed to credit their evidence and arguments until Stampp forced the issue. Once, however, he had put a spike in the southern apologists' stance, his book was followed by such additional important works as John W. Blassingame's 1972 *The Slave Community: Plantation Life in the Ante-Bellum South,* Eugene D. Genovese's 1974 *Roll, Jordan, Roll: The*

World the Slaves Made, and, in the same year, Ira Berlin's *Slaves With-out Masters: The Free Negro in the Antebellum South,* all three of which exposed the strength of African American culture under slavery. One result of such additional works was that the earlier, usually overlooked studies of Woodson, Du Bois, and Franklin gained new traction among scholars and drew equal in esteem with Stampp's important work. All of them, as well as many others, cinched the case that, despite the restraints that withheld freedom and opportunity from African Americans, both slave and free, before the Civil War, these people were agents on their own behalf who succeeded in building their lives and communities as best they could.

But the book that best illustrates the critical impact of fresh ap-proaches to old subjects was Robert W. Fogel and Stanley L. Engerman's 1974 bombshell *Time on the Cross: The Economics of American Negro Slav-ery.* It argued, on the basis of econometric theory and statistical evidence, that American slavery—the main source of southern wealth as well as a system of human bondage and race control—was, when put up against other slave systems, a comparatively benign form of labor, a viable sys-tem of economic production, and on the whole profitable for the south-ern states. It is easy enough to imagine why such an argument would cause an outcry, even though the authors clearly stated and maintained their abhorrence of bond servitude. Slavery a system of production rational in economic terms? Southern slaveholders smart enough to understand correctly their economic interests? The economic value of slave labor measurable in the same terms as free labor? Slavery possibly less onerous than previously thought, especially in contrast with slavery elsewhere in the New World? Using aggregate data and econometric methods to measure an immoral institution? The book's contents and claims imme-diately roiled the community of historians of the South and of slavery; and the authors' arguments, subjected to sometimes brutal attack, sus-tained damage severe enough to render their work historiographically something of a dead end.

Yet in the decades since their book's publication, the questions they opened to investigation have never lost their salience, even if few historians of the Civil War and the American South now feel a debt to *Time on the Cross.* The American South and coerced racial slave labor are now seen as a dynamic capitalist society, not the static anticapitalist culture that Genovese envisaged. Historians now agree that, due to its antebellum expansion into the Southwest as well as to the growth of sugar culture, slavery was stronger and the price of slaves higher in 1860 than had been the case. As recent historians like Walter Johnson (in *River of Dark Dreams: Slavery and Empire in the Cotton Kingdom* of 2013), Edward E. Baptist (in his 2014 *The Half Has Never Been Told: Slavery and the Making of American Capitalism*), Sven Beckert (in *Empire of Cotton: A Global History* of the same year), and Wendy Warren (in her 2016 *New England Bound: Slavery and Colonization in Early America*) have argued, slaveholders and slave traders proved themselves through their use of coercion to be every bit the income-seeking capital-savvy equals of their northern free-labor, commercial, industrial counterparts: up-to-date capitalists enmeshed in international commercial markets, entrepreneurs of staple crop production, and experts skilled in the efficient exploitation of enslaved laborers. If confirmation of the economic value of slaves is needed, we need look only at the evaporation after the Civil War of billions of dollars of southern capital sunk into the ownership of slaves who had been freed. But more than this, these historians have argued, slavery had undergirded and dominated the entire prewar American economy, and slaveholders had directed American foreign policy for much of the nineteenth century. Consequently, even if slaveholders sought their profits within an international capitalist system without fully adopting capitalistic ways (in the terms laid down by Genovese and others), their exploitation of bound labor was critical to the expanding strength of the United States. If they had been alive to read these works, Charles and Mary Beard would have claimed vindication of their earlier, less fully developed views.

All of this said, in one of the ironic turns with which the history of history is littered, the capitalism-centered interpretation of these recent historians strengthened the case for a moral interpretation of the Civil War, one offered only intermittently in earlier decades. The chief exponent of this renewed line of reasoning was Princeton historian James M. McPherson. In his influential *Battle Cry of Freedom: The Civil War Era*, published in 1988, McPherson bore down on the conflict of the 1860s as a great moral struggle between North and South, a struggle undergirded by their opposing social systems and ideologies. Placed in context with the works of Baptist, Beckert, Johnson, and Warren, McPherson's grand moral rendering of the war can now nestle comfortably with neo-Marxist interpretations in a kind of truce in the long struggle among historians to close the gaps between them.

Moreover, once we consider the implications for historical understanding of such unorthodox arguments as those of Fogel and Engerman, we see again how permeating of historical understanding even sharp challenges to what has become conventional historical thinking can prove to be. For instance, if, as Fogel and Engerman averred, plantation slavery made economic sense, then how, without a war, could that system have been eradicated?[7] Their argument once again made the Civil War seem to be a "necessary," "irrepressible" conflict—a position first enunciated by James Ford Rhodes, resuscitated in new form by the Beards, and sustained by Allan Nevins in 1947, when the first segment of his multivolume history of the origins and prosecution of the Civil War (under the general title of *The Ordeal of the Union*) appeared. If slaveholders were economically rational in their assessment of slavery's profitability and if, as neo-Marxist Eugene Genovese would long argue, they held to their position as paternalistic leaders of a social class whose power was rooted as much in their social and cultural position as in their economic strength, then might not slavery, as Lincoln's Republican Party so feared, have spread elsewhere in the United States, especially into those areas where large-scale monoculture could prosper, as eventually it did in lands as far distant as the Imperial Valley of California, Cuba, and Brazil? Might slavery not have adapted itself even to urban industries, as it already had done in the pre–Civil War iron industry of Richmond? If so, why not also in other industries, such as mining? And if slavery was so profitable in the existing United States, was it not ratio-

7. As if in proof that no historical interpretation goes long without challenge, the recent works by Baptist, Beckert, Johnson, and Warren quickly have come under strong attack from some economic historians who, working from the evaluation of aggregated data culled from manuscript sources roughly similar to those used by the others, have challenged the assertions of the less data-driven histories of Baptist and others. How divergent interpretations drawn from the same materials but exploited differently by historians of different skills and methods can drive historical controversies is here perfectly illustrated. How soon and on what grounds this particular battle will be resolved remains to be seen.

nal, as many antebellum southerners had sought, for the United States to try to secure more territory beyond the nation's borders so as to profit further? In other words, after Fogel and Engerman's work appeared, it was again possible to argue that a genuine and economically strong Slave Power—that is, the southern slave states united politically around the maintenance of bond servitude and its expansion beyond southern borders and agriculture—had actually existed and that northerners had not been delusional in thinking so. It could also again be argued, as it had not been argued for decades, that the abolitionists, rather than being over-emotional haters of the South, had been onto something: their radicalism and their calls for armed force had been both rational and justifiable, given the grounds on which slaveholders defended themselves.

Much of this new history of the South and of slavery developed within the larger post-1945 debate in many intellectual disciplines about modernization—the process by which societies make the transition from small-scale agriculture using one or more forms of bound labor (serfs, slaves, and tenants) to urban industrial means of production using wage labor, a long process accompanied by changes in ideas and culture as well as in the means of production.[8] Shorn (although never fully) of its connotation of progress, modernization theory provided a fresh way of measuring and comparing the differing cultures, labor systems, and market orientations of the North and South before the Civil War. In this context, there arose over a half century's time yet more ways of understanding what might have caused the armed conflict between the two sections. Genovese saw the South as an old-fashioned, neofeudal paternalistic culture built around the social authority of slaveholders holding out against modernizing free-soil interests, commercial agriculture, and urban industry in the North. Marc Egnal offered a neo-Beardian approach that put economic forces, not slavery, at the center of the Civil War's causes. In congruent studies, Bertram Wyatt-Brown and others portrayed the South as bound to the ethical tenets of personal, patriarchal, family, and sectional honor threatened by abolitionism. Other historians depicted the North as the more advanced economy and

8. The debate over modernization was distinct from controversies over modernism in literature, art, music, and culture generally.

culture, whose commercialism, free-soil agriculture, and free labor were
the aggressive forces that gave the South no option but to defend itself
with arms. It was also argued that southerners, their vast store of capital locked in land and slaves and thus comparatively illiquid compared
with northern wealth, were prepared to shift their assets into industry
and nonagricultural commerce when that made economic sense, as it
could have should slavery have begun to prove fully adaptable to urban
manufacturing. Perhaps, after all, the Confederacy's society was not premodern—neither standing still nor standing in the way of the North's
vital modernizing system. Historians also discovered, when they applied
various measures of modernization to North and South, that neither
section was holding on to old ways or changing to new ones without
economic tensions within each section, tensions that would play out
on the road to civil war, affect fighting and politics during the war, and
lead to major changes after the war. All of this greatly challenged some
historians' conclusions that North and South were two distinct civilizations, one modern, the other premodern. Instead, went this argument,
both sections, differently commercial and capitalistic, were vying for
victory on Civil War battlefields after having each ventured, in its own
way, down different paths of economic development.

If, as it appears, historians are still not in full agreement about
such a critically important issue as the causes of the Civil War more
than 150 years after the first shot at Fort Sumter was fired (although
most would now put the issue of slavery's continuance and spread at the
center of their explanations), how can anyone else be? Some perplexity
is understandable. But there can be no doubt that the results of these
various recent approaches to the origins of the Civil War, as divergent
as they have been, have had two enduring consequences for the history
of the subject. First, and quite simply, they have revolutionized understanding of slavery and the South, neither of which will ever return to
the characterization of them embodied in the interpretive schemes that
existed before 1945. In the opening decades of the twenty-first century,
by wide agreement slavery is understood to have been an ever-changing,
expanding institution in a diverse, itself-changing section of the nation,
an institution that, by means of the three-fifths clause and the equal
apportionment of Senate seats, had effectively held the nation's politics

in its grip for seventy years after 1789. It was an institution that varied in different parts of the South, a tinderbox always ready to explode from slave resentment, a system based on coercion, functioning only because of the hegemonic violence of the slaveholders and the quietism of enough slaves who nevertheless somehow maintained their own agency, integrity, and dignity—yet not entirely without a sound economic basis on slaveholders' terms. Consequently, the conviction that slavery was in fact the fundamental cause of the Civil War—the South defending it, the North determined to halt its spread—is now the almost universally held view among historians, even as they admit onto the list of the war's causes many other, less fundamental immediate triggers of the conflict.

Second, this interpretive stew reveals how historians struggle to get to the root of things, how difficult it is to do so, and therefore why it is essential that, by differing on matters large and small and by thinking their way through questions not earlier asked and discrepancies in evidence and argument not yet encountered, historians are always taking issue with one another, offering revisions of previous interpretations, and never flinching from coming at their subjects freshly and fearlessly. That is their intellectual world.

∾

Does this mean that we must anticipate an endless succession of changing interpretations of the causes of the Civil War and of every other historical subject and that a resolution of interpretive differences should be assumed to be inconceivable and unachievable?

The answer to this question, one likely to trouble some people, is "Probably." It is not because some historians think that there is nothing better than to go over and over the same ground. Instead, a full resolution of all interpretive differences, especially of major issues, is probably outside the boundaries of what can be achieved. It is in the nature of human thought to be imperfect and incomplete; of human beings to be argumentative and widely diverse in thought and disposition; and of most knowledge to be provisional. It is natural to flinch at this thought, and all historians themselves harbor at least a modest hope that the interpretations they accept—that, indeed, the interpretations that they may have had a hand in constructing in the first place and seen widely accepted—are final, authoritative, certain, unassailable, and likely to endure forever. But that, too, is an illusion, for it overlooks the diversity of minds, temperaments, and interests that exist among historians as among everyone else. Some people are drawn by personality to the constant and unchanging, others to the variable and impermanent; some think best within established structures of ideas, others from outside them; some reason that it is best to suffer the difficulties of the known world than to set forth in search of another one. In the case of historical knowledge, the odds are that those comfortable with uncertainty, ambiguity, and the unknown will be satisfied before those more contented with stability and the known. To offer that conviction is not to take sides; it is rather to state, on the basis of all that we know about the long history of historical interpretation (which I take up in Chapters 2 and 3), what has always been the case and is likely always to remain so—that understanding of the past is inherently contingent on the circumstances external to the historians who study the past and under whom its realities come into being.

Even if it were possible, as it is not, to transform the internal logic of historical thought, there is no reason to desire the end of revisionist history. Look at the advances in understanding that different interpretations of the coming of the Civil War have brought us precisely because of differences among historians. Yes, some of these views have required a major reorganization of our understanding of nineteenth-century America, to say nothing of the Civil War; many of them have proved disturbing to those who resist the alterations in understanding that always result from the advance of insight and knowledge; some have even proven wrong (that is, if historians are ever justified in fully ruling out any possible interpretation of past events). But historians have come far since the days of James Ford Rhodes in thinking about the causes of the Civil War. They have narrowed the grounds of dispute and have come to understand and accept the resulting differences of view that will always attend emotionally and historically freighted subjects. While historians disagree and will probably always disagree in some measure about the war's origins—for instance, how central the battle over slavery's existence and spread was to the onset of civil war—we should welcome those disagreements as reflective of the enduring benefits of the vitality of argument in a free society.

In any event, why expect historians, any more than others, to be impervious to the society and culture in which they live and work and to advances in research methods, available evidence, and interpretive schemes? Why should we expect them to frame their questions as historians did a century ago or to present their findings in terms used in the past? After all, people do not ask Picasso to paint in the manner of Tintoretto; they do not expect Philip Glass to compose in the tonalities of Mozart; they do not complain that Madonna does not sing as Ella Fitzgerald did. Historians, like artists, address the world in which they live, not other worlds. If they did not write in terms their contemporaries could recognize and understand, they would serve little useful intellectual or social function. Moreover, historical knowledge gains purchase in people's minds most readily and comes most alive when it relates to readers' own minds and felt needs, when it makes sense in their lived circumstances. In every successive era, societies face fresh challenges that require fresh knowledge and understanding. Such was the case in the immediately post–Civil War decades, when still raw emotions invited historical defenses of each section's responsibility for the conflict. Such was the case in the first third of the twentieth century, when the costs of industrial capitalism evoked a new look at the values, such as they were, of slave society. And such has been the case since the advent of the civil rights movement, when urgent public needs called forth a review of the historical realities of racism, race relations, protest, and the role of government in the United States.

But professional historians do not without thought simply reflect back on society its own beliefs. They struggle to immunize their thinking from as many current intellectual conventions as possible. But since members of the larger society are never, any more than historians themselves, uniform in their own views, individual historians will always find themselves, often unintentionally, more closely associated with some parts of society and with some schools of thought than with others. The test for historians' interpretations is not their consonance with any existing political or ideological views; the test is their interpretations' consonance with known evidence, their plausibility, and their strength—their ability to withstand the criticism to which knowledge and ideas are always subjected.

In the end, a historical battleground like that over the causes of the

Civil War has to be considered a comprehensive interpretive arena that incorporates and embodies somewhere within it, like a Russian doll, the residue of every argument that has been offered since the outbreak of argument about that subject. Each set of differing interpretations about a subject creates a distinct, bounded, intellectual universe in which historians and general readers alike debate one another, gradually add to knowledge and understanding, and approach, even if only asymptotically, that treasured if elusive goal we call The Truth. It is a universe in which historical knowledge advances, disputes are begun and concluded, scholars decide on what is most important to focus on next, and ideas are refined. An informal universe of permeable and shifting borders, this intellectual universe is a kind of professional home where collegiality usually (but not always) reigns, strong scholarly partnerships are born, and institutions and publications support its members' work. While tempers may occasionally flare, bitter tensions surface, and stalemates of sorts occur (as surely they did in more than a century and a half of thinking about the causes of the Civil War), slowly but surely historians of good will reduce their areas of dispute, come to some agreement, accept their colleagues as tillers in the same rocky fields of research and thought, and learn from one another. This is a world of thought whose participants accept as part of its inherent nature the changing nature of its interpretive schemes. Revisionism is thus the normal baked-in condition of historical thought. It never has been and never will be otherwise. In fact, the ancient origins and enduring life of historical dispute will become clear as we turn, in the following chapters, to the long history—more than twenty-five hundred years of it—of revisionist history.

For Further Reading, Chapter 1

An adequate account of the historical literature about the causes of the Civil War, to say nothing of writings about the war itself, would require an entire book. To write that book is not my intention here, for I use this subject to introduce dimensions of the realities of revisionist history, not to cover Civil War historiography. Fortunately, a book on Civil War historiography does exist, even if only through the early 1950s. That work is Thomas J. Pressly's comprehensive *Americans Interpret Their Civil War* (Princeton: Princeton University Press, 1951). Although my use of it differs from Pressly's purposes and is thus not so detailed about Civil War literature, my debt to his work will be obvious. Its coverage, however, must now be supplemented to account for additional thinking about the subject over the seventy years since Pressly wrote. A work that brings the literature about slavery into the late 1980s is Peter J. Parish, *Slavery: History and Historians* (New York: Harper and Row, 1989). Incisive reviews of Civil War historiography since then include Edward L. Ayers, "What Caused the Civil War," in Ayers, *What Caused the Civil War: Reflections on the South and Southern History* (New York: Norton, 2005), 131–144, and James M. McPherson, "And the War Came," in McPherson, *This Mighty Scourge: Perspectives on the Civil War* (New York: Oxford University Press, 2007), 3–19. The most detailed and analytical recent surveys of the vast, ever-growing scholarly literature on the subject are Frank Towers, "Partisans, New History, and Modernization: The Historiography of the Civil War's Causes, 1861–2011," *Journal of the Civil War Era* 1 (2011): 237–264, and Michael E. Woods, "What Twenty-First-Century Historians Have Said About the Causes of Disunion: A Civil War Sesquicentennial Review of the Recent Literature," *Journal of American History* 99 (2012): 415–439. But even Towers's and Woods's exhaustive treatments are already somewhat out of date because of the appearance of yet more recent studies, some of them noted in the body of this chapter. Others include Calvin Schermerhorn, *The Business of Slavery and the Rise of American Capitalism, 1815–1860* (New Haven: Yale University Press, 2015), and Sven Beckert and Seth Rockman, eds., *Slavery's Capitalism: A New History of American Economic Development* (Philadelphia: University of Pennsylvania Press, 2016). Schemerhorn's *Unrequited Toil: A History of United States Slavery* (New York: Cambridge University Press, 2018) is of equal quality and importance. Recent work that offers insight into the complexities of a single school of Civil War and Reconstruction historiography can be found in the essays in John David Smith and J. Vincent Lowery, eds., *The Dunning School: Historians, Race, and the Meaning of Reconstruction* (Lexington: University Press of Kentucky, 2013).

TWO

The Ancient Origins of
Revisionist History

As the historiography of the causes of the Civil War makes clear, historians argue with one another. They always have. Since to be taken seriously their arguments must arise from historical evidence—from such materials as documents, artifacts, and interviews—the arguments that follow from that evidence must be evaluated for their accuracy and plausibility. But often not all evidence is known; often what evidence is known is incomplete; and the known evidence can usually be used in different ways. Therefore, historical arguments are almost always partial. They arise out of a particular, single historian's mind at a particular time in a particular society and culture and thus necessarily reflect that mind, that historian's intentions, that time of writing, that society and culture. Historians use evidence for specific, not all possible, purposes.

Accordingly, the historical argument of this and its following chapter is a partial one, a reality that every reader should keep in mind while reading it. It is an argument based on my angle of vision and on one of the intentions of this book: to explain that history has always been revisionist and to offer evidence to support that statement. I review the long history of historical thought from that perspective—not, as many other historians of historical thought have done, as an analysis of changing historical thought. I do not try to write a full history of written history; I do no more than review that history's well-known figures and schools and the highlights of their written histories for my own purposes. Rather than emphasizing the great merits of their works, I pull out from what they wrote what serves my aims here: to show how the writing of history through the ages can be read as a continuing journey of intellectual adjustments to new circumstances, new knowledge, and new minds—that is, as a long record of revisions to previous ways of doing history and to previously held understandings of the past. For from the very beginning of history in the Western world two and a half millennia ago, historians have taken different approaches to the past, offered sharply different interpretations of long-ago events, felt free to attack each other, and given us a tradition of written history filled with ruptures, sharp turns, and a constant accumulation of fresh ways to look at what preceded them. As the historian Frederick W. Maitland once wrote, there is no settled way to do history or to think historically. "An orthodox history seems . . . a contradiction in terms." And so it has been since the beginning. This chapter and the next are intended to show how a single way of doing history—that is, a universally accepted history—has rarely existed; and how, when it did, it existed for an only comparatively short period before being overtaken (even if not fully replaced) by new ways of research, new evidence, new understanding, and new argument. Written history is nothing if not a record of unending renewal.

❧

Before the writing of history commenced in Greece around 450 BCE, there was epic poetry—the narrative legends of grand human themes and heroic figures. Epic poems were written history's seedground, the soil from which grew what we recognize today as history. Epics were tales of the past—of the origins of tribes and peoples, of battles between men and women and of their struggles with fate, of tragedy and triumphs over great odds, of pagan gods' quarrels with humans and among themselves, and of cycles from order to disorder and back to stability again when human affairs were set right. The greatest of the ancient epics, the origin-works of Western literature, were Homer's *Iliad* and *Odyssey*. Because of their compelling portrayals of human situations, the songster's majestic tales helped define the course of thought that remains the dominant, if no longer exclusive, cultural inheritance of those living in the West. They told of the deeds of ancient heroes—Achilles, Agamemnon, Hector, Odysseus, and Penelope—whose valorous exploits of fortitude, honor, revenge, and fidelity during the era of the Trojan Wars became etched into Western consciousness.

Yet these great creation epics are not history; they are myth. Embellishments of simpler tales based no doubt on the actual exploits of some real people, intended to please their hearers and arouse in them the ambition to accomplish similar great deeds, and meant to teach lessons of virtuous behavior and warn of the costs of pride and vengeance, the two Homeric epics—"quest romances" and "mythistory," they are sometimes called—have appropriately been taught as great works of literary art, not of history. They gain their force not from being woven around kernels of historical fact (which surely they are) but by their claims to universality and by taking on dramatic shape over countless generations by the bards who, in telling them, filled them out with the stories that make them unsurpassed as art and move to reflection all who read them now. No sense of possible other ways to tell these tales intrudes into their story lines; nothing in them is provisional. If "Homer" actually existed, he related his tales as fact without inquiring into their plausibility.[1] Gods and humans interact and affect each other, but the link between cause and effect is weak and often, at least to our day, hard to credit. When Homer turns to explaining what happens to his heroes, he frequently invokes the gods; they, not humans, pull the strings. And he leaves no evidence by which the validity of his claims about the epics' human characters and their exploits can be evaluated. We know that people like Homer and his contemporaries, no doubt like others about whom he wrote, possessed the basic intellectual ingredients of history—concepts, even if not ours, of time and change and the impulse to tell stories. We know, too, that ancient Greece was peopled by men and women who had the human qualities and emotions Homer gives his characters. But we cannot independently assess Homer's claims

1. In addition to uncertainty that Homer ever existed, it is by no means clear that "he" was a single person. Also, "he" may have been blind. Moreover, for over two centuries scholars have debated the historical value of Homer's epics—whether any store can be placed in their factual validity, especially in the *Iliad*.

about his poems' specific characters and their deeds, even when these figures act without the gods' intervention, and he offers us no help in doing so.

Most non-Western cultures of the time, like the culture of these ancient Greeks, lacked a sense of history. The contents of what tales they told were principally chronology and genealogy. The singular exception were the ancient Hebrews, whose Bible is a unique early instance of the record of change over time, a record in many cases of real events, a linear account of human existence from the creation of the world, and a self-conscious narrative of the history of a people. Yet even the Hebrews did not write what we would recognize as believable, verifiable records of what had happened in their past and why it had done so. Homer and the Hebrews compiled chronologies—lists of events in sequence but without causal links. History did not intrude into their consciousness as being the result of human and natural causality, the vehicle of change, or the result of progress or decline; their history was ever the same, a cycle of events that followed a known pattern. And in the tales these chroniclers told, humans had little role in the working out of their fates. Gods, mostly fickle gods taking arbitrary actions, were in the saddle and spurred mankind along. If there ever existed a prelapsarian age of historical consciousness—an age before written, contentious historical argumentation—it was the age of Homer. By the fifth century BCE, that age ended at the hands of other Greeks.

What we know as history commenced when inchoate ideas about the past, about chronology, and about genealogy gave way to an intellectual structure concerning the past that was shared across populations and generations, a time when explanation supplanted mere chronology, and, equally significant, when a critical mind went to work on tales about fate, the gods, and the cycles of time. That is, history as we know it appeared when someone began to be skeptical about stories like Homer's, searched for the human foundations of human events, used evidence rather than poetic imagination, and related human cause to human effect—when someone went beyond Homer to supplant fiction with fact. The first person to show those qualities in an extended narrative was Herodotus of Halicarnassus (the town, now Bodrum, on the eastern shore of the Aegean Sea in Asia, in which he was born around

484 BCE).[2] In his celebrated *Histories,* the first fully wrought Western work of prose about any subject that has survived in its entirety, Herodotus wrote about the wars that broke out in 480–479 BCE between Greeks and (as he and his contemporaries called them) "barbarians," the non-Greek peoples like the Persians among whom Herodotus lived before moving to Athens. His intentions differed from those of the rhapsodists whose traditional accounts of the Trojan Wars had reached their peak with Homer and who had peopled their tales with divine and mythological characters. Herodotus offered his research, he stated in the opening words of the *Histories,* "so that human events do not fade with time"—that is, to preserve the record of known human acts, "some brought forth by the Hellenes, others by the barbarians," as well as the acts of the gods. He also set out to tell of "the causes that led them to make war on each other."[3] It was a simple aim but, as the future would reveal, one fateful with promise. By choosing with bold confidence as an identifiable Greek, writing in the first person, to accept responsibility for the stories he told, Herodotus opened the door to a new genre of what the Greeks called *historiē*—inquiry, or intellectual endeavor. That term eventually came to mean inquiry into the past. By stepping outside the tradition he inherited and investigating questions on his own, Herodotus was inaugurating the writing of history. And by writing in prose, he separated the province of history—whether purposefully or not we do not know—from the cultural dominance of imaginative literature. Not for nothing did Cicero call him "the father of history."

What made Herodotus a historian and not a mere chronicler of human acts were the particular elements, ones not seen before, he brought to his work. He was by nature a geographer, anthropologist,

2. There were historians, or at least protohistorians, before Herodotus both in Greece and, earlier, in Egypt and Sumeria, of whose protohistories Herodotus and others were aware, but little of them is now known, and little of their work, save for inscriptions, chronologies, and genealogies, survives.

3. Historians do not just argue and take issue with each other. Like poets, composers, and artists, they pay tribute to their predecessors and always have done so, usually in citation, often by incorporating their predecessors' earlier reflections into their own works, but sometimes simply with a silent nod. Here, Herodotus, the first historian, sets a precedent in this regard by seeming to tip his hat to his great forebear Homer, who, in book 6 of *The Iliad,* has Helen of Troy appeal for Hector's love "so that we may live in song for men to come."

zoologist, ethnographer, and folklorist as well as historian.[4] Traveling widely, he spoke with contemporaries to secure evidence of what had happened before and during the Persian Wars, conflicts that had taken place during Herodotus's youth and within the living memory of many whom he interviewed. In doing so, he inaugurated the active, engaged historical method that, while long serving as one among many ideals of historical research, also created what would prove a fruitful tension between on-site and archival work. (It was he, for instance, who provided the classic description of the Tower of Babel that has since served as the basis of all illustrations of it.) Two and a half millennia before the French *Annales* school and such historians as Fernand Braudel laid claims to having pioneered pathbreaking interpretive approaches to the past, Herodotus foreshadowed their histories of *mentalité* (for which the English word "mindset" is probably the best equivalent) and their emphasis on large swaths of the past (what has come to be called *la longue durée*).[5]

Herodotus set forth large themes—the struggle between West and East (Greece—that is, the West—wins) and between freedom and tyranny (freedom—Greek freedom—again wins), a struggle that has echoed through the West's memory and culture ever since. His historical characters argued over the relative benefits of democracy, oligarchy, and monarchy—an argument inherited also from Aristotle's *Politics* by Enlightenment political thinkers and of deep concern to the founders of the American republic. A participant in a polytheistic culture, he comfortably reported on claims about gods' interventions and the oracle at Delphi but gave to historical figures—humans known to have lived—their full scope of human qualities. Even though he was unable fully to dismiss the gods' influence over human affairs, as philosophers had al-

4. The Classical scholar Edith Hamilton called him "the first sight-seer."

5. The *Annales* school gained its name from the title of the celebrated French journal *Annales d'histoire économique et sociale* founded in 1929 by Lucien Febvre and Marc Bloch. Through the historians whose works were published in it, the journal exercised outsized influence on Western historiography in the latter half of the twentieth century. That influence continues to be felt in works of social, cultural, and economic history as well as in works of "deep" and world history, whose authors follow the lead of Braudel, a leading *annaliste*, in emphasizing not events (*l'histoire événementielle*) but vast, timeless forces of climate, geography, and social development (*la longue durée*).

ready started to do, Herodotus began to remove them as causative agents on earth. Causation, he thought, lay in human events and decisions, not with capricious deities, and he thus laid down one of the permanent criteria by which a work is judged to be history or not: he sought to explain, not just to record, how the Persian Wars had come about. And while writing as a Greek who brought to life in his pages the public realities of Greek city-states, Herodotus echoed Homer's evenhanded treatment of the characters in his tales by seeking to balance his own loyalties to Greece with a tolerant understanding of the Persians and other peoples who filled his history—of, as he put it, the "great and wonderful deeds, manifested by both Greeks and barbarians." Thus were humane understanding and moral themes incorporated into historical texts at their birth, as were the figures and events that live on in Western memory: the Persians' invasion of the Greek city-states under the leadership of "barbarian" leaders Croesus, Cyrus, Xerxes, and Darius, and great battles such as those of Salamis and Thermopylae. Herodotus purposefully aimed to run down the wars' origins using the widest range of methods, evidence, and explanations available to him. He also tried to assess the wars' significance for Mediterranean civilization. He was the first person known to us to make study of the past the subject of rational inquiry.

Yet Herodotus was a historian not simply because he undertook his own research to explain the causes of the Persian Wars. Nor was it because he wrote thematically, put humans and not gods at the center of his history, linked events and decisions causally, and adopted a stance that we can recognize as one of trying to be objective and unpartisan. He was a historian because he described his sources, such as what he heard and saw among the people whom he encountered and whom he had learned from ("There were other things, too, which I learnt at Memphis in conversation with the priests of Hephaestus"). He also told his readers how distant he was from those sources (for instance, second- or thirdhand). Here was someone who recounted history for those who had not been present—an achievement in itself—while at the same time pioneering in historical methods.

Like a skeptical reporter, in the *Histories* Herodotus also lifted his eyebrows at the claims and stories of the past he found wanting in credibility and plausibility, and he felt free to reject them. (Of the Chaldeans' belief that "the god enters the temple [of Babylon] and takes his rest upon the bed," Herodotus remarks, "I do not believe them." "My business," he remarks elsewhere, "is to record what people say, but I am by no means bound to believe it.") Dismissive of much myth, he inaugurated the displacement of legend by the ascertainment of fact. In mild rebuke of Homer, he corrected what he thought were the errors of the great poet who had lived (or so we think) four hundred years earlier.[6] A skeptic, he felt free to offer his own judgments while accepting responsibility for explaining how and why he arrived at them. Words and phrases like "perhaps," "they say," "according to some authorities," and "so far as knowledge goes" filled his account. By offering a history that differed from the epics and chronicles of events that preceded his work, Herodotus was taking the first steps toward trying to alter his contemporaries' understanding of the past. He was also suggesting that different versions of the past could exist. His *Histories* made history a practice in which historians would assess sources, seek confirming or new evidence for what they wrote about, offer fresh views of the past, and feel free to criticize others for their errors, limitations, and commitments. In fact, simply by taking up an early version of field research, Herodotus inaugurated the future course of historical inquiry.

Right at the creation of Western historiography, then, the seeds of what would become the revisionist tradition within the writing of history took hold. Once Herodotus had created historical criticism, it could never be suppressed, nor could anyone ever escape its influence. Thus it was that not even this first great historian could avoid attack from his successors any more than he could resist questioning the work of his predecessors. It did not take long for Herodotus himself to be assailed and his *Histories* to be derided. In fact, so influential was the criticism of his work that his *Histories* were effectively ignored for two and a half millennia.

It was Herodotus's younger contemporary, Thucydides, who

6. In this respect, Herodotus differed from his near contemporary Plato. In *The Republic*, Plato banished poets—and here he was thinking in particular of Homer—from his ideal polity for wielding malign influence over its citizens. Herodotus went more easily on his great predecessor, no doubt thinking that his epics were more than poetry and that somewhere inside them were reflected long-lost historical facts, albeit facts used to create art.

inaugurated their dismissal. The *Histories* were, Thucydides scornfully wrote, "a prize essay to be heard for the moment," a work not to be studied and one unlikely to endure. "So careless are most people [that is, Herodotus] in the search for truth," wrote Thucydides, "that they are more inclined to accept the first story that comes to hand." His own views, by contrast, could "safely be relied on." Not for him was history to be "attractive at truth's expense."[7] In throwing down the gauntlet to anyone who did not adopt his own different focus and possess his own distinctive intentions, Thucydides turned interpretive differences into interpretive battles and opened what has proved to be a never-ending struggle over the past—over what is good history, useful history, and artful history and, above all, over what are the "correct" interpretations of past events, the "correct" subjects of inquiry, the "correct" evidence to use, and, above all, what are the "correct" aims of written history. By establishing criticism of predecessors as a legitimate practice in moving historical thought forward, Thucydides' words also served notice to his successors that the struggle over how to do history and what the past should mean would not always be good-natured and free of conflict.

What was at issue? Herodotus, a cosmopolitan possessed of limitless inquisitiveness, had written what we now recognize as a kind of universal cultural history, one that takes in all human possibilities. He saw and accepted the world's vast diversity of customs, beliefs, traditions, and acts and found all those dimensions of the world fascinating and worthy of study in their own right for that very reason. As for the world's condition at the time he wrote, he believed that it could not be understood without reaching as far into the past as necessary to explain its origins and the roots of its events; if the contemporary world was worth studying, then all the more reason to understand the historical earth in which it had germinated. No ethnocentrist, he believed that the thinking and culture of every people, none of whom he dismissed as

7. Under Thucydidean influence, Polybius later took issue with some of his predecessors whose works are lost to us, and during the Roman Empire Plutarch (whose *Lives* focused on politics and warfare) derided "the malignity" of Herodotus. But their criticisms proved to be mild compared to some later attacks. The sixteenth-century Humanist historian Juan Luis Vives, differing entirely with Cicero, called Herodotus "the father of lies." So much for the gentility of historians.

beyond interest or significance, have a bearing on that people's actions and that all kinds of questions about the past could validly be asked and all subjects considered potentially relevant to explaining everything else. One can imagine him puzzled by efforts to limit history's subject matter or to elevate one kind of history over another as people have done from then on.

By contrast, Thucydides thought Herodotus's approaches and his subject matter altogether defective. Born between 465 and 460 BCE into the wealthy Athenian elite, Thucydides was less the curious, disinterested investigator that Herodotus was and more a man of action and strategic thinking, one whom today we would call a defense intellectual, someone caught up in the events he sought to understand. A youth when the first Peloponnesian War—a civil war between Athens, Sparta, and their Greek allies—began in 460, he wrote his unfinished work in his twenties after having led a defeated Athenian naval force and then been exiled. While striving hard to be objective, he brought a participant's observations, associations, and commitments to bear on what he wrote. In his tight focus, his rationalism, his sternness, and his stated aspiration to be objective, Thucydides turned history in the direction against which all subsequent histories, ones that follow other approaches and have other aims, have had to contend.

For instance, his classic *History of the Peloponnesian War* was devoid of gods quarrelling away on Mt. Olympus and intervening in human affairs; instead, Thucydides grounded his tale entirely among living humans; and he thought prayer of no help in distress. (During Athens's plague, he wrote, no acts availed in stemming the disease's spread. "Equally useless were prayers made in the temples, consultation of oracles, and so forth.") This was not the last time historians would try to banish all deities and unverifiable claims from their accounts, but it was the first time one made the attempt and thus of enduring significance. No mythic, otherworldly explanations qualified in Thucydides' mind as rational bases for historical inquiry and interpretation. Equally fatefully, and implying that he felt daunted by the hope of knowing how and why everything had happened, Thucydides took as his subjects a far more limited set of topics—warfare, politics, statecraft, and diplomacy—than had Herodotus; one explained war and the relations among states, he thought, not by looking at religious beliefs or burial customs but rather by examining military battles and military leadership. He also inaugurated the practice of contemporary history by writing of current events and of the war in which he had fought, thus bringing into written history the elements of memoir. A historical portraitist, he made major contemporary figures like Pericles—for whom he wrote celebrated speeches whose contents and lessons continue to bear reading—play leading roles in his work. Humans (at least male humans) and not large, abstract forces, he believed, made history. All of this placed Thucydides, like Herodotus, among the very first to sense that a historian's task is to reconstruct the past as it happened, not as others wanted to believe it had happened.

With similar consequences, Thucydides believed history to be a kind of human "science" whose study would provide warnings and lessons to its students. For example, given to generalizations, he argued that wars usually commence from an absence of forethought. "Action comes first, and it is only when [people] have already suffered that they begin to think." Most significant, he intended his work to be "a posses-sion for all time. . . . Future ages will wonder at us, as the present age wonders at us now." To him, history was not meant primarily to please, commemorate, and edify, although he thought of his beloved native Athens as being "an education to Greece." Rather, historical knowl-edge was an instrument for use, one indispensable to those who would master human affairs and statecraft and would direct public policy. In Thucydides, history became the history of public affairs; and, as we would expect from a contemporary of Sophocles and Euripides, tragedy as a theme of historical events entered the picture. To Thucydides' way of thinking, since human nature is uniform, even if its regularity is not the uniformity of scientific reality, historians are justified in drawing general conclusions from what they learn from study of the past. In his and others' hands, historical knowledge could lead to wisdom. Many after him have thought so, too.

For our purposes, Thucydides' great history has a particular signifi-cance. In the authoritative words of Donald Kagan—a leading historian of the ancient world who terms himself "a revisionist historian of the Peloponnesian War"—by taking issue with Herodotus's approach to history Thucydides was "the first revisionist historian." Thucydides earns Kagan's commendation as a revisionist on many grounds, large and small. He sought to teach rather than to please (a Herodotean aim). He asked questions rather than told stories. Like Herodotus, he wrote of individual leaders, but unlike his predecessor he tried to plumb the nature of the leadership and statecraft his leaders employed; he spent few words on the common people. This led him to draw historical truths about man's nature, good and evil, and the workings of fortune from what he observed. He had no difficulty dismissing popular causal explanations for what he believed to be stronger ones. (The fundamental cause of the Peloponnesian War, "though it was the least avowed," he wrote, "I believe to have been the growth of the Athenian power, which terrified the Lacedaemonians and put them under the necessity of fighting.") He sought to place his work on a firm factual basis and exclude anything that could not be verified. Thucydides thus laid claim to the utility of historical knowledge for understanding human affairs. And he inaugurated the long battle between historians who emphasize large forces over vast reaches of space and time and those who focus on more limited affairs. In opening this fissure between historians of what the French call "*l'histoire totale*" and those who focus on discrete, closer events, or "*l'histoire événementielle*" ("event history"), he changed the subject of historical inquiry from society and culture (Herodotus's interests) to war and foreign relations. It would be difficult to get more revisionist than that.

In undertaking that last effort, Thucydides had his most lasting impact. With only a few exceptions, like Tacitus's writings on the German tribes, not until the eighteenth century would people studying the past again turn their attention to society and culture and try to recapture for history the realities of the lives of those not involved in politics, military affairs, and the relations between states.[8] And even then historians' return to the inspiration of Herodotus was relatively

8. One telltale American example: encouraging the education of his son John Quincy Adams, John Adams urged him to read, among others, Thucydides, not Herodotus. And in their late-life correspondence, the senior Adams and Thomas Jefferson reflected on their readings of Tacitus and Thucydides but never Herodotus. The *Histories* of Herodotus were not considered preparation for statecraft.

brief. The nineteenth-century German scholars who laid the foundations for history's emergence as a subject of professional training and research kept history focused on those same Thucydidean subjects, from which it would not veer strongly again until the second half of the twentieth century. Thus this "first revisionist historian," by the power of his words and arguments, forced all historians who subsequently differed from him to take up their own "revisionist" approaches. From then on, every historical interpretation that significantly and clearly differed from interpretations offered earlier could validly be termed a revision of others that had preceded it.

Of course, the term "revisionist" is anachronistic when applied to a work of ancient creation; it is a word of the late nineteenth century, not of distant coinage. Yet applying the term to the intellectual and methodological space that Thucydides put between himself and Herodotus offers us the chance to understand what, even long ago, historians were up to and always since have been. To do so, we have to give up many of the notions that we may have absorbed in early life. Then we are taught, often unintentionally, to think of historians as people who relate the facts of the past and little else—as people who teach us what feudalism was, when the Declaration of Independence was released, what caused the French Revolution, and how the Great Depression unrolled—and who then leave it at that. History thus becomes, and we too often incorrectly think of it as, a parade of facts—lists of events recorded just because they happened. But a mere relation of facts is not history. A parade of dates with events attached to them is but an annal, as a list of kings—another early form of recording time and its passage—is but a roster of rulers and nothing else. A chronicle—facts related, sometimes but not always, in chronological order without causal links—is only slightly closer than an annal to being what we know of as history.

But history is not annal or chronicle. History is what emerges from chronicle—when facts are used for a purpose. Thus Herodotus's *Histories* and Thucydides' *Peloponnesian Wars* transcended chronicle and became history because their authors tried to explain the causes and outcomes of the wars of which they wrote, because they were linking events, acts, and motives causally and for a purpose. Here is where we begin to see what historians, distinct from chroniclers, always try to achieve. Historians do not compile lists or simply relate a narrative of bare events. Instead, they seek to understand the relationships between the facts that are to be found on a chronicler's list. We know, for instance, that the British government adopted the Stamp Act in 1765; that is a fact. We know that the British closed the port of Boston in 1774; that, too, is a fact. We know that British troops battled their way through Lexington to Concord and back to Boston the following year; that is another fact. And we know that the Declaration of Independence was agreed to by members of the Second Continental Congress on July 2, 1776, and made public two days later; those, too, are facts. But those facts do not make up history when listed simply as facts; they remain nothing but declarative statements until historians relate those facts to explain how and why those events resulted in the American Revolution. Once those facts are linked to one another and seen as leading somehow one to the next, once the understanding of them held by contemporaries is added to the mix and then interpreted in a particular way—then we have history, not chronicle. That is to say, with facts alone we cannot have history. It follows that with facts alone we cannot have different interpretations of history. We get different interpretations of the past when different perspectives on existing evidence emerge to create the possibilities of new understanding and new meaning.

For centuries after Herodotus, the perspectives that he and Thucydides brought to their histories resided within a relatively stable intellectual universe. The ancient historians argued among themselves and criticized one another, yet they shared the same general canons of thought and presentation, and their histories reflected the same general aims. If, by taking on and besting Herodotus in the sweepstakes as to how to do secular history, Thucydides established the conventional contents of that variety of history—public affairs—so too his major stroke of revisionism—his successful attack on the contents of Herodotus's work—was to be the last such major alteration in historical writing until secular history itself was challenged. Thucydides' successors as historians, Greek and Roman, told different tales, offered different emphases, and drew conclusions different from one another without in any substantial way altering or dismissing their predecessors' ways of proceeding or shattering the intellectual order within which their forebears had written. As a result, the Classical Age of history, like that of architecture, sculpture, and drama—the age of Herodotus and Thucydides—imprinted the West with ineradicable structures of historical thought and art. The mode of history these early historians' works embodied (most of those works, save for those of Herodotus and Thucydides, coming to us as mere fragments), the contents they conveyed, and the rhetoric in which their histories were cast lasted unimpeded and mostly uncontested for centuries while passing from Greek to Roman historians along the way. They were embedded in the tales that formed the basis of Western moral and political thought into our own time. The works of these historians— Xenophon, Polybius, Sallust, Livy, Plutarch, Tacitus, and Josephus being the most renowned among those whose works survive—formed the curricula of schoolchildren and collegians well into the twentieth century and stocked the minds of the statesmen, clerics, and poets who read and memorized their words and cherished the examples of which they wrote. The Renaissance—a rebirth of learning—would not deserve its name without the reawakening of these ancients' authority as moral and civic guides. Until modern times, military figures studied these ancient historical texts for their lessons. Rare were members of the Continental Congresses and the Constitutional Convention who failed to summon references to these ancient historians in their debates or to subscribe to the lessons they taught as they founded a new nation. Classical histories composed the very foundation of the thought of those who established the United States.

Differences among these early historians of course existed, differences in subject matter, style, tone, and emphasis. But what their works shared, not how they differed, is what they most consequentially bequeathed to the future—and what set up the intellectual quake that followed. To them (save for Herodotus), history was political and military history almost exclusively, the rest being only contributory to the larger purpose. This led them to portray the past as unchangeable save in its details and in its cyclical course; wars and interstate conflicts were normal, and progress as we have come to envisage it was nonexistent. Though they could look back to the origins of their subjects (as in Livy's depiction of the founding of Rome), they all felt most comfortable with recent and contemporary events since evidence of the distant past was hard to come by. With exceptions (Thucydides), they passed along as proper to history the worship of gods (the Jewish historian Josephus crediting "divine providence" with influence), an emphasis on oratory (Thucydides again being the greatest exemplar), education by historical example (Thucydides and Livy), an attachment to biography (Plutarch), an emphasis on great men, great events, and the state (all of them), warfare (Herodotus, Thucydides, and Julius Caesar being the leading authors on this subject among them), and the inevitable falling off of statecraft, morals, and manners (Polybius, Livy, Tacitus, and Sallust). The political philosophy of the Americans who founded constitutional government is unthinkable without the example of Rome's disintegration described and explained by Livy and Tacitus. And where else but from them did Edward Gibbon first learn of the decline and fall of the Roman Empire? From Herodotus on, they argued that history teaches by the records of virtues and vices it provides, and no readers could miss the proud patriotism toward cities and states that their histories exemplified. Theirs were accounts fit for the Mediterranean world in the centuries after written history first took the form that we recognize as history. It was history of discrete historical developments and events.

And so if any statement about written history can be said to be axiomatic from the very founding moment of history in the West and from what we can learn of the relationship between Classical history and Classical times, it is the proposition that every age, every culture, and every belief system produces its own history—one that is distinctive, partial, and, to members of its own community, often unquestionable. The historians of the Greek and Roman worlds wrote histories that made sense above all to inhabitants of their ancient lands, reflected the eras in which they were written and the intellectual culture of the historians who wrote them, and helped contemporaries understand the times in which they lived by exploring how those times had come to be. But those histories were unlikely to prove fully satisfying to people who, for one reason or another (tribal origins, geographic location, different life experiences), did not occupy secure positions within the Greek and Roman worlds or whose belief systems could not accommodate Greek or Roman worldviews—and vice versa.

∾

Such was to prove the case within the small but slowly growing community of Christians—most of whom were Jews slowly altering their religious beliefs—who lived in the late Roman world. Imagine yourself in their place as they considered their young faith in the context of the history known to them. Existing written histories of the Hellenized Roman world, histories that reflected the perspectives of the Roman elite if not of all Roman people, were steadfastly pagan. Yet having gradually been purged of the gods that had peopled mythic histories, these histories had as their subjects humans who were responsible for their own destinies. Such Classical works offered neither a date on which human history was said to have begun, an overall meaning to human history, nor a scheme that explained how history operates or what history's general purposes might be. They stuck closely to, say, the wars of the Greek states or the origins of Rome; they did not claim to be a history of all history, only of specific geopolitical segments of it. They surely offered no story of progress or redemption. Given these historiographic realities, it is difficult to imagine now that a new kind of history, a history reflecting the historically novel belief system of the pious Christians living in the pagan Roman Empire, would not have appeared from within this young group of believers. Three centuries after the birth of Jesus, such an interpretation emerged.

The history eventually produced within the Christian community —a history that answered to Christian faith, not to pagan beliefs— wrought a decisive transformation in the way the past, present, and future were perceived and written about in the West. That new way imprinted Western history with a new chronology and, most important, with a new story line. In fact, its most lasting consequence was to transform the multiple narratives by which historians had told Greek and Roman history into a single, new one. Its creators clearly sensed what historians have come to consider a truism: that those who control the narrative of the past influence, even if not fully control, the present. The enormous depth and significance of the substitution of Christian for Classical chronology and story—a genuine revolution in historiography as well as in human affairs—is conveyed by the simple fact that Westerners have not escaped its consequences since the fourth century CE. It was to be the secularists and those who clung to older ways of viewing historical human affairs who would from then on be on the defensive—and, in the West, on the defensive for roughly a millennium and a half. If any people had cause to indict the history to which they did not subscribe as "revisionist," it was the heirs of the Greco-Roman pagan historical tradition, who were left behind by the Christian historiographic revolution. That revolution's permeating effects on the very foundations of Western thought and history have never been surpassed, nor have those effects ever been fully eradicated from Western historiography, no matter how altered are the ways in which formal history is written now. That is to say, there has never in the West been a revision in the conceptions, methods, and contents of history greater than the one wrought by Christian thought and faith.

Like the origins of many great intellectual and spiritual movements, Christianity was born among then historically obscure people, in this case Jews—some Hellenized, some Romanized, some unaffected by the surrounding major culture—on the shores of the Mediterranean. Their beliefs were captured first in the record of Jewish origins and life presented in the Old Testament, with the Jew's single god, who now makes his appearance in historiography, working his way on earth through a covenant with the tribes of a chosen people. Those beliefs were then expanded in the books of the New Testament into the Christian narrative of the incarnation of God on earth. The Bible itself constitutes a history of sorts. It relates a story, and it offers causal explanations of events. It resembles Classical historiography, especially that of pagan history's earliest variety in Herodotus, in offering up tales of miraculous occurrences, albeit at the hands of a single purposeful deity, not many capricious ones. It narrates a tale of origins, leaders, events, and wars, as well as of transgressions, punishment, atonement, and redemption.

Yet as history has come to be defined in the West since the eighteenth century, the Bible is more a source for history than a history per se. Differing from the Herodotean approach, it is not inquiry. And while in kinship with Thucydidean history it offers lessons, they are moral lessons, not those of statecraft. Historians mine the Bible for the facts that, combined with information drawn from archeology, philology, and kindred disciplines, have yielded knowledge of biblical times that could be gained in no other way. And unlike Classical histories, the Bible is a composite history, one whose books were written by many people at different times, then gathered into a canonical text; it lacks a single author's overview, perspective, and style; and, for many reasons, it excludes many other texts that existed at the time of creation of the Bible's conventional contents.

Great early Christian thinkers, such as church fathers Origen and Tertullian, had offered oblique interpretations of the past as their young Christian community struggled to create a narrative of its existence that made sense in Christian terms. But, biblical commentators and religious thinkers, they cannot be considered historians in any true sense. Instead, the first exceptional Christian historical talent was that of Eusebius, a fourth-century bishop of Caesarea, a Mediterranean coastal town in the Roman province of Judaea in Palestine, today's Israel. A contemporary of, and adviser to, the Roman Emperor Constantine, whose conversion to Christianity in 313 CE altered the course of Western history, Eusebius saw the need to give his newly official religious faith a narrative grounding in historical scholarship. "This work," he wrote in his *Ecclesiastical History,* "seems to me of especial importance because I know of no ecclesiastical writer who has devoted himself to this subject; and I hope that it will appear most useful to those who are fond of historical research." Like the Classical historians before him, he sought to "preserve the memory of the successions" of his chosen examples, in his case "the apostles of our Savior," the fathers, saints, and bishops of the young church. Acknowledging that he was "the first to enter upon the subject," he begged his readers' indulgence for any errors he may have made while stoutly stating his principal intention: "to give the names and number and times of those who through love of innovation have run into the greatest errors, and, proclaiming themselves discoverers of knowledge falsely so-called have like fierce wolves unmercifully devastated the flock of Christ."

Yet the result of Eusebius's work was more than setting the record straight on his terms. History itself gained a new grounding. Eusebius gave the past a firm chronology, one dated from Abraham. Moreover, a sacred, not secular, account of the past since "the days of our Saviour to our own," his *Ecclesiastical History* was effectively a history of God's imperium on earth starting with Jesus and the apostles and continuing into Eusebius's own lifetime, an approach that the historian Donald R. Kelley argues warrants calling Eusebius "the Christian Herodotus." Its breadth made his work the first to lay claims to being a universal, as well as a confessional and Eurocentric, history. His Mediterranean world stood in for what he thought of as the entire world. It was also a history of Christianity triumphant—again, in Kelley's words, history as "preparation for the Gospel," one that reconciled Roman history to sacred history and helped establish in historiography, as well as in fact, the primacy in the monotheistic Christian Church of the bishop of Rome and the centrality of what came in the centuries ahead to be the Holy Roman Empire. It was Constantine, wrote Eusebius, who "reunified the Roman Empire into a single whole." Also unlike most previous historians—take for example Herodotus, who relied on interviews, and Thucydides, who made up edifying speeches—Eusebius, following the Roman historian Polybius in his *Histories,* quoted extensively from documents known to him. He thus brought to history a reliance on surviving written sources—the feature that has been fundamental to historical reasoning ever since. He also followed Polybius in taking up the grandest of themes—which in Polybius's case had been the rise of Rome to dominance in the Mediterranean world.

In other respects, Eusebius's *History* was to prove more problematic. It was partisan and polemical, treating Jews, Classical historians, and heretics as enemies of The One Truth. Although Eusebius considered his work to be one of universal history, it set aside the theme of a common humanity in favor of a scheme that divided good people from bad. It established within the Roman Church a tradition of historiographic orthodoxy that proved as powerful as its doctrinal counterpart and as difficult to change. And while absorbing the Classical approach to historical periodization around wars and states, it substituted for that chronology episcopal history, one based on the line of succession of the bishops of Rome. By domesticating secular to sacred history, Eusebius also moved the history that the pagans had recorded into contemporary times and thus concluded a marriage between Christian (later Catholic) and Imperial Rome, papal and Roman institutions, Christian and pagan people, sacred and profane belief systems, and divine and human histo-riography. But it was very much history on Christian terms, one that in the future would force any new kinds of history that sought intellectual authority to battle against a way of interpreting the past that sent its roots deep into Western consciousness and life and has maintained a longer and more tenacious hold on Western thought than the pagan one ever did. Consequently, any distinctively new historical methods or perspectives that arose once Christian history became the Western norm would necessarily be "revisionist" in this larger Christian context. Grand revisions were to pile up on revisions: first Christian of pagan, then secular of Christian.

In addition to being a history of triumphant Christianity and making the history of Rome part of sacred history, Eusebius's revisionist narrative set forth a divine plan for human existence. History was now linear and progressive; and if Classical belief in recurring cycles of his-tory remained embedded in Christian historiography in the form of cir-cuits of individual human achievement, sin, fall, judgment, redemption, and deliverance, History in the largest sense now had a goal as revealed by Scripture—itself a profound revisionist invention. For the first time, the chance of earthly progress and development toward enlightenment as well as redemption on a large scale under God's watchful eyes took on intellectual, as well as religious, authority. Ever since then Western-ers have remained the children of progress, confident that human life and society were capable of improvement and growth. And ever since then, historians have had to battle against the tendency to see the pres-ent as nothing more than the fulfillment of the past—what the historian Herbert Butterfield termed "the whig fallacy."[9]

In Butterfield's formulation, whig history enshrines the tendency "to praise revolutions provided they have been successful, to emphasize

9. Coined by Butterfield in his influential 1931 book *The Whig Interpretation of History*, the terms "whig history" and the "whig fallacy" (alternatively written as "Whig history" and the "Whig fallacy") drew on the vital tension in modern British history between Royalists—those who supported the monarchy—and, as they were known, the Whigs, those who sought greater power for Parliament and, by extension, the people. Thus the Whigs were usually seen as the paladins of "progress" and of the fulfillment of history's inevitable improvement—the kind of history that Butterfield was criticizing.

certain principles of progress in the past and to provide a story which is the ratification if not the glorification of the present." The whig historian "busies himself with dividing the world into the friends and enemies of progress"—its enemies being those who are unenlightened for not knowing what we do. Instead of asking how religious liberty arose, the whig historian "by a subtle organisation of his sympathies tends to read it as the question, To whom must we be grateful for our religious liberty?" These historians seek demonstrable truths in, and lessons from, the past and scorn analyzing "mere processes"; that is, they scorn "watching complication and change for the mere sake of complication and change," which, remarks Butterfield, "is precisely the function of the historian." Instead of "imaginative sympathy" for the past, "There is the hint that for all this desire to pass moral judgments on various things in the past, it is really something in the present that the historian is most anxious about." In Butterfield's terms, Eusebius's history can be seen as an early version of James Harvey Robinson's "new history"—history written with the present in mind.

Historical thought after Eusebius was forever to be characterized by this assumption of directionality—that history moves ahead—an assumption not to be challenged with sustained force until our own time.[10] Now a single god ruled, and the pagan gods acting in arbitrary fashion according to their varying whims were relegated to outposts in fiction and fantasy. Thus commenced, in Eusebius's and his successors' telling as foretold by the Bible, the thousand-year reign of Christ on earth. For centuries after Eusebius, most Western histories (most of them being little more than chronicles of events) were derivative of this master's reworking of history's story line.

It would, however, be a mistake to see this historiographic revolution as a full rejection of pagan history. All past schemes of thinking and writing about the past become embedded in new ones, however deeply hidden, even forgotten, they may be. Struggle as they sometimes try, historians, like everyone else, are incapable of jettisoning every as-

10. In fact, Donald R. Kelley terms Eusebius "the original Whig historian" for finding in the past the roots of what came to be Christian civilization in the West—as if that civilization were predetermined, the direction of history were unquestionable, and no possible alternative outcomes existed.

pect of the intellectual and cultural world (many dimensions of which they are unaware) into which they are born. The ghosts of histories past always maintain their residence in history's house. In early Christian times, those ghosts wore Greek and Roman sheets. Christian historians absorbed much of the history of Rome related by earlier writers into the history of the world since Genesis. They did not ignore the role of outstanding figures in the record of God's kingdom. Great men (and occasional great women) filled Christian as they did Classical chronicles, this time however often in saintly garb. Miracles took the place of the pagan gods' often inexplicable acts. Peoples fought peoples as in Classical accounts. And not to be overlooked, the history of God's rule on earth was told through the history of His church and its bishops as in the past it had been told through the rule of the Greeks' and Romans' gods at work in Greek and Roman cities and states. Even though not directly and probably not even consciously, Christian historiography took form in terms set by ancient historians: great figures, conflicts, institutions, and lessons to be learned.

In many respects, the history of Christian history after Eusebius is the history of Western thought. From the fourth century until the fourteenth, history was centered on the church when it was not enraptured of the Crusades, the lives of saints, and fantastic Arthurian tales and chivalric scenes. While the knightly codes and acts of warfare and the more theatrical tournaments depicted by chroniclers like Jean Froissart contain factual reportage and can be used as historical sources, they left little residue in the ways history came to be conceived. Some medieval scholars—most notably Gregory of Tours in sixth-century France and Bede (long the Venerable, now Saint) in eighth-century England—created notable changes in historical perspective (and, in Bede's case, in chronological dating) by writing influential accounts of Christianity in their respective dominions. In that way they added to Western historical thought an emphasis on the history of individual nations and inaugurated yet another departure from the way historians had written earlier. But no less than any other historical tradition, Christian historiography itself eventually proved susceptible to change and, more significant, to conflict. Divisions within Christianity—between Christian polities, Christian theologians, and Christian sects—may have taken some time to make themselves apparent; yet if their depth and consequence did not rival the deep and permanent split within the Christian community of faith that came with the sixteenth-century Reformation, they were consequential enough to indelibly affect the course of historical thought and constitute revisions to the interpretive scheme inaugurated by Eusebius.

That was because the early Christian lands and societies of which Eusebius and others wrote in their histories proved no more immune to alteration in their earthly circumstances than any others. So when assaults on the rapidly spreading Christian community did arise, the intellectual and religious system that grew to sustain Christian beliefs had to develop beyond its original Christian formulation to respond to these attacks. Most difficult to understand and justify in Christian eyes was the gap between the claims of God's rule on earth and the realities of life. And nothing more was needed to bring home the intellectual, theological, and historical significance of that gap than the Visigoths' sack of Imperial Rome in 410. How was the city that Eusebius and his successors had incorporated into their Christian chronicles—"Eternal Rome" to its ancient inhabitants, the seat of the bishop of Rome, and thus the center of Christianity to believers after Constantine—how was this Rome to be understood if Christianity's fortunes were so closely tied to so vulnerable a capital of empire? On the other hand, how could Christianity be understood if freed from its Roman context?

The most significant intellectual response to these questions, forced on Christians by the Visigoths' invasion of the Eternal City, came from the bishop of Hippo (in today's Algeria), the figure known since then as Saint Augustine. Augustine's *City of God,* written sometime after 410, was historiographically almost as revolutionary as Eusebius's *Ecclesiastical History,* although Augustine laid no claim to be writing history.[11] Wrestling like so many others in this great book to make sense of the destruction of the seat of the church, Augustine, who had directly encountered refugees from destroyed Rome, distinguished between a "city of man," like the ruined community on the Tiber, and a "city of God." The former, the earthly city, Augustine portrayed as the home of human

11. Nor can Augustine be considered a historian in the line of those who preceded him. For instance, he did not seek evidence through interviews and travels as Herodotus did, and he did not use documents, as Eusebius did.

life, of sin, evil, and confusion, where mundane history takes its course. The other city, the heavenly city, is the locale of the sacred—of divine order, justice, forgiveness, and love. In the first, he writes, "The princes and the nations it subdues are ruled by the love of ruling; in the other, the princes and the subjects serve one another in love." While the two cities sometimes intermix, humans live in only one of them and can hope for access to the other only through divine intervention and redemption. But even if relegated to an earthly city, humans are subject to a providential plan, whose spiritual course it becomes historians' role to reveal and explain. Following Eusebius, Augustine thus gave additional authority to the notion of progress while adding renewed responsibility to historians' professional and intellectual obligation to explain the deeds of humans to other humans.

Like all ideas, whether grand or modest in scope, Augustine's two-city scheme embodied unanticipated and inadvertent consequences— ones of such magnitude that, had Augustine himself foreseen them, he might have turned his mind in other directions. These consequences were at first subtle and slow to take effect, and the span of time between Augustine's intellectual innovation and the first signs of what was at stake was more than a millennium. Not until the fifteenth-century Renaissance did the significance for historical understanding of Augustine's distinction between two realms of experience first make itself fully visible. While intended as a theological strategy, Augustine's intellectual move laid the groundwork for a historiographic revolution as far-reaching as the earlier shift from Classical to Christian interpretations of the past. That revolution was the slow disenchantment, demystification, and de-Christianization of history—the exiling of God, as well as of magical spirits, animal and household gods, ghosts, and other supernatural beings, from human affairs.

Yet so gradual and extended was these pagan characters' departure from the intellectual construction of the world that one must ask whether such a momentous alteration in thinking that is not historical in intent, is so slow to be realized, and takes so long to become the modus operandi of historians ought to be encompassed in a history of alterations in historical thought at all. Can nonhistorians affect historical thinking? Can a development like disenchantment and the waning of the role of divine intermediaries in human life have a justifiable place in a history of historical revisionism? Both questions can be accorded historiographic function as long as we free ourselves from some twenty-first-century assumptions about historical studies. Today, challenges to existing interpretations of the past come thick and fast. They originate in the opening of new evidentiary sources (genetic samples, for instance), the development of new methods for exploiting old evidence (LiDAR airborne remote sensing to locate buried structures under jungle canopies), the broadening of what is taken to constitute valid historical evidence (wall drawings in caves, for instance, or the contents of landfills), and the spread of new ways of thought and modes of interpretation (gender studies being a good example). But they also arrive, as did Augustine's if much more rapidly due to accelerated communications, from alterations in thought outside historical scholarship. Thus the centuries between Augustine's great work and the earliest glimmerings of its nontheological consequences in the Italian Renaissance can seem for that reason alone (to say nothing of the fact that his *City of God* was a theological work) to put his theological scheme outside the history of history. But measured not by intellectual intention or historical proximity but rather by the eventual deep intellectual consequences on historical writing of Augustine's thinking, his book has to be considered yet another major turning point in the way the past was conceived. We are its legatees.

∾

Augustine's *City of God* distinguished between two spheres of history—the earthly and the divine, one preparatory for the other. That suggested the possibility of writing, even the church's permission to write, separate histories of both, each distinct from the other, and it exposed a fault line that would eventually allow the idea of historical progress to be cast in secular as well as Christian terms. It was a possibility first fully grasped in fourteenth- and fifteenth-century Italy, where churchmen and others rediscovered the significance of the texts of Classical Greece and Rome. This rebirth of learning, this rediscovery of literary and historical writing—the Renaissance—opened the way to the gradual redirection of Western thought toward human rather than godly affairs. Historical study gained renewed authority in this great age of humanistic thought and reflection.

With hindsight, it is tempting to see the emergence of this first serious challenge to Christian ways of historical thinking as inevitable. But if historical developments were inevitable, historians would be out of work and could turn their labors over to soothsayers and planners. Instead, such developments require explanation and interpretation after they occur. No doubt, since those who write history are of the same broad diversity as the rest of humankind, a divergence from the Christian story line would have occurred at some time simply because human minds different from those of Eusebius and Augustine would have taken up writing about the past. But why did this happen in the fourteenth and fifteenth centuries—a question that incorporates its counterfactual: why did it not happen earlier or later?—and why did it happen where it did, in Italy, principally in Tuscany?

Within a few centuries after the Emperor Constantine had signaled the end of hostility to Christianity within the Roman Empire and allowed the young religion to gain adherents, the Italian states had developed into a collection of distinctive, frequently warring and secessionist, jurisdictions rent by succession crises and changes of regimes. Often these states were coveted by the leaders of other states, many of those from outside Italy. Whether republics, like Venice, or ducal and princely entities, like Milan and Venice, these statelets were geographically contained, all centered on cities—thus "city-states." To maintain their freedoms, they had developed cadres of skilled politicians and diplomats and given birth to patriots who affirmed their loyalties firmly to their cities or those cities' ruling families. Religion was far from these men's concern. As if taking permission from Augustine, they understood their situations in secular terms; and in consonance with their growing nonreligious outlook on the world, they developed a deep appreciation of the writings of Classical antiquity, especially of Classical historical texts. Out of this crucible of historical coincidence arose two developments that were critical to establishing what would slowly emerge from them to be conventional in historical thought—in the first place, an acceptance of alterations in historical interpretations and arguments among historians and, in the second, an adoption of the conventions by which those arguments would be carried out. Each would forever affect the way in which the past was understood and historical inquiry pursued.

The first creative breakthrough came from the philological studies of Lorenzo Valla, a peripatetic Italian priest and scholar deeply affected by the fourteenth century's reawakened examination of the texts of Classical antiquity. Philology, the historical study of languages, already existed as a reputable subject of inquiry; and the rebirth of interest in Greek and Latin Classical texts had reanimated the study of the languages in which they were written. In 1439, Valla shocked the medieval world of learned men, both within and outside the church, by demonstrating in a slashing attack that a purportedly fourth-century document, the so-called *Donation of Constantine,* by which the Emperor Constantine had supposedly given authority over Rome and the western part of his empire to the pope, was a forgery. By promoting that fake, wrote Valla, the later church had engaged in "dishonoring the majesty of the pontificate, dishonoring the memory of ancient pontiffs, dishonoring the Christian religion, [and] confounding everything with murders, disasters and crimes." His virtuoso performance of linguistic scholarship and forensic inquiry demonstrated that the *Donation* could not have been written, as had long been asserted, in the century after Constantine but instead, because it incorporated words that had not existed in the fourth century CE, had been written much later. What had conventionally been taken to be the document by which Constantine bestowed the church's authority on the pope was no such authority at all.

Valla's discovery, one rooted in the analysis of historical documentation, revealed not only that a revision of received historical wisdom was possible but that such an altered history could be dangerous to established power and tradition, its danger being one of the reasons that "revisionist" history has always been controversial.[12] Valla's research also established a new, and thenceforth foundational, criterion for historical argument: every historical interpretation must pass muster on an evidentiary basis. To purge written history of error was as much historians' responsibility as was writing history afresh. To be considered

12. It should however be noted that Valla's discovery did not alter the situation of the papacy. This should comfort those who see revisionist history of any sort as an inescapable threat to power. While people get exercised by challenges to received or conventional interpretations of the past, these challenges rarely result in rapid or deep alterations in institutions, practices, or relationships. Those changes may come, but usually only gradually.

authoritative, arguments over what had actually happened in the past would now have to take place on the basis of factual evidence, not mere claims. Moreover, while being more than a simple matter of criticism, Valla's achievement also prospectively evened the field of historical argumentation by placing as much weaponry in the hands of any defense of received knowledge as in that of any attack on it. No revisionist history could in the future win out simply because its claims were attractive. Those claims now had to survive the heavy tests of empirical validity and acceptance by other expert historians. They also had to withstand the complicating fact that evidence itself could be contradictory, incomplete, and unclear.

Yet Valla's achievement embodied an even more portentous development in the history of history, one that has never gotten its due. It demonstrated that to be a historian did not require one to be a participant in the history of which he or she wrote. Previously, that had been the situation of every historian—from Herodotus and Thucydides through Eusebius and Augustine, to medieval figures like Gregory, Bede, and Froissart; close-up participant history had been the conventional, orthodox form of historical writing. By contrast, Valla liberated historical knowledge from firsthand observation. He demonstrated that thinkers and scholars could be free of direct engagement with the subjects of which they wrote, could examine the remains of their history in surviving documents and church archives, and could reflect on them at their writing desks, all the while building plausible narratives and offering authoritative interpretations. Even if inadvertently, Valla opened the door to pure intellectual inquiry about the past and thus to independent, often clashing, sometimes irreconcilable, and thus ever-changing interpretations about earlier times. His investigative work led to the emergence of the goal of balanced, perhaps even "objective," assessments of past events based on research in the archives of religious institutions and powerful families.[13] In the long parentage of

13. Valla thus strengthened the distinction between reportage—"the first draft of history," on-the-scene observation of contemporary events, which, in effect, the earliest historians, from Herodotus on, had pursued—and professional history, the calmer, more distanced, more reflective, archivally based interpretations of the past undertaken long after events had occurred and their participants had died.

revisionist history, Lorenzo Valla deserves a place among its greatest figures. Every historian is in his debt.

Valla's bombshell discovery was followed by a second, equally decisive new approach to the past during the Renaissance. Significantly, it was not based on Valla-like disenthralled research in archives. And it had to contend with the pervasive Christian reading of the past, the Christian community's dual foundations in the Flood and Rome, that had characterized historical thought after Augustine in what the Renaissance Humanists termed the Middle Ages. In most respects this reawakened approach to the past followed age-old historical custom: the attempt to understand the very circumstances in which the people writing history were involved as men of affairs. What differed was the new historians' point of view, one that inaugurated an approach to history from which there has been no turning back, even though, unlike Valla's, it has been contested ever since. It was history focused on the historian's commune, his city-state, of which Florence received the most gifted attention.

The local history of Italian communities had been pioneered by Humanists Giovanni Villani and Leonardo Bruni, the latter Valla's teacher. But the two historians who brought it to its highest achievement—by replacing chronicles of local events with analytical history—were Niccolò Machiavelli and Francesco Guicciardini, both Florentines. The two participated in the public life of their city, Machiavelli as a diplomat and supporter of republican efforts to oust the Medici family from control, Guicciardini as a diplomat in that family's service (and thus deeply acquainted with documentary records, which, following Valla, he exploited). Like Augustine faced with making theological sense of the sack of Rome, both were deeply troubled by the French invasion of the Italian states in 1494; and like Livy earlier meditating on the fall of Rome, both sought to extract principles of governance, behavior, and practice from the history of their own and past times. Machiavelli did so most famously and enduringly in *The Prince* (ca. 1515), which emphasized the role of force in politics and statecraft, and in his *Discourses on the First Ten Books of Livy* (1519), a work concerning the conditions for the maintenance of republican government, which he extolled. The Venetian republic, he wrote, "both for its institutions and for its importance, deserves to be celebrated beyond every other Italian state," and he tried to show how it gained, then lost, its preeminence. In both of his principal works, Machiavelli assumed Thucydides' mantle and urged statesmen to study history to learn the causes of success and failure in war and diplomacy. "As to exercise for the mind," wrote Machiavelli in *The Prince*, "the prince ought to read history and study the actions of eminent men, see how they acted in warfare, [and] examine the causes of their victories and defeats in order to imitate the former and avoid the latter." Guicciardini referred to "laws" that history followed and that must be studied. As much as they differed with each other, in the eyes of both history was a useful science filled with lessons that could be learned. In the words of the distinguished historian Felix Gilbert, in their works "explanation of the 'why' took precedence over narration of the 'what.'"

Like most Humanists, the two historians found their inspiration in Classical histories and reanimated the ancients' concern with republican virtues and service to the commonweal. But their histories— Machiavelli's pessimistic 1525 *Florentine Histories* (sometimes known as the *History of Florence*) and Guicciardini's equally dark-spirited 1540 *The History of Italy,* both written in vernacular Italian—were works that, like Herodotus's and Thucydides', sought to make sense of their times, the former's drawn from his long interest in power and his deep Florentine patriotism, the latter's based on his understanding of the relation between city-states and the necessity of a balance of power among them. Adapting Thucydides' and Livy's concerns with politics, war, and foreign relations, of which in various ways, like Thucydides, they were practitioners, they recaptured for history the ancients' tight focus on specific, not all, dimensions of human affairs. Like Thucydides, too, they stuck close to recent history and sought in the past those examples of human action that offered instruction in appropriate and injurious conduct, in statecraft, and in moral philosophy—the last being the subject in which history would long remain embedded in educational curricula.

Moreover, Machiavelli and Guicciardini broke sharply from ancient, medieval, and Christian historiography in their thoroughgoing exclusion of conventional religious explanations for human affairs and in their refusal to seek some providential purpose in the human past. Their approach owed much to their conviction that successive popes had been responsible for the troubled state of Italy in their lifetime. They had no compunction about criticizing the church. In doing so, they deepened the foundation of an enduring intellectual, as well as political and constitutional, tension between church and state in the West. In that respect, their histories were something new. Where the Classical historians had been, in Western terms, pagan—polytheists, or believers in many gods—these Renaissance Humanists, even while in religious matters Christians, were in historical matters secularists. They felt no attachment to the medieval determination to reveal the hand of Providence in human affairs. Neither God nor gods (with the exception of "Fortuna," or Fate, now increasingly a metaphor for the inexplicable) appeared in their historical works. Their subjects were of this world, as were their explanations of events and the lessons they drew from them—in the Classical and Humanist tradition, from "philosophy teaching by examples," the examples not of clearly defined conduct but of a philosophical attitude toward human fortune and misfortune.[14] Made by humans, history had to be explained in human terms. In this regard, their histories moved into the opening unintentionally provided by Augustine's distinction between the cities of man and of God and marked a break with histories going as far back as that of Herodotus, who credited deities with agency on earth, and with that of Eusebius, whose God presided over His terrestrial dominion. The implicit attitude of these two historians was that God was inessential to historical explanation. Their shift to a secular approach to history was fateful, even if it took centuries to secure itself as a core feature of Western historical studies. Few alterations in the ways history was earlier pursued can rival it in its enduring consequences.

14. "History is philosophy teaching by examples" was the celebrated formulation of Dionysius of Halicarnassus, one invoked by countless thinkers since. It is not that Machiavelli and Guicciardini completely dismissed large forces, especially Fate, from their explanatory schemes. But in accepting the role, indeed the power, of Fortuna in human life, they had principally in mind those forces that were beyond the power of humans to affect—forces of such magnitude and complexity that humans could not fully understand them. This did not, for these historians, entail a belief in a direction for human affairs, a purpose to history's course, or a plan instituted by God. But it was fully compatible with confidence in rational explanations up to the limits of historians' knowledge.

One other aspect of this Renaissance change in Western historiography must not escape attention. Today, when historians and their
readers think of "revisionist history," they often have in mind ideological battles (or at least battles that take ideological form, like that over
the wisdom of dropping atomic bombs on Japan), a new perspective—a
feminist one, for example—on an old subject, or new interpretations
occasioned by the discovery of new evidence (such as DNA findings).
Most of these fresh perspectives are intentional; their authors make clear
their grounds for challenging or adding to previous views of a subject
in a particular direction, with a particular argument, or because of the
discovery of new facts. Machiavelli and Guicciardini can be classed with
such more recent historians. They adopted a secular approach to the
past because of the challenge they set for themselves—to bring down to
earth, in a Christian culture, an explanation of the discouraging events
of recent times in their beloved Italian states. They thus began the process of freeing historical study from theology and from the assumption
that, being in the hands of God, the past as well as the present was
beyond comprehension. Neither believed that he needed to go beyond
ascertainable fact to explain the historical past. Both believed, writes
Felix Gilbert of Guicciardini, that "historical writings could disclose insights which could be expressed in no other way." For them, history was
an independent branch of knowledge that yielded its own distinctive
understanding of human life.

Already by the early years of the Reformation—for the two Florentine historians were writing their historical works after Martin Luther's
challenge to the Roman Church in 1517 and after Christopher Columbus
had stumbled on the Western Hemisphere—historical thought and
writing were showing early signs of the diversity of interpretation and
sensibility that would eventually open history to the multitude of varied
approaches we know today. And how could they not have? The Reformation and the European discovery of lands to the west engendered yet
another revolution in historiographic interpretation, one so abiding
that, thenceforth, the period before 1517—between the origins of the
primitive church and the early sixteenth century—came to be known,
in the Christian West at least, as the Dark Ages. From a few formative
Classical texts, themselves not of a single voice, were emerging distinc-

tive tangents, distinctive styles. Already, history was straining against the tendency to resolve itself into the expression of a single perspective, a single sensibility, or a single inquiry. In other words, historical thought was on the verge of modernity.

For further reading, see next chapter.

THREE

Revisionist History in the Modern Era

T he opening to European consciousness of a new world on the western edges of the Atlantic after 1492 and the division of Western Christianity into warring religions (and, conse- quently, into increasingly warring states) after 1517 eroded the existing, general historical conventions and traditions that had come to exist by then. With Europeans discovering lands, peoples, and customs they had not earlier known, new national and imperial rivalries taking form, and the old Western Church being assailed from within and without as never before, history was thenceforth to be rewritten from every perspective—out of new evidence, new thinking, new conflicts, and new intellectual needs. Accordingly, changes in historical thought and argumentation began to speed up, and the variety of historical genres, though still owing much to the Classical and pagan founders of written history, grew in number and kind. Already it was clear that the past looked different from different vantage points and that its inter- pretations and presentations were never again to remain uncontested. Not that history had ever been walled off from the rest of society; from the beginning, it had had to accommodate itself to powerful, outside influences. But from the late fifteenth century forward, those influences began to mount in number, diversity, and force. The accommodation of historical thought to external reality was nothing new; rather, its need to accommodate to that reality, given the accelerating divisions and conflicts in Western society, was simply intensified. From then on, history was to be characterized, if by nothing else, by variety, debate, and change.

The European discovery of a new world to the west was the first major jolt to historical thought in the early modern world. How could the existence of strange civilizations be squared with Christian origin stories, especially if the tribal cultures of the Western Hemisphere had their own tales of their beginnings? How significant was the past of the "Old World" when set against the different past of the "New World?" Could this New World be encompassed within narratives that gave primacy to power and warfare in the Thucydidean tradition, or would Herodotean relativism and the acceptance of the equal importance of different civilizations fit better with the discovery of new realities? Future answers to these and countless other questions of similar magnitude would accelerate the erosion of the certainties that had underlain historical thought for centuries.

While the process was slow, the adaptation of old knowledge to new (and vice versa) constituted a lasting revision in historical perspective, one whose influence has never waned and from which fresh understanding continues to flow. As more was learned of the history and culture of all peoples throughout the world; as the realization of the influence of geography, the environment, and biology on the human past gathered steam; as it became clear that different peoples possess distinct convictions as to their origins, see the world in distinct ways, worship distinct gods, speak in languages that create distinct modes of thought—as the consequence of all such factors, the Christian and Western certainties of historical thought that existed at the opening of the sixteenth century were bound to disintegrate. In their place arose histories more varied and more subject to dispute.

Not surprisingly, it was the Reformation, usually dated from Martin Luther's direct challenge to the Catholic Church in 1517, that provided the second spur to a rethinking of the Western past—the spur to what Donald Kelley calls "a massive project of revisionism." First for Lutherans, then for other Protestants, the conflict (armed as well as theological) within Western Christianity necessitated new historical narratives, a fresh emphasis on national pasts, and an intensified turn to archival sources. The Protestant Eusebius was the Strasbourg historian and diplomat Johann Sleidan, not much recalled today, who, in as balanced a fashion as he could summon (and thus earning the enmity of some fellow Lutherans), laid out in his 1555 *Commentaries on the Condition of Religion and State Under Emperor Charles V* the historical case for the Lutheran Reformation. Other Protestant historians, followers of Luther, John Calvin, Philip Melanchthon, and Ulrich Zwingli, then joined Sleidan to, as they saw it, cleanse history of the theological errors that had infested the True Church since the days of Constantine. This necessarily gave rise to deeply polarized and polemical works and battles between Protestant and Catholic apologists over which religion's history possessed the theological and moral upper hand. Each religion, then each denomination and sect, would now have its own historians— or at least propagandists writing in historical terms. And if that were so, then what nation, what city, what party, what people would lack its historians, many of them partisans, too? History was becoming a battleground of argument as well as a field of inquiry, and a battleground it would remain.

Relevant here is that so much of the rivalry between Western confessions was played out in historical as well as theological terms. Given the lock that the Roman Church and Roman history had for so long secured on the way the past was understood, the spreading breaches with Catholic Rome released other peoples, like the Germans, French, and English, to break free of the Italian yoke and try to interpret their histories in national terms, sometimes even to the point of entirely ignoring the Greek and Roman past—and increasingly, like Machiavelli and Guicciardini, God too—in their search for historical origins. Such histories, now written in vernacular languages, became accessible to those without competence in Latin, so that historical issues began to be of significance as they never had been before in debates outside the circles of scholars and educated professionals like doctors and lawyers. History, taking on presentist colorations, was becoming a factor in the rise of national patriotism and a general possession of the increasingly growing reading public and political classes, which it has remained ever since. Interpretations of the past thus became revisionist battlegrounds between national states—nation-states that would be at one another's throats until the conclusion of the Thirty Years' War in 1648.

The appearance of these national histories only strengthened the accelerating tendency of historical thought to take on secular hues and was an early example of the breakup of histories claiming to be universal in favor of increasingly specialized, ever more confined topics. Moreover, not for at least four centuries did the historiographic division between Catholic and Protestant views of the past inaugurated by Sleidan and others abate. Only in recent decades has it been possible to read histories of religion whose aims are not to vindicate one confession over another. And while written history's role in justifying religious differences—at least those between the great Western religions—has diminished, its role of serving as the terrain on which ideological, methodological, and other rivalries play out has never ended.

This development, dating from the early sixteenth century at the latest, should alert us to another feature of historical thought that had its initial impact, one also never diminished, within the century before 1648, when Europe's religious wars came to a close. It is what professional historians know of as "historicism": the recognition that there exists no fixed point—geographical, chronological, cultural, national, ethnic, ideological, or any other—from which to ascertain truths about the past.[1] If Catholics and Protestants; Germans, French, and British; colonists, African slaves, and Native Americans; Whigs and Tories; males

1. The shape-shifting term "historicism" requires explanation. Philosophers of historical knowledge use it, as Karl Popper did, to refer to the supposed laws of history—that "history is controlled by specific historical or evolutionary laws whose discovery would enable us to prophesy the destiny of man." Georg W. F. Hegel, Karl Marx, Oswald Spengler, and Arnold Toynbee were adherents of this view. By contrast, most practicing historians employ the word to mean the method of placing the development and reality of everything in the past in its full context of culture, society, institutions, politics, language, and the like. Few historians today are not historicists in that meaning of the term; they are contextualists. But to complicate matters further, there exists a third meaning of the term, one that, since the days of twentieth-century historian James Harvey Robinson, has attracted many historian adherents—that historical knowledge can help solve current problems. As should be clear, one has to use, and read, the term "historicism" with due caution.

and females—if each of these could try to bring distinct perspectives to bear on the historical past, then where lay the certain, recoverable truth about the past for whose search historians had taken on the responsibility? Once loosed on the intellectual world, historicism—radical doubt about historians' ability to find the full, perhaps single, story about the past and agree about it—was never again to be contained. If anything was inevitable, it was that, from the seventeenth century on, history was to be a terrain on which contending interpretations of the past would struggle for ascendancy.

Yet the argument that all history is potentially revisionist history risks being indiscriminate. From the days of Herodotus, it was the conceit of historians that they were seeking The Truth about the past, not one of many truths. (Cicero termed the search for truth the "first law" of history.) So even when their histories took on the role of justifying a particular national regime or religious view, historians laid claim to the ideal of fidelity to evidence. Such truth claims were historians' admission tickets to the community of other historians. These claims were also what separated them from storytellers and poets and made the results of their endeavors more kindred to fact than to fiction. Such claims, however, did little to stem disagreements among historians, for no agreement they might reach as to the validity of evidence automatically extended to the evidence's significance and meaning. They could agree, for example, that the Thirteenth Amendment to the Constitution ended slavery in the United States. But what had the legal end to American slavery meant in fact for blacks and whites alike? The search for truth could separate as well as bind historians.

In that sense, historians were always arguing about the comparative strength of interpretations and about those interpretations' fidelity to the truth, however they might define the truth. Even when arguing about the relative merits of different interpretations, historians had also to ask: If all written history makes equal claims to truth, then on what grounds are those claims to be assessed, and who is to assess them? If appeal to some external authority—to religion, national regime, ideological camp, or interpretive approach—cannot bring historians to agreement, what is to do so? Over time, the answer was this: agreement could be arrived at only through the accumulation of experience and the arrival at a kind of informal assent about the acceptable use of evidence able to create a set of standards governing historians' endeavors. At the same time, historians would eventually understand that nothing could eradicate disagreement among them. They could at best seek comity—an agreement to live with their disagreements and to argue without end, all the while hoping to narrow the grounds of their disputes.

Moreover, as time passed, these disagreements increased with the growth in the number of practicing historians and in the kinds of minds at work on the past. Schoolchildren experience the result in their history textbooks, where, at the start, large events and developments unscroll at a somewhat leisurely pace, until they are replaced by an increasing rush of facts, dates, and names that create an often lasting frustration with history courses in schools. Coverage becomes difficult to control. Even an illustrative sketch of the history of historical thought, a sketch like this one intended to develop a considered line of argument, can only with many omissions avoid breaking up into strings of brief sketches of historians and works of history once it reaches the Enlightenment and then the nineteenth and twentieth centuries, when historical thought had disintegrated from the relative coherence of assumption, approach, and method that characterized it in the West through much of the previous centuries. The incorporation of ever more subjects under historians' gaze and the reduction of large historical time periods into ever shorter ones for interpretive purposes, along with the proliferation of distinct interpretations, create a kind of inexhaustible, sometimes exhausting, availability of partly valid ways of looking at the past. This has become another feature of intellectual modernity.

Historians will disagree as to when, sometime between the seventeenth and nineteenth centuries, historical studies crossed the threshold into this fully modern existence. But without doubt, by the late seventeenth century, early in the period of the Enlightenment, signs of many of the characteristics of what we now think of as professional history had made their appearance. Following the example set by Lorenzo Valla's unmasking of the forged *Donation of Constantine*, seventeenth-century historians began to keep an eye out for anachronism and to integrate source criticism regularly into their methods, especially when assessing assertions about secular history.[2] In this aim, historians were aided by the gradual opening of state and church archives. They quarreled also over the purposes of historical scholarship and methods of historical research. Especially in seventeenth-century France and England, they contested the relative authority of old and newly discovered evidence and old and newer approaches to research and argumentation in what became known as the Battle between the Ancients and Moderns—between those who looked to the past and those who looked to the present for knowledge and authority. The very argument that new knowledge could supplant old understanding not only meant that ancient views could be criticized; it also assumed the legitimacy of arguments over which particular histories were valid and worthy of acceptance.

Historical agreement was also threatened by skepticism. Historians tend to assume that skepticism—about claims, sources, and methods—is natural to their work, although some historians may be more skeptical than others. Yet as part of every historian's intellectual toolkit, skepticism has its own history. From the time of Herodotus, historians had discounted many of the claims that people and written sources made about historical events and developments. René Descartes had made radical doubt a constituent of Western philosophical thought. But as the normal stance of historians—a method of critique, a regular, necessary approach to evidence—skepticism owes its origins to the eighteenth century and to two men specifically. The first prominent thinker who elevated doubt about past historical claims to a principle of thought was David Hume, known now principally as a philosopher but controversial in the late eighteenth century for his six-volume *The History of England,* whose publication commenced in 1764. The second, one who applied skepticism as a basic method of extended historical inquiry, was England's Edward Gibbon, a cosmopolitan figure par excellence of the eighteenth century's self-styled Enlightenment and one of the greatest, most erudite historians of the modern era.

2. Providential history still tended to escape from the day's emerging tests of evidentiary validity due to the nature of its claims, but Baruch Spinoza's refusal to accept the Bible's supposed divine origins set in motion an enduring criticism of biblical assertions.

In many respects, Gibbon's great work, his six-volume *History of the Decline and Fall of the Roman Empire,* whose first volume appeared in 1776, fit well within the day's conventions of written history. It concerned major figures, politics, institutions, laws, conflicts, and wars. As embodied in its title, it followed other works, in the tradition of Giambattista Vico, by adopting the Classical and Christian conceit of cycles in history and of the progress of decadence and descent. And it was not without its Thucydidean lessons drawn from the past: "The decline of Rome was the natural and inevitable effect of immoderate greatness." Yet while it addressed a question central to the church and every European state—why Imperial Rome, whose history was the template for Europe's past, and the church, whose seat was Rome, had ceded power and influence to other forces—it did so in new ways. Among them was Gibbon's acceleration of the liberation of Western historiography from its Roman shackles, a liberation begun by Valla, Machiavelli, and Guicciardini and a change of emphasis as significant as it was determinative of written history's future direction. He did so with fresh, distinctive approaches—venturing, for instance, into cultural history, and thus, along with Voltaire and Johann Gottfried von Herder, reawakening the Herodotean approach to history after centuries of Thucydidean thralldom. By following the lead of his predecessors, like Machiavelli, Guicciardini, Hume, and William Robertson, who freed history forever from the history of Rome and on-the-spot reportage, Gibbon also removed Rome's past from the center of Western history, greatly broadened the scope of histories of the Western world, and encouraged other historians to explore other subjects and establish other standards for measuring the past. He was the earliest historian to make ironic wit a method of argumentation, one all the more influential for its stately pace and magisterial style.[3] He was unsparing in his criticisms of the church

---

3. For instance: "The various modes of worship, which prevailed in the Roman world, were all considered by the people, as equally true; by the philosopher, as equally false; and by the magistrate, as equally useful." Of the removal of antipopes by the Council of Constantine: "Of the three popes, John the twenty-third was the first victim: he fled and was brought back a prisoner: the most scandalous charges were suppressed; the vicar of Christ was accused only of piracy, murder, rape, sodomy, and incest." Unfortunately, Gibbon's sly humor did not set an example. Wit is rarely found in historical writing today.

and its leading figures even when he wrote elegies to what he considered to be the beauty of so many religious practices.

Gibbon also brought to the past a turn of thinking rarely seen before among historians, even if possessed by others in the eighteenth-century republic of letters. No one before Gibbon mined such a breadth of published sources as he did or questioned with as much skepticism, in Valla's spirit, oft-used and oft-quoted sources, especially religious ones. "The theologian," he reflected about historians' responsibilities when writing about religion, "may indulge the pleasing task of describing Religion as she descended from Heaven, arrayed in her native purity. A more melancholy duty is imposed on the historian. He must discover the inevitable mixture of error and corruption which she contracted in a long residence upon earth, among a weak and degenerate race of beings." Largely under the influence of Gibbon's example, history would continue its journey toward becoming an empirical human science, a never-ending argument over the validity, meaning, and significance of evidence. Most important, Gibbon brought a rationalistic independence to the past. Making clear that he was not taken in by the centuries-old claim that Rome—Rome, that is, as the center of Western civilization—was saved by Christianity and its influence preserved by the church, Gibbon famously saw Rome's fall as "the triumph of barbarism and religion," the triumph, that is, of uncivilized invaders and the Catholic Church, whose corruptions hastened Rome's fall.[4] Yet it may be that Gibbon's most lasting influence inhered in his ironic turn of mind. For Gibbon, the historical record revealed unintended consequences, the folly of grand schemes, and the baselessness of too many previous causal explanations. The task of historians, he urged all coming after him, was to free themselves of received opinion and let evidence guide their narratives of the past and their explanations of how that past came to be.

By the time Gibbon had completed his multivolume work, he had secured scholarly history's position as a human science. While not alone in doing so, his deeply revisionist approach to the two, great subjects of history that had long before secured classic status—the history of

---

4. Needless to say, Gibbon's work inaugurated a debate among historians and churchmen over Rome's fall that has never ceased.

Rome and of Christianity—opened a new era of historical thought and practice. Although he owed much to the ancient historians of Rome, as well as to Machiavelli and to British opposition writers and politicians of the century in which he wrote, Gibbon opened most subjects as fair game for future historians' evaluation and reevaluation. Piety about the contents of the past needed no longer to be maintained. If they followed Gibbon's example—and of course not all did so—historians were now free to bring their individual interests, perspectives, methods, and ideologies to bear on any subject of their choice.

∾

By the opening of the nineteenth century, after the assaults of new scientific knowledge, the revival of Classical learning, the rupture within the Western Church, the discovery of the New World, the accumulation of new documentation, and the advances of textual criticism, history as it had been written for centuries after Constantine's conversion of the West to Christianity had changed almost beyond recognition. The venerable, unified Christian view of the past had disintegrated, the hold of traditional subjects on historians' attention had substantially weakened, and the monopoly over historical methods and styles of belletrists, even ones as great as Gibbon, was under threat. So, too, were venerable traditions of politics, statecraft, and war—the classic subjects of Thucydidean history. Most volumes of Gibbon's *Decline and Fall* appeared between the era's two great revolutions, the American and the French. Like the events that bracketed it, his work marked both the culmination of old ways of doing history and the inauguration of new ones, so that while historians would never stop writing sweeping histories with literary artistry, slowly their grand works were displaced by histories of lesser scope, greater focus, and new intentions—everything from the professional aim of creating new knowledge based on archival research to the more public purpose of helping forge the nation-state. By the time the Napoleonic Wars had drawn to a close in 1815 with the French emperor's final defeat at Waterloo, the world in which historians lived and worked had been deeply altered. Not surprisingly, equally affected were the histories they wrote.

The next chapter in the history of historical thought and practice, one that bears on the growth of the kind of revisionist history that has become standard to historical studies in our day, took place east of Britain and France, the two countries that in the eighteenth century had been the center of developments in history's history. The following hundred years proved a German century of historical studies, for it was in the then still-un-united German principalities, church territories, and free cities that so many of the attributes of what we think of today as the world of professional history had their origin. The German states' defeats in the Napoleonic Wars had aroused a desire, especially in Prussia, to awaken German political and intellectual life. For historical studies, German universities, principally in Berlin and Göttingen, were to be the major sites of that awakening. Paradoxically, changes in the intentions and practices of historians originated in a nationalist reaction to the revolutionary, universalist, and rationalistic ideas of the French Revolution. That is, the revisionist impulses of academic historians gained their enduring roots within a traditionalist, conservative context. In one of history's many ironies, modern historical revisionism owes many of its strengths to a reaction against liberalism.

This new stage in history's history required more than changes in perspective and approach. It required the creation of an independent, learned discipline—a domain of knowledge with its own methods, subjects, purposes, structures, and practices in which at least some of its developments would arise immanently—that is, out of prior historical inquiry by professional historians working within the discipline itself as well as from outside influences. To become that discipline, history had to free itself from being an adjunct to the study of rhetoric, oratory, religion, and law and become autonomous—institutionally as well as intellectually. The discipline had to create its own dedicated practitioners, people who called themselves professional historians and "did" history. It had to be built on the model that Gibbon had offered, one in which the interpretation of sources and the evaluation of arguments were uppermost. It called for, and thus called into being, the protocols of preparation and the institutional structures that would nurture and support practitioners of the historian's craft. It needed in these practitioners a confidence in the legitimacy of their individual researches and interpretations, in their sense that they were free to follow evidence and argument where each might lead. And it assumed the idea of progress, that great Enlightenment faith in the possibility of improvement in human knowledge as well as in human affairs.

Yet the idea of progress was at a considerable discount after the failure of the radical revolution in France and of the brief Napoleonic Empire that succeeded it. The hope for any kind of universalistic history had suffered a keen blow when the rationalistic, secular ideals of the French Revolution and the advances of Napoleon's imperial armies proved to be failures. The history of individual nation-states, not of an overarching Western civilization built on Rome's example, now seemed to an increasing number of people the likely source of guidance toward improvements in human life. If gains in the human condition in individual countries—indeed, if improvements in the fortunes and power of individual countries—were possible, then historical knowledge could be key to assessing where progress had occurred and where it had not. History now became a potential political as well as intellectual instrument in the emergence out of separate lesser jurisdictions of new nation-states like Germany and Italy and in the modernization of older ones. In fact, nationalism became a major historical force shaping historical scholarship in post-Napoleonic Europe. The stakes involved in historical arguments consequently rose; and "mere" erudite, pleasing, Herodotean history, especially to those for whom history came to be the bedrock of national self-consciousness and self-assertion, came to seem limiting. Social and cultural history, which had enjoyed a renaissance of sorts with Voltaire and Gibbon in the eighteenth century, now again took a back seat to historical concerns with the nation (the people, the *volk*, and race), the state (the political unit), and interstate relations, all subjects that lodged at the core of historical research and argument for the next hundred years. History, as was to become apparent, was once again to be "useful," however its utility might be defined.

The leading figure in the creation of the basic elements of academic history as we know it today, probably the most influential historian of the past two centuries, was Leopold von Ranke, professor of history at the University of Berlin in the heart of Prussia, the core state of the emerging modern Germany. University-based professors of history had existed here and there before Ranke took up his professorship in 1825; and positions of royal historiographer at many princely courts, as well as semiprofessional positions at royal, church, and other archival collections, had helped provide the foundations for modern historical research. As for the distinct subject-specific academic departments within university faculties that today we take for granted, existing schools of law and medicine within universities already pointed the way.

But it was Ranke more than anyone else who is associated with the founding of the modern history professorship, history department, and approaches to preparing other historians for scholarly careers; it was he who did the most at this early moment in history's professional development to turn historical study and writing from an occupation into a vocation. He firmly institutionalized the seminar as the central feature of professional education in history, thus creating a system of student preparation that ensured that historians' influence might be enduringly felt.[5] Emphasizing the value of objective history—the historian's duty being, in his celebrated formulation, to discover the past "as it essentially was" ("*wie es eigentlich gewesen war*")—he influenced every succeeding generation of historians by having his students write tightly focused monographs instead of sprawling narratives, a form of presentation that required a dependence on known evidence embodied in manuscript and published sources.[6] "Go to the archives!" and "State the facts!" became imperatives ever after. The emphasis on evidence was accompanied by a consistently critical suspicion about the contents of documents and a growing reliance on neutral, rather than literary, prose, the kind often criticized today as "academic." The canons of research and writing that Ranke established eventually led to the inau-

5. In the United States, his example was followed first at Johns Hopkins and Harvard universities in the late nineteenth century. Now, of course, the research seminar is a standard feature of all graduate school preparation in many other disciplines.

6. Much ink has been spilled over the correct English translation of Ranke's celebrated phrase. It can also be translated as "as it actually happened" without significantly altering its meaning. However, some believe that the better translation is "as it essentially was" or "as it essentially happened." The alternative translation removes from Ranke's words the implication that the past can be known or re-created in its objective reality, an implication that, in some minds, makes Ranke a naïf. Instead, the translation "as it essentially was" allows for the more modern—or, as some would have it, postmodern—understanding that no objective reality can be recaptured and that there can never be a single way of understanding any part of the past.

guration in 1859 of the *Historische Zeitschrift*, the first journal devoted solely to historical scholarship in the Rankean mode. Like that of most of his contemporaries among historians, Ranke's scholarship and that of the students he taught focused on the nation-state, albeit without the mystical, spiritual, theological, and narrowly nationalistic trappings that came to characterize, with such dire consequences, much later German thought about the realm (*das Reich*). Ranke's work also emphasized interstate relations, especially the shifting balances of power between nations. As if these influences were not enough, Ranke also insisted that all eras and subjects of history were "immediate to God" ("*unmittelbar zu gott*"), a conviction that would gain widespread resonance in the second half of the twentieth century. Such convictions formed the basis of what came confidently to be called "historical sciences" (*historische Wissenschaften*), Ranke himself terming history an "empirical science," a body of knowledge secured by its own independent methodology.[7]

While one risks overemphasizing Ranke's influence, it is impossible to overlook the fact that almost every historian coming after him had to contend with what he and his contemporaries established. As is common with institutions, practices, and intentions everywhere, the ones Ranke fully developed first had a tendency to endure. After him, to step away from state relations and political and diplomatic history came to be seen as heterodox even when one protested that those subjects and such narrative style were not written into a historian's Decalogue but were merely artifacts of the archives one consulted and the intention of one's work. Consequently, to deviate from Ranke's norms came to seem novel, perhaps dangerous. Questions raised about the goal, even skepticism about the possibility, of "objective" history offered in monographic form was likely to be met with disbelief. Even if one quoted Ranke's conviction about every subject's immediacy to God—even if, say, one insisted on the role of manual laborers, women, and slaves, as

7. The setting in which Ranke helped create the discipline of history—the University of Berlin—could not have been more congenial to his purposes and, being in Prussia's capital, more influential. That institution was founded in 1810 by a group of men, led by philosopher Wilhelm von Humboldt, as the staging ground of a wide range of *Wissenschaften*, formal and systematic forms of inquiry, or what we call disciplines. History was among them. Humboldt's creation is now the Humboldt University of Berlin.

well as warriors and statesmen, in the development of human societies and tried to recapture their contributions to the past—heavily fortified professional conventions, expectations, and practices stood in the way of departures from Rankean norms. Is it any wonder that the term "revisionist history" came to convey connotations of resistance (on the revisionists' part) and disbelief (on the part of those troubled by any questioning of existing interpretations)? In some circles, it would be like *lèse majesté*—an unacceptable criticism of constituted authority and practice; in others, it would seem refreshing ideological or political challenge.[8]

Yet given the curiosity and disputatiousness of human nature, neither contempt for, nor adherence to, tradition could ever extinguish the impulse to use fresh evidence and advance fresh argument. This became clear in another development in Germany, one more defiant than Ranke's, an interpretation of the past that, while altogether different in intent, consequence, and practice, had an impact on historical thought analogous to the impact of Augustine's writings 1400 years before. This fresh interpretation's author was Ranke's contemporary Karl Marx, who, like Augustine, is not typically granted membership in the company of historians. Like Augustine's writings, Marx's did not have an immediate impact on historical thought. Only in the twentieth century did Marxism, as the vast congeries of thinking and writing deriving from Marx came to be known, become an unavoidable element of historiography, an element that had to be acknowledged and confronted whatever one's position on the political or ideological spectrum.

Some would proscribe Marx, as they would his ideological and

---

8. This became clear in nineteenth-century Germany, where a sharp battle (the *Methodenstreit*, or "dispute over method," as it became known) broke out between on the one hand Ranke and his followers, especially Friedrich Meinecke, and on the other Karl Lamprecht and kindred champions of cultural history (*Kulturgeschichte*), who, following the earlier lead of Jacob Burckhardt, in the 1890s challenged Rankean political history. Although the Rankeans effectively won that particular battle among historians and thus kept historical scholarship focused on the emergence of a strong German nation-state and the awakening of the German people and the German "race" (with deep repercussions in the future Third Reich), Lamprecht foretold the turn that historical studies would take seventy-five years afterward, especially in France but also, somewhat later, in Germany, Great Britain, and the United States.

writing partner Friedrich Engels, from historians' ranks on the grounds that they were political economists. But in many of their works—and directly in Marx's *The Class Struggles in France, 1848 to 1850* and Engels's *The Peasant War in Germany* and *Revolution and Counterrevolution in Germany*—they undeniably wrote history, even if with more than historians' interest in the past. As early examples of what came to be called social scientists, unlike most modern historians they sought patterns and laws in human affairs and took less interest in discrete events and relationships. While historians try to identify causes and effects, none would be inclined to write, as Marx did, of "the logic of economic development," which relegated humans to the implementation of inevitable historical change. But from the beginning, it proved impossible to fence off their works from historical thought or to prevent their writings from affecting the way the past was conceived, if only because their works made universal claims, were suffused with historical examples, and ventured to explain the past as well as to predict the future. For those reasons, their challenges to orthodox and Enlightenment history were encompassing and deeply influential.

Marx tried (unsuccessfully, it turned out) to expunge all philosophy and metaphysics from what he considered to be the central, legitimate foci of historical understanding: human agency. In his mature writings, he denied both to the Judeo-Christian God and to pagan gods—mere human imaginings, he thought—any responsibility for human affairs, and he reduced religion ("the opiate of the people"), human consciousness, and ideas, all three of which he considered mere reflections (the ideological "superstructure") of more basic material realities, to secondary roles in human life. He believed that humans and humans alone, whether through the chains they forged on themselves or the freedom they gained after breaking the chains put on them, created their world via their modes of production and the social conditions and relations (the "structure") that emerged from those modes. "Life is not determined by consciousness," Marx wrote with Engels in *The German Ideology*, "but consciousness by life. . . . In direct contrast to German philosophy, which descends from heaven to earth, here we ascend from earth to heaven." Modes of production, argued Marx, create the classes, the divisions of labor, and the material relations that constitute society (hence, Marx's emphatic "historical materialism" and his conviction that "the nature of individuals . . . depends on the material conditions determining their production"). And so when social relations and forces of production contradict a belief system, that belief system, that ideology, must change. In such a circumstance—in the change of relations between ideas and realities—are laid the seeds of "class struggle," which will alter relations between classes and destroy capitalism by bringing about the "dictatorship of the proletariat." That in turn will require a transformation in the apparatus of the state, which is nothing but a reflection of the oppressive power held by the exploiters over the exploited. When that transformation has occurred, when capitalism has collapsed because of its inherent contradictions and the state has withered away, history as it has been known will come to a close and a society of cooperation, tranquility, and the common ownership of property—"from everyone according to his ability, to everyone according to his need"—will take its place.[9]

If Marx's and Engels's futuristic theorizing seems antithetical to the ways that historians today address their subjects, it is not unlike that of Eusebius. Like the great Christian historian, the two Germans identified and sought to understand the historical roots of a phenomenon—the clash of capitalism and labor—that was the principal conflict of their time. They imagined the realization of a historical paradise emerging from the resolution at some future date of the contradictions of the nineteenth century. They sought to give meaning to the day's unprecedented circumstances and confusions. While such an aim is now considered to be outside the historian's remit, the arguments, drawn from the past, of these two "Marxist" theorists imprinted themselves ineradicably, as did those of Eusebius, on the thinking of an increasing proportion of Western historians.

But more than these theoretical, metahistorical, prophetic innovations would alone suggest, Marx laid down another kind of challenge, one specifically relevant to historical thought. Without directly taking on the historical orthodoxies of his day—those represented by studies of

9. Needless to say, while a large proportion of historians are progressives and, like Marx, condemn injustice, few share Marx's confidence in either the arrival of some Elysium at the end of days or, as it has been more recently termed, also prophetically, the end of history.

the state, of diplomacy, and of war, the venerable concerns of historiography since the days of Thucydides—Marx instead trained his attention elsewhere. Following the lead of Voltaire and Gibbon in pursuing cultural and social history, he opened the door to the history of capitalism, property holding, workers and labor relations, manufacturing, business and commerce, and, above all, class—the history of the entire economy, all dimensions of which were implicated in modes of production and the relations among different groups of people. In turning a lens toward class, Marx magnified the importance of questions of tradition, culture, dependence, and freedom. And he converted the idea of the state from a necessary source of order and the rule of law to an instrument of one class's power over the others. These emphases were accepted no more widely by historians than they were by most of the Western public. But they introduced new and critically significant subjects of inquiry into historical thought and laid the groundwork for extensive modifications to traditional historical understanding. They also sowed suspicion about the very integrity of historians' endeavors. History could now be seen as an ideological tool, and every historian could now be suspected of class, and later ethnic, race, and gender, bias.

That Marxism never replaced conventional, progressive historiography and that it never gained the same inclusive adoption in the West as had Christian historiography in earlier centuries should come as no surprise. By the nineteenth century, few were the dictators like Constantine or absolute rulers after him, save for such totalitarian despots in the USSR, China, and North Korea, who were in a position to determine the single permissible faith of a realm or population, nor could a single historian, like Eusebius, command Western culture's entire historiographic field and set the pattern for most subsequent thinking. Western historical thought had advanced to the point that increasingly varied intentions and methods characterized historians' work. By the time of Marx, no "Marxist" history or any other kind of history, even when it gained some purchase among scholars and thinkers, had the field to itself or fought for precedence unopposed. Moreover, Marxism's eventual association with totalitarian Soviet communism cemented its controversial status in the West, the status from which it has never escaped. Yet Marxism's influence within historical circles eventually proved immense—and not

just among self-declared Marxist historians. It helped organize and satisfy historians' mounting desire to balance political with social history
and to respond to the world's transformation after 1945. By the 1960s, no
historian could legitimately avoid acquaintance with scholarship into
such subjects as class and labor relations, industry and commerce, and
the extrapolitical consequence of state power; by the 1970s, none could
avoid conversance with Marxian terminology or its cognates. One did
not have to invoke "the means of production" or "the proletariat" to
write histories of working people or economic interpretations of politics. In the last third of the twentieth century, Marxist questions had
become commonplace among historians, even among non-Marxists.
Consequently, just like Christian history when compared with pagan,
any work of history that incorporated a Marxist framework necessarily
became "revisionist" against the background of the histories that were
being written in an orthodox or conventional manner. This juxtaposition of the new against the conventional was probably inevitable. But by
the twentieth century, that juxtaposition had become commonplace.

∾

It is here, well along in my effort to outline the long history of revisionist
history, that I must finally spell out how and why the term "revisionist
history," anachronistic when applied to pre-twentieth-century historiography, came finally to be widely applied.[10] The reason is that not
until late in the nineteenth century, and only in reaction to Marx's theories, did the term "revisionist" come into general use in regard to any
intellectual works. And not until the twentieth century did historians
employ the term in any way close to its current uses. No other term
of similar meaning and acceptance existed before the late nineteenth
century, and none has since been coined to refer to pre-nineteenth-
century alterations in earlier histories of any subject. Consequently, it
has seemed unnecessary to avoid using the term "revisionist" for works
of history or any other subject written before 1900 that diverged from
earlier or conventional interpretations or to eschew the term's appli-

10. Such use of other contemporary analytical terminology (such as class, gender, social
structure, and economic mobility, to name only a very few) to refer to realities that existed
long before the new terms existed is routine among scholars in the humanities and social
sciences.

cation to any era of historical writing. In any event, as the examples of Kagan's and Kelley's application of the term to the works of Thucydides and later historians shows, historians have not shied away from doing so. The term's wide application to histories in any historiographic tradition is now inevitable and seems fully appropriate and legitimate.

Yet whatever may be one's reservations about employing the term "revisionist" when applied to works of history before the nineteenth century, there is no denying that the term's use began to have an identifiable history starting with its birth within European Marxist circles in the late 1890s. Its coinage arose around dissenting Marxists' criticisms of orthodox Marxist thought, especially criticisms advanced by Eduard Bernstein, one of the founders of democratic socialism. Orthodox Marxists who adhered more closely than did Bernstein to the original thinking of Karl Marx were the first to use the term "revisionist" against Bernstein and others who deviated from foundational Marxist propositions. It bears emphasis, however, that Bernstein accepted the term's application to his criticisms even though his critics employed the term negatively. No doubt because of its association with Marxism, the term "revisionist" has never fully lost its derogatory and negative connotations, nor has it kept clear of purposeful pejorative use, especially among some members of the general public, who, when they use it or hear it used, hear and use it mostly in negative terms. Most historians, however, now accept and use the term, both descriptively and critically, with ease.

In any event, historians' adoption of the term in relation to works of professional history did not occur in Bernstein's era. Its widespread use remained in the future. In fact, it is still impossible to determine precisely when "revisionist" was first used in relation to a work of history. But if we must shift focus exclusively to the United States as a stand-in for histories written in other countries, there can be no doubt that the first widely contested work of academic history in the United States—a work that now easily warrants the descriptive tag "revisionist"—was Charles Beard's 1913 *An Economic Interpretation of the Constitution,* a scholarly and public thunderbolt when it appeared. Beard's book argued that both the Framers of the Constitution and their opponents had adopted their respective positions because of the kind of property they owned, not out of deep Enlightenment or constitutional principles. Attacked and celebrated equally, Beard's argument heralded a new phase in the written history of American history, one characterized by a robust confidence in the advantages of revisionist historical stances.

Beard's work on the Constitution made the splash it did because it sharply differed from earlier interpretations in two ways not previously seen in American historical circles: it introduced a strong democratic socialist theme into the literature of American history; and, also for the first time, it took on the reputation of the Founding Fathers and their previously unquestioned unselfish acts of civic principle. As Beard wrote, "It cannot be said . . . that the members of the [Constitutional] convention were 'disinterested.' . . . They knew through their personal experiences in economic affairs the precise results which the new government that they were setting up was designed to attain." In addition, Beard's book had the distinction of being a tightly focused monograph based on a close examination of selective surviving evidence rather than a large, sweeping, multivolume approach. It was a thoroughly academic work, one written in the Rankean manner by a university professor of history who offered his book as meeting the demanding standards of the academic world. It was as such that it was evaluated.

The shock of Beard's study arose from its single, narrow claim, based on previously unexploited Treasury Department records, that, even if actuated by concern for the young nation's survival, the men who framed the Constitution in the summer of 1787 drafted it in a way favorable to property owners like themselves. This would not have been a novel claim—and does not strike us today as being one—had Beard simply pointed to the not surprising likelihood that the Framers' thought was bounded by their status in society; as members of the wealthy landed and urban professional gentry, they would not have been inclined to undermine their own station or interests through a set of constitutional provisions that would endanger either. After all, the Framers assumed that these interests were identical to the interests of the general free population, or at least of those within it who shared the Founders' values and aspirations. But Beard presented evidence showing that a substantial percentage of the Framers gathered in Philadelphia in the summer of 1787 were townsmen, not farmers; lawyers, not storekeepers; and—here was Beard's most striking claim—creditors, land speculators, investors, and holders of public securities. Of the Framers, he claimed, "At least five-sixths were *immediately, directly, and personally interested* in the outcome of their labors at Philadelphia, and were in a greater or lesser extent economic beneficiaries from the adoption of the Constitution." And he went further still by making a more specific claim: that the Framers sought intentionally to protect the interests of three groups of Americans: those who had bought existing Revolutionary-era debt at a discount from those in need of cash; those who had sought to prohibit the states from issuing paper money that would lead to monetary depreciation (including the depreciation of money—theirs—out on loan); and those who were seeking to protect the interests of commercial, manufacturing, and landed property.

In short, argued Beard, the Constitution was the product of a particular class of men who were in a position to enshrine in the nation's new constitution their own interests—interests they believed were threatened by the state-centered system established by the Articles of Confederation they hoped to replace. While Beard was a professed admirer of the Founders, his analysis of the evidence could only be read as being critical of them. It could also be read as arguing either that the Framers were trying to benefit directly from the government they constructed (the kind of charge that came naturally to the Muckrakers of Beard's Progressive Era) or that their interests determined the manner in which they viewed public issues (a more nuanced socioeconomic interpretation of their motives). While Beard always felt more comfortable defending the latter rather than the former interpretation, both approaches left the previous view of the Framers—of their being somehow above the sordid fray of life into which other humans plunge—more difficult to accept than before. No historian of the nation's founding who came after Beard could ignore the challenge his book laid down— the challenge of explaining both the Framers' motives and the words they embodied in the Constitution as somehow beyond self-interest.

Beard's reinterpretation of early constitutional history was in every respect an example of how every work of history reflects its time and author, no matter how hard the writer works to sterilize the work from outside influences. A distillation of intellectual and cultural currents running strong at a specific moment in the United States, Beard's

Economic Interpretation grew not only from his sensibilities and social conscience but also out of his intellectual and political engagements, those shared with many Americans. While the book must be read as a work about the past, it was also a work of Progressive, "New" history suffused with reformist hopes as well as anger at industrial conditions and social inequities. Furthermore, it was a reflection of the determination of some historians, the leader among them being Beard's Columbia colleague James Harvey Robinson, to make historical knowledge relevant to its times. (Thus its designation, the New History.) It also showed the influence of another of Beard's Columbia colleagues, the economist E. R. A. Seligman, whose ambitious anti-Marxist 1902 work, *The Economic Interpretation of History,* made a deep impression on his Morningside Heights colleague. Furthermore, Beard's monograph reflected then-current strains of a new realism, a "revolt against formalism," in political science and jurisprudence and a search, in those and other disciplines, for an empirical basis for all claims and arguments. Perhaps the best example of the effort to ground every jurisprudential assertion in ascertainable fact was the celebrated "Brandeis Brief," the long document of statistics and social science arguments filed with the Supreme Court by attorney Louis D. Brandeis (not yet a member of the Court) in the 1908 case of *Muller vs. Oregon.* Nor can one read Beard's book without being struck by its tone of muckraking zest—the pleasure of getting behind the obvious facts and exposing the darker side of public affairs. The Progressive stance of deep skepticism about the civic and economic claims of commercial, financial, and industrial interests, as well as about those interests' intervention in politics, was unmistakable in the pages of the *Economic Interpretation* as Beard went about unmasking what he argued were the realities behind the Framers' constitution—the Constitution, no one was allowed to forget, under which the nation continued to be governed.

Yet it is important to note in this context that Beard's interpretation did not survive critical attack from other historians for misconstruing the evidence he used and ignoring other evidence. Beard's book may have been, as Richard Hofstadter termed it, "the most controversial historical work of his generation," but that only made Beard's unorthodox view of the Founders a more inviting target of efforts to undermine it. No history, and certainly not one so determinedly revisionist, is ever exempt from second readings and new scrutiny. Beard's was no exception. The distinction between the Framers' personal and real property holdings that Beard thought established his points proved untenable. While he never showed any class animus in his works—he was the son of solidly middle-class parents—the dualism inherent in Beard's economic interpretation, especially the stark divide between property holders and others—a reflection of a lingering American Populist inclination to see the world in dualistic terms—became less persuasive as decades passed. The materialist and deterministic assumption behind Beard's arguments —that economic interests led straight to constitutional provisions— were also eventually seen to be the result of faulty psychological and sociological assumptions and thus largely unsupportable. Scholars' study of new documents that have been unearthed since Beard's work also opened the way to other and subtler lines of interpretation about the Framers' motives. Yet despite its defects, despite the fact that the *Economic Interpretation*'s influence on scholarship about the Constitution's origins has now weakened, Beard succeeded in demonstrating once again, if demonstration were needed, that a historian's work—that historical knowledge itself—could be made pertinent to the day's politics and by extension that the day's politics could not always be kept out of historical scholarship.

One of the features that made Beard's pathbreaking work so influential is that it brought together academic protocols of monographic scholarship and an acute political sensibility. This lent to his specialized historical research, as well as to much of the same kind of research that succeeded his own, a relevance outside academic walls, thoroughly in the Robinson "new history" mode, that it had rarely possessed before. Consequently, the application of historical knowledge to buttress ideological claims achieved a legitimacy in academic scholarship that such use might have had to wait longer to gain. Scholarship also came into wider public view and was now more widely understood to have an extra-academic payoff. The result was that probably never again could historical scholarship be immunized from application to the widest range of subjects by nonscholars. And as the century-long controversy over Beard's arguments has subsequently revealed, scholars themselves could battle, add to, revise, and dismiss the work of colleagues with the same gusto as political combatants engaged in partisan conflict. History had begun to come into its own as a normal factor of public debate in an open, democratic society.

Yet even given the scholarly tumult that it evoked, Beard's book fell short of arousing a controversy in which the past would play a direct role in current public affairs. While the debate over the *Economic Interpretation* leaked into the public press, it never engendered a full-throated argument among those whom today we term public intellectuals—among them newspaper writers, essayists, and pundits, as well as scholars. That stage was reached only in the 1920s during the spirited dispute over the causes of the First World War.

It was when that controversy escaped from the academic precincts in which the dispute over Beard's book had largely been fought that the term "revisionist" became widely employed for the first time in a rancorous public debate about the past—a debate that was very much about the present.[11] From then on, the notion of "revisionist history," previously a term restricted to the historian's trade, became part of intellectual discourse generally. From then on, too, the term became the sport of political and ideological combatants who invoked or dismissed "revisionism" as their own aims inclined them to do and took on the diverse connotations, positive and negative, that it has possessed since. What also made the controversy over the causes of the First World War noteworthy is that it contained all the elements—evidentiary, ideological, partisan, and personal—that characterize the most lively and significant of such disputes. With it, we enter the contemporary world of revisionist history.

∾

In American historical circles, the descent of Europe into war in 1914 and then American entry into the conflict in 1917 were bound to be

11. A Google Ngram search (a rough measure only) of the terms "revisionism" and "revisionist" reveals a very modest use of both before 1920—that is, in the few years after the publication of Charles Beard's *Economic Interpretation of the Constitution*—and then a substantial rise between 1920 and 1940, when the controversy over the causes of the First World War was at its highest. Some, although probably very little, of the terms' use in those decades can be attributed to post-Bernstein debates within Marxist circles or to references to those debates.

seen from the vantage point of American conditions. The nation had seen its way since 1901 through a period of vital political reform under the presidencies of Theodore Roosevelt, William Howard Taft, and Woodrow Wilson, and in campaigning for reelection in 1916 Wilson had famously promised to keep the nation out of war. But the assassination in Sarajevo in August 1914 of Archduke Ferdinand, heir to the leadership of the Austro-Hungarian Empire, the resulting bloody cataclysm that followed, and the German declaration of unrestricted submarine warfare against the United States and other nations had made the Wilson administration and much of the American public gradually turn their attention away from domestic to foreign affairs and then to the increasing likelihood that the United States could not avoid joining the European conflict. Wilson succeeded in keeping the United States on a neutral course among the combatants for three years. But by 1917, given repeated German provocations at sea—including the notorious German sinking of the British ocean liner *Lusitania* in 1915, the so-called Zimmerman telegram of 1917 proposing an alliance between Germany and Mexico, and the danger that the military stalemate on the ground in Europe would result in a victory for Germany and its allies and thus upset the European balance of power—most Americans, including a reluctant Wilson, were ready to toss in their lot with the Entente, or Allied Powers (France, Britain, and imperial Russia) against the Central Powers, sometimes also called the Triple Alliance (Germany and the Hapsburg and Ottoman Empires). Many Americans (at least enough of them to back Wilson's reluctant call for United States entry into the war) had come also to believe that Germany was responsible for the war and that therefore the United States no longer had any option but to join the conflict, as it did in April 1917. At the war's end in November 1918, after American troops had helped tip the balance against the Central Powers at the cost of thousands of dead and wounded, American opinion had hardened even further against Germany, and a majority of Americans had accepted the by then conventional view, argued most effectively after the war by historian Bernadotte E. Schmitt, that, guilty of bringing on the war, Germany had to pay for what it had wrought. This, essentially, was to remain the popular, conventional view of the causes and burdens of the First World War, a view captured most effectively in Barbara W. Tuchman's celebrated 1962 best-selling history, *The Guns of August,* a book that has faced sharp scholarly assault since then.

But a volatile mix of new evidence, reawakened Progressive reform currents, and domestic politics ensured that this view did not remain unchallenged for long after Schmitt wrote. For one thing, in promising to exempt the United States from the European war in his 1916 presidential reelection campaign, Wilson had satisfied the isolationists and those, like German-Americans, for whom war with the Central Powers was anathema. He had also aroused unfulfilled expectations among those who believed in his promise that he would work hard (as he had) to keep the United States out of war and succeed (as he had not) in doing so. By the war's end, their hopes dashed, millions of Americans felt betrayed by the administration and embittered against it, and they were prepared to credit any evidence that suggested that they had been sold a bill of goods. Moreover, to demonstrate that they did not alone bear the burden of war guilt, the defeated Central Powers opened to examination their prewar diplomatic archives, which provided evidence that Britain, France, and imperial Russia shared responsibility with Germany and the Hapsburgs for creating the conditions for war (a view that Germans, and German historians, had hammered home throughout the conflict). For their part, having gained control of the Russian government after the October 1917 revolution and having pulled Russian troops from the battlefield, the newly empowered Bolsheviks were eager to do all they could to demonstrate the tsarist government's complicity in the outbreak of hostilities. Accordingly, it became increasingly difficult for scholars to maintain with confidence that the Central Powers alone bore responsibility for the European carnage, even if they had been forced to accept legal responsibility for inaugurating the war in the peace treaty that followed it. If Britain and France could be held at least partly blameworthy for the start of hostilities, then the justification for American involvement to make the world safe for democracy through cooperation with the Allies was significantly weakened, and isolationist sentiment might be vindicated.

Old populist and progressive suspicions about corporate influence ("the interests") and the profiteering of "arms merchants" while thousands paid with their lives also added to fresh doubts about Germany's war guilt, especially after the American economy dropped into recession in 1920. Anger rose, too, over the suppression of free speech under the wartime Espionage Act, which Attorney General A. Mitchell Palmer put to use after the war's end to jail and deport people accused of Communist adherence following the victory of the Bolsheviks in Russia. Those who had earlier come around to the view that entry into the war would preserve the future of Progressive politics felt deceived. Now that the war had ended, the normal wartime impulse that had led Americans to pull together in support of the nation's fighting forces also dissipated, and old political battles renewed themselves. For many, the costs of the recent war seemed increasingly unjustifiable. How should war guilt be apportioned, domestically as well as abroad? Who was responsible for the Great War, and who was accountable for the entry of the United States into it?

It was in such charged circumstances that a debate over these freighted questions broke out. It did so even before the adoption in 1919 of the Treaty of Versailles (from whose negotiation Germany had been excluded) and the inauguration of the League of Nations, which the United States failed to join and with which many leading American figures, who felt duped by the peace terms, quickly became disillusioned. Unlike the debate just a few years earlier over Beard's analysis of the framing of the Constitution, the arguments over responsibility for the war spilled into the public prints, engaged some of the nation's leading public intellectuals, and eventually had a role in arguments over the American posture toward international relations before the Second World War. Consequently, debate over responsibility for World War I was to prove no mere academic kerfuffle, nor one without lasting political and ideological ramifications. A battle over the way to interpret recent world history now took on as much weight as the earlier interpretive battle over the causes of the Civil War. The difference this time was that professional academic historians, not amateurs and belletrists, were front and center in the debate.

This was a dispute that had engaged Americans since the Spanish-American War, one conditioned by old Progressive Era battles, a dispute about power, wealth, and justice at home. Also, from the perspective of 1920, the war's outbreak not long before gave the conflict an immediacy

and relevance that hot debates over Beard's interpretation of the Philadelphia Convention could not possess. Consequently, the new controversy quickly drew many people into a bitter battle that had originated
even before U.S. entry into the war, when writers like Walter Lippmann
and Herbert D. Croly, the philosopher John Dewey, and historian Carl L.
Becker, as well as Beard himself, who had favored entry, went head-to-
head with war opponents like isolationists Randolph S. Bourne and Wisconsin Senator Robert M. La Follette. Few should have been surprised
when their often sulfurous debate continued more or less in its original
form after the war and when the disputants summoned ready-at-hand
Progressive arguments about the dangers of German might, the traves-
ties of the Morgans and Rockefellers, and the subjugation of the majority of Americans to a selfish plutocracy. Also by 1919, everyone had to
reckon with the trove of newly opened diplomatic archives that made
the Progressive terms of the old debate untenable.

The first heavy salvo in this postwar battle came in 1920 from Smith
College historian Sidney B. Fay, who, writing in the *American Historical
Review,* then as now the nation's leading scholarly journal of history,
presented new evidence that the clause of the Paris Peace Treaty that
held Germany responsible for starting the war and doing so purposefully could not stand up to scrutiny. Taking a cue from John Maynard
Keynes, who attacked the Versailles Treaty in his 1919 *The Economic Consequences of the Peace,* Fay argued that the peace treaty's requirement that
Germany alone pay reparations to the victorious nations for its culpability in setting off the war was without justification—a contention (the
"dictated peace") that Adolf Hitler in the years ahead was to exploit to
arouse Germany against its treatment by other nations. Many read the
implications of Fay's argument as little more than a political move to
press the United States to pay additional sums for the reconstruction of
Europe and lessen Germany's reparation payments. (If Germany were
forgiven some of its reparations to Britain and France, it was argued,
those payments would instead go to repay American loans to Germany
held by wealthy people and banks.) But it was Fay's fellow academic,
Harry Elmer Barnes, who was to emerge as the leading "revisionist"
scourge of those who defended the Allies' innocence in precipitating the

war. Eventually arguing that American intervention in the European catastrophe had been a colossal mistake, Barnes was to become a favorite of such popular magazines of opinion as *The Nation* and the historian most responsible for turning many serious opinion makers, as well as historians like Beard and Becker, into critics of the standard view of Germany's responsibility for the war and of American innocence in its origins.

In fact, so effective was Barnes in reaching a large audience with often inflammatory arguments—especially in his widely read 1926 *The Genesis of the World War: An Introduction to the Problem of War Guilt,* which challenged this standard view—that the very idea of "revisionist history" itself gained the capacity for the first time to stir up protest and resistance. Many members of the public, previously unaware of "revisionist history" in any form and new to the idea that historians could differ among themselves about evidence and interpretation, found it difficult to evaluate and absorb the new evidentiary findings that challenged interpretations that, until recently, had been unresisted in popular understanding. It was in such circumstances that the first public spat over rival historical interpretations put the very concept of "revisionist history" into play. It also became clear that professional academic historians like Barnes were going to have to share the field with a growing set of critics and public figures outside academic precincts—for example Charles A. Lindbergh on the right and Norman Thomas on the left—whom historians themselves had alerted to serious problems with the until-then orthodox interpretation of the recent past.

As is often the case, circumstances external to arguments within the community of historians also kept the public debate alive. When French and Belgian troops invaded Germany's industrial Ruhr Basin in early 1923 as compensation for unpaid German reparations, revisionist interpretations that had downplayed Germany's responsibility for starting the war gained renewed strength—not because of any new evidence but because the French-Belgian incursion cast already-published fresh historical arguments into new perspective: no longer could it be maintained that Germany was alone responsible for events in Europe. One could now argue backward that it had been simply a matter of time after

1910 before one European nation or another had maneuvered others into precipitating the conflict that everyone had predicted anyway. In addition, the rising chorus of revisionists—academic historians, magazine editors, and newspaper writers alike—no doubt owed much to dissatisfaction with the political conservatism of the Harding era of the 1920s. But one had also to guard against discounting the always close-to-the-surface suspicions of any and all British motives by Irish-Americans and German-Americans ("hyphenates," as they were called) who felt that their views had been ignored in the lead-up to war, and the anti-Semitic sympathies of those for whom Jewish bankers were symbols of wartime profiteering. To make matters even more complicated, none of this says anything of the deeply Anglophilic loyalties of much of the American population, whose representatives continued to hold most political power and who had felt few inhibitions about going to war in aid of Great Britain in the first place. The result of these deep and broad cultural prejudices was that by the late 1920s, debates about evidence and its meaning, debates normally fenced within academic circles, had broken free of any such confinement. A political and rhetorical donnybrook took the place of academic discussion.

In addition to Barnes, who continued to lacerate those who defended U.S. involvement in the war, historian-economist C. Hartley Grattan breathed fresh life into older isolationist impulses in his 1929 book *Why We Fought*. Grattan took advantage of new evidence that reduced Germany's responsibility for the Great War and further undermined the justification for American entry as a moral crusade against Teutonic perfidy. But he also challenged the position that American entry had failed to gain the assured security it sought; in his view, American security had been strengthened by joining the war. Thus another large question came to the fore: what was best for the United States in world affairs—to enter them or to stand aloof? An even more highly charged issue—who profited by war?—soon arose in another arena: hearings chaired by Senator Gerald P. Nye on the role of munitions manufacturers in supporting the American war effort. In fact, by the mid-1930s, few aspects of American foreign relations and domestic politics had evaded reexamination in the terms that Sidney B. Fay and Harry

Elmer Barnes had introduced in 1920. Equally important, the ranks of influential and ordinary Americans willing to defend America's entry into the Great War had dwindled to a level unlikely to have been reached without the evidence offered by—the term becoming increasingly accepted—"revisionist historians." With a 1937 Gallup Poll showing that 70 percent of those surveyed thought that American entry into the war had been a mistake, revisionist history had clearly come of age. In fact, in the words of Warren I. Cohen, the most authoritative historian of this historical contest, revisionist history emerged "triumphant" for having escaped the scholar's study and entered general discourse.

But that was not to be the end of the story. Even as yet another historian, Charles C. Tansill, was joining the lists against the 1917 American intervention with strongly argued, anti-British positions in his 1938 *America Goes to War,* events had another fate in mind for his kind of argument, an argument that he, like so many others, believed should serve as a warning to those who would involve the United States in the duplicitous dealings of foreign nations. That fate was, of course, revanchist, militant Nazism. It would be difficult to invoke any better example of the extent to which historical interpretations can be caught up in external events than the public reactions to the onset of a second world war in Europe even before Japan's attack on the United States at Pearl Harbor. While historians like Beard, Grattan, and Tansill, along with public figures like Lindbergh and Thomas, remained firm in opposition to a second American involvement on the Continent, Soviet Russia and Nazi Germany had begun in 1939 to divide up Poland, and German troops had entered Paris in 1940. So even though historians had earlier had their chance to change the terms of debate over war and foreign policy and had done so to great effect, they would have no such chance this time. Those, like the influential journalist Walter Millis, who had long criticized the belief that war could make the world safe for democracy, now in 1941 were forced by events to become ardent military interventionists, while those who detested Franklin Delano Roosevelt for his politics as well as for his efforts to come to the aid of Britain before 1941 were left with no choice but to fall in behind the president, who had been striving to keep the nation free of armed conflict for fear that it would endanger the New Deal.[12] When the United States declared war on the Axis powers in December 1941, two decades' worth of efforts to keep the nation out of war, efforts undergirded substantially by revisionist historians and sustained in part by them, evaporated overnight. Most revisionist historians granted the necessity of this new war despite their deep misgivings. This time, there was to be no sustained debate over who was responsible for war or over whether the United States should enter it. And since Germany was the clear aggressor in Europe, any chance to keep alive the old debate about war guilt and the wisdom of the 1917 dispatch of American troops to Europe also died when Japan attacked Pearl Harbor.

At least they died in public, so that after Pearl Harbor no one was going to risk contesting American entry into World War I any more than into World War II. But the limits on the power of events to affect historiographic controversy and fresh thinking about past events are also revealed in what has happened since 1945 to the interpretive literature about World War I: rather than returning to its original 1919 mold of blaming Germany for the war's commencement, that literature has remained entirely revisionist in cast, in large part because historical sources strongly support the revisionist view. To be sure, consonant with a conviction widely held in 1914, Germany is now conceded primary responsibility for bringing on the Great War, this conclusion gaining wide acceptance principally due to the 1960s work of Fritz Fischer, who, in *Germany's Aims in the First World War,* once again squarely placed blame for inaugurating the war on Germany's shoulders. But the view that somehow the other powers, especially France and Russia, bore no responsibility for the conflict has lost credibility under the scrutiny of those who have continued to find new evidence implicating the other powers and to develop new perspectives for interpreting it. The context

12. This greatly compresses the complexity of these developments. Strong anti-interventionist and antiwar sentiment extended to the December 1941 Pearl Harbor attack, which rendered anti-interventionist arguments irrelevant. Yet revisionist thinking remained alive to affect the ways in which Americans viewed and responded to World War II and its aftermath. The revisionist views of historians and activists placed some limitations on FDR's conduct of the war; and disillusionment with the outcome of the Treaty of Versailles of 1919 and the League of Nations deeply affected post-1945 American policies toward the rest of the world.

of World War I's origins has expanded to include the Moroccan crises of 1905 and 1911, tensions between Italy and Turkey, and conflicts in the Balkans well before the 1914 assassination of the archduke. Historians now recognize that domestic politics in each of the warring nations contributed significantly to their responses to the Sarajevo assassination in the summer of that year. For the moment at least, the weight of historical consensus—consensus being about the best that can be expected in any historical debate—is that the revisionists have won the interpretive contest over World War I. They have done so, however, largely out of sight of the kind of popular publications and cultural commentators dominating debate in the 1920s and 1930s.

This should not be taken as evidence that historical interpretations that fly in the face of conventional views or provoke members of political camps have lost their sting. Nor should it give anyone confidence that all revisions to conventional historiography can withstand the criticism that they are bound to receive and thus take a place alongside other views acceptable as legitimate by historians. Instead, we ought to see the course of the controversy over World War I war guilt and American entry into the conflict as a sign of the maturation of historical debate in contemporary times. From being seen as an outrageous assault on the knowledge and insight of those who held to received wisdom after 1914, the combined corrosives of new historical evidence, fresh arguments, and actual events have gradually eaten away at those certainties to provide a richer and far more nuanced and complex understanding of the origins of World War I than existed earlier. Just as the passage of time and the accumulation of new knowledge have challenged the classic histories of Herodotus, Thucydides, and Eusebius, so those same factors have subjected the initial convictions of contemporaries of the Great War to alteration—and done so in a remarkably short time. In addition, the fires of ideology have been banked as the years have passed and as events have followed events to change the shape of the world, domestic politics, and international relations. In our altered universe of travel and communication, of deepened scholarly research, of an increase in the number of practicing historians, and of broadened historical methods and interpretive options, exchanges of views and information have brought about the speedier resolution of at least some scholarly issues

and fuller agreement about what is known and what remains to be
known. Even if these conditions have failed to end all scholarly debate,
even if they can never insulate historians from attack by nonhistorians
or from historians' need to address public concerns, even if they cannot
prevent the intrusion of nonhistorical considerations into historical controversies that touch on sensitive and immediate public issues, historians
have provided new conditions for carrying on the never-ending search
for historical understanding and applicable historical knowledge through
scholarly and public debate about critical issues of public concern.

∾

A compressed review, like those contained in this and the previous
chapter, of roughly two and a half millennia of changing historical interpretations cannot be expected to touch on every major alteration in
historical understanding or every important historical reinterpretation
over that span of time. But even though I have taken up only some of
the high points of the long history of revisions to existing historical
argument, it is hard to resist the conclusion that challenges to the ways
any people at any time view their past are inescapable—that those who
study the past, whether they be professional historians or others, inevitably bring their own distinctive sensibilities, attitudes, and situations
to what they write and how they see the world, both present and past.
It has therefore proved impossible, and thus foolish, to expect humans
generally or historians particularly to come to uniform agreement about
even minor components of any period, development, or set of events in
the past—no matter how firmly their interpretations are hawsered to
the available evidence about them. Similarly, there can be no doubt that
in some countries any questioning of widely accepted interpretations
about the past bring risks in its wake—risks running from mere criticism to ridicule, to banishment, even to death. When are intellectual
innovators not met with hostility and contempt? Yet most historians
have accepted the risks of having their work found wanting in the arena
of professional and public opinion; only by historians' venturing to
use new evidence or to employ existing evidence in new ways can fresh
knowledge and fresh understanding originate. And so from Thucydides
on, historians have seen the seduction of certainty worse than the risk
of infamy. With a determination to understand the past more deeply

than their predecessors did, they have dug into the sources and applied their individual minds to historical problems with fearlessness and high spirits. After all, are historians to accept any view of the past as inarguable any more than other humans have proven themselves capable of agreeing about anything else?

Argument and disagreement are routine among historians, and provisionality of interpretation is the norm, especially over long spans of time. Like normal science—the term coined by historian Thomas S. Kuhn to describe scientific research pursued within conventionally accepted explanatory frameworks—historians' labors usually proceed more or less as they always have through methods roughly analogous to those in use since the nineteenth century and in consonance with modes of argument accepted by them all. Consequently, what is likely to challenge conventional thinking most quickly and strikingly are not new methods or a new logic of inquiry but new tangents on old problems, new tangents so striking that they constitute what Kuhn, in his classic 1962 work *The Structure of Scientific Revolutions,* termed a "paradigm shift" in the interpretive scheme of things. Kuhn gave this term to any major break with orthodox scientific understanding, a break brought about by the gradual piling up of anomalies and unanswerable questions—what elsewhere I have referred to as the sedimentation of interpretation—originating from fresh research and fresh thought not comprehensible within explanatory conventions standard at the time. He also included among the causes of such shifts the changes in the larger culture that reorient old thinking and raise new questions.

This does not however mean that, once advanced, a specific way of seeing a subject of history cannot quickly gather momentum and acceptance and infuse a large subject with eventually widely accepted fresh thought, nor does it mean that historians will deny themselves the opportunity of using evidence and fresh thought to try to alter the world of scholarship, perhaps of thought and action generally, along lines of deep significance to them. The challenge thrown down by James Harvey Robinson in his early-twentieth-century call for a "new history" has shown itself to be too influential and too productive of good to put those who advance fresh ways of seeing the past on the defensive. Historical knowledge is now a democratic, public possession.

In recent decades, Robinson's kind of new history has diffused itself into traditional historical interpretation as new scholarship and understanding of the role of gender, sexuality, race, ethnicity, and religious
belief have come to the fore. It has done so in ways that probably would
not have been possible until after World War II, when, after a more diverse population of people had entered the ranks of professional historians, revisionist history had proven its general public applicability. While
subjected to sometimes hard-to-withstand criticism, not all of it offered
in good faith, such historical scholarship has hugely broadened understanding, just as it has increased the stakes outside the academic world
of the application of scholarly knowledge to the larger world of social
relations and political arrangements. Once, from the 1960s on, fresh
arguments about the historical contributions of previously scorned,
overlooked, and devalued people like women, workers, immigrants,
gays and lesbians, and adherents of unpopular beliefs—whom scholars
term "subaltern" groups—gained traction among them, historians generally were brought to the conclusion that no history that continued
to omit people outside the traditional schemes of political, institutional,
and diplomatic history (which effectively meant, at least for histories of
the West, all but white males) any longer had much value. In this sense,
history was reconciled to citizenship. The hope of advocates of the New
History that historical knowledge would prove relevant to public concerns, that all people should and could find themselves in accounts of
the past, was vindicated. It also turns out that, in addition to opening
up vast new areas of historical inquiry, introducing these previously
ignored people into the written history of venerable historical subjects
like diplomacy, politics, and public policy has greatly altered even those
long-thought-to-be-reasonably-well-understood topics.

By the early twenty-first century, tension between scholarly authority and popular attitudes has become a normal component of public affairs. Professional historians have often exhibited a tendency to see
amateur opinion as a derogation of their greater knowledge—greater by
depth of research and breadth of understanding—just as some citizens
sometimes see scholarly historical knowledge as a presumptuous intrusion on established or patriotic thought. Historians need occasionally to
remind themselves that they ought to bring the same humility toward

public debate about the past, if not always its contents and claims, as they do toward scholarly controversy. Both kinds of argument are always provisional and partial; and historians should know that the contents of public debates about the past are revealing evidence of the realities of every era in which they occur—those eras being the very subject of historical inquiry. For their part, members of the public need not defer to scholarly knowledge, nor agree with one another any more than historians do. But they should at least recognize the potential cost of ignoring what historians, who wrestle with fact as well as interpretation, think are the soundest conclusions to be drawn from evidence.

A culture without argument is a culture without life, and historical study without conflict is historical study without vitality. We should hope that citizens try to govern themselves by the same liberal premises that most historians apply to their search for knowledge—knowledge that will serve as the basis of understanding and as a guide to action. That has been the touchstone of historians since the days of Herodotus; and as long as it is, there will be no end to battles over the past.

For Further Reading, Chapters 2 and 3

The literature about the history of historical thought, writing, and method is vast, and any attempt to suggest a few works of particular relevance and merit necessarily excludes most others that could join the selection. A strong candidate for the starting point is the group of works about origin myths. Here, the classic study, among many others of his writings, is Mircea Eliade, *Myth and Reality*, trans. Willard R. Trask (New York: Harper and Row, 1963). An important more recent work is Joseph Mali, *Mythistory: The Making of a Modern Historiography* (Chicago: University of Chicago Press, 2003.) Mali takes Herodotus's side in the unending dispute about the relative value of primordial beliefs and stories and the Thucydidean tradition of empirical knowledge. He, like Eliade, sees myths to be foundational to civilization and to the collective identities of people, implicitly challenges the notion that all tradition is "invented" (at least beyond empirical determination), and is sensitive to the role of myth in marshaling thought and belief toward action. See also Donald R. Kelley, "Mythistory in the Age of Ranke," in G. G. Iggers and J. M. Powell, eds., *Leopold von Ranke and the Shape of the Historical Discipline* (Syracuse, NY: Syracuse University Press, 1990), 3–20. Such historians insist that within every memory lies the irrational and subconscious, whose task it is mythistory's to bring to light.

Two useful compilations of excerpts from the writings of major figures in the history of history are Donald R. Kelley, ed., *Versions of History from Antiquity to the Enlightenment* (New Haven: Yale University Press, 1991), and Fritz Stern, ed., *The Varieties of History from Voltaire to the Present,* rev. ed. (New York: Random House, 1972). Nothing can substitute in content, quality, and style for the greatest works themselves, starting with those of Herodotus and Thucydides. Accessible, attractive editions of each of their seminal histories are *The Landmark Herodotus: The Histories,* ed. Robert B. Strassler; trans. Andrea L. Purvis (New York: Pantheon, 2007) and *The Landmark Thucydides,* rev. ed., ed. Robert B. Strassler; trans. Richard Crawley (New York: Free Press, 2008). There are many other translations of both. A fresh edition of Eusebius's history is *The History of the Church: A New Translation,* trans. Jeremy M. Schott (Oakland: University of California Press, 2019).

In the modern literature, the most erudite, comprehensive, and searching are the three linked volumes of Donald R. Kelley: *Faces of History: Historical Inquiry from Herodotus to Herder* (New Haven: Yale University Press, 1998), *Fortunes of History: Historical Inquiry from Herder to Huizinga* (New Haven: Yale University Press, 2003), and *Frontiers of History: Historical Inquiry in the Twentieth Century* (New Haven: Yale University Press, 2006). Two single-volume surveys of the same large subject, more encyclopedic than Kelley's volumes, though necessarily of less depth regarding any single historian or era, are Ernst Breisach, *Historiography: Ancient, Medieval, and Modern,* 3rd ed. (Chicago: University of Chicago Press, 2007), and Daniel Woolf, *A Global History of History* (Cambridge: Cambridge University Press, 2011). A fourth study is John Burrow, *A History of Histories: Epics, Chronicles, Romances, and Inquiries from Herodotus and Thucydides to the Twentieth Century* (New York: Knopf, 2008), a discursive, lively, opinionated, and learned journey through its ages-old subject. To these four, a short introduction to the topic should be added: Jeremy D. Popkin, *From Herodotus to H-Net: The Story of Historiography* (New York: Oxford University Press, 2016).

Those who wish to dip into the history of historical writing in the entire world from 600 BCE should consult the scholarly essays that constitute Daniel Wolff, genl. ed., *The Oxford History of Historical Writing*, 5 vols. (Oxford: Oxford University Press, 2011–2012). Everyone interested in the link between historical knowledge and its written presentation should turn to Peter Gay, *Style in History* (New York: Basic, 1974), an erudite, stylish set of essays on its subject through the works of four great historians. Taken together, these studies make as clear as anything can the alterations in and variety of approaches and interpretations that have characterized historical thinking and writing throughout time.

Singling out specific, more limited, yet appealing and authoritative studies in the always growing literature of historiography is not easy. But among them some stand out. One is Donald Kagan, *Thucydides: The Reinvention of History* (New York: Viking, 2009), in which the author makes a strong case, which I find compelling even if requiring some qualification, that the Greek historian was the first revisionist historian. A classic on its subject is Felix Gilbert, *Machiavelli and Guicciardini: Politics and History in Sixteenth-Century Florence* (Princeton: Princeton University Press, 1965). Peter Gay, *The Dilemma of Democratic Socialism: Eduard Bernstein's Challenge to Marx* (New York: Columbia University Press, 1952), is the standard study of this major Marxist revisionist. The literature on Charles Beard generally, and on his interpretation of the Constitution's framing, is large. Still the best general appraisal of Beard and his work is part 3 of Richard Hofstadter, *The Progressive Historians: Turner, Beard, Parrington* (New York: Knopf, 1968). The standard treatment of the controversy over responsibility for the First World War and for American entry into it is Warren I. Cohen, *The American Revisionists: The Lessons of Intervention in World War I* (Chicago: University of Chicago Press, 1967), although Christopher Clark, *The Sleepwalkers: How Europe Went to War in 1914* (New York: Harper and Row, 2014), has superseded it. Cohen's work ought also to be supplemented by pp. 207–224 of Peter Novick, *That Noble Dream: The "Objectivity Question" and the American Historical Profession* (New York: Cambridge University Press, 1988), which reveals the private, personal animosities and currents that flowed beneath this historical controversy, as they do beneath so many others. One way through the vast literature on this subject is through the concise essay-length overviews of the circumstances of each nation involved in the war's origins found in Richard F. Hamilton and Holger H. Herwig, eds., *The Origins of World War I* (Cambridge: Cambridge University Press, 2003). A fine summary of current scholarly thinking about "war guilt" in 1914, as well as about the vast literature, revisionist and otherwise, on the subject is Samuel R. Williamson, Jr., "July 1914 Revisited and Revised: The Erosion of the German Paradigm," in Jack S. Levy and John A. Vasquez, eds., *The Outbreak of the First World War* (New York: Cambridge University Press, 2014), 30–62.

The large matter of revisionist history is part of the venerable debate over presentism in historical understanding. The classic work in this debate is Herbert Butterfield, *The Whig Interpretation of History* (New York: Norton, 1965), first published in 1931. A wise book, it never fails to warrant careful reading. A sly riposte to Butterfield by a leading scientist is Steven Weinberg, "Eye on the Present—The Whig History of Science," *New York Review of Books,* December 17, 2015, pp. 82–84. Weinberg argues that the history of some sciences, such as physics, is necessarily whiggish because progress in them can be planned, seen, and measured.

FOUR

Varieties of Revisionist History

As should be clear by now, each work of history is best approached as if it were, in one respect or another, a revision of some previous one. Starting from the simple fact that each history differs from all others if only in nuance and wording, the differences between works on the same subject grow in number and kind until some threshold into revisionist history is crossed. But where is that threshold? Some historians will argue that histories that merely add new details to what was previously known are probably not, in any important sense, revisionist; others will disagree. But most histories advance new contents, arguments, perspectives, and details about their subjects and in doing so reorient a subject and move it in a new direction. A few throw down major challenges to previous interpretations. Occasionally, a true revolution in historical understanding occurs because of the force and authority of a single work, a closely related group of works by a number of authors, or vast and largely irresistible cultural forces that lead historians to surrender to those forces' momentum and enlist in the ranks of those interpretations' adherents. But when does orthodox history of a subject end and revisionist history begin? It is difficult to say, which is why it is best to assume that every work of history is revisionist in some manner—that is, that it is potentially destabilizing of existing interpretations of an existing subject—and then to try to determine in what respects and to what degree it alters prior understanding of the past.

Revisionism is not inherent to any work or group of works. All general distinctions among works about the past are adventitious and can be determined only by placing each work into its express historiographic context; every written history must be evaluated on its own for its contribution to knowledge. Moreover, since approaches to evaluation change over time so that what seems revisionist in one era may not seem so in another, critical approaches to works of history are never uniformly applied, and historians are never likely to be unanimous in their acceptance of the validity of those approaches. The needs of the present, changing thinking about the craft of history, a fuller appreciation of dimensions of past and present, even intellectual fashions all play a role in determining what works of history, at any specific time, are considered to be within the normal historiography of a distinct subject or are something significantly fresh enough to constitute revisionist history. It therefore cannot be strongly enough emphasized that no hard-and-fast rules exist for determining the placement of any work of history within its literature. A single work's intellectual fate and influence is often not known until its author is long dead. Works once thought of major consequence may appear less so with the passage of time. Thus it makes no sense to assume that any single category—like "revisionist history"—serves effectively to make sense of the many varieties of revisionist history that have long existed. Every history has to be considered on its own, in context with others, and in the larger perspective of all written history. Any categorization of revisionist histories must be fluid, and the placement of any single work on any scale of revisionist history must itself be considered provisional.

Until now, the undifferentiated blanket term "revisionist history," the one I have used, has stood in for what constitutes many kinds of history. Without separating the single category into some more specific subgenres, we risk overlooking much that revisionist history encompasses and many of the distinct intentions and approaches of the historians who write it. What follows is therefore an attempt to disaggregate the general phenomenon of revisionist history and to differentiate its varieties. Treating each kind of revisionism as a distinct mode of approaching historical subjects ought to help lay bare the grounds on which historians arrive at their interpretations of the past; it ought also to reveal dimensions of historians' purposes and their finished works that often go unnoticed. Yet in no way do I wish to offer a formal typology of revisionist history or to suggest that any particular work about the past can or should find a secure place in some schema of historical literature. That literature is too diverse and the experiences of scholars and readers of history too varied to justify the construction of any architectonic classification of revisionist history. Nor do I mean to suggest that rigid lines demarcate from one another the categories I propose here. What follows instead is the sketch of a spectrum, not a rigid scale; and just as historians argue about how to view the past, so there will be disputes about where on the spectrum of revisionism specific works of history belong. My intent is rather to provide some signposts by which the impact of works of history can be identified and therefore more fully understood. They are not meant to serve as a measure of the relative worth of particular historical works or as the basis of comparison of the insight and skills of individual historians. In the context of reflections on the general phenomenon of revisionist history, I offer this informal taxonomy only as an aid to broadened understanding of a complex phenomenon.

∾

As I have indicated earlier, Thucydides can justifiably be considered the Founding Revisionist for taking sharp issue with Herodotus. But when compared not simply with the historians who may have preceded him (little of whose works, save those of Herodotus, survive) but also with those bards who sang and wrote some of the great works of ancient literature that are known to us, Herodotus must be given chronological pride of place in the pantheon of revisionists. Simply by inaugurating a new form of prose writing he termed *historiē*, he struck out in a radically new direction, so that when his *Histories* are put up against the epics of Homer, Herodotus's work appears starkly different in art and intent from those great poems. But precedence in time should not be allowed to determine precedence in the measurement of significance of reinterpretation. Another metric by which to assess the relative significance of alterations to preexisting historical views—the depth and scale of those changes—is likely to prove more useful. Yet the fact that Thucydides was the historian who inaugurated the enduring tradition of taking clear and purposeful issue with existing historical approaches and offering alternatives to them does not mean that his departure was greater or more significant than those of all historians who succeeded him.

When compared strictly with all historians, the honor of surpassing historiographic greatness in the West surely belongs to the history of the Western Church conceived and written by Eusebius who, with his Christian successors, ushered in a lasting reimagining of the Western past through the creation of a new grand narrative of past, present, and future. They did so by dislodging the previously dominant Classical historiographic tradition. That act was one of transformative revisionism—an interpretive revolution that forever altered the entire culture of a major segment of the world's population. But in one of the complications that characterizes all historiography, in addition to transforming the way the past was interpreted Eusebius and his followers were as much founders of a new line of historical reasoning as revisers of an old one. The creation of new and the alteration of existing historical understanding sometimes go hand in hand. Like Eusebius, a historian can be a transformative historian of one school of history while being a founding historian of another.

Historical understanding cannot exist without a sense of continuity between past and present. But Eusebian historiography came as close as can be imagined to rupturing the links between the ways people before the early fourth century CE understood their beginnings and the ways their successors did. What preserved the psychological, as well as historical, balance between the pre- and post-Eusebian eras for the few people who thought in formal historical terms was the simple fact that, starting in the Hellenic Mediterranean world and moving gradually into the farthest reaches of the West (one that would become known, because of this very transformation, as the Christian world), the transformative re-envisioning of the past that Eusebius inaugurated was slow and lacking in uniformity. The British Isles, the last major European redoubt of pagan belief, did not fall entirely to Christianity for three centuries. In addition, enough elements and practices of non-Christian tribal and ethnocultural groups were absorbed by Christianity that the transition between one historical system and another was eased; and Christian and non-Christian historiographies continue to exist parallel to each other in many areas and communities of the West.

Nevertheless, the Eusebian revision represented a permanent alteration of an entire intellectual and cultural world—a change in historical understanding, following a change in religious belief, so penetrating and thorough as to force a reconsideration and reformulation of each of its adherents' sense of the past and future. Historians will see in this interpretive rupture a "paradigm shift." It is probably the closest that we can come to fully applying a concept originally used in relation to revolutions in scientific understanding to historical thought without slipping into the concept's misapplication. No other change of such depth and permeating consequences in historical conceptualization has ever occurred in the West. No other scheme of reorganizing past, present, and future has so deeply affected thought and understanding. In fact, nothing on this scale and with the same penetration into the deepest recesses of the mind and spirit in a large portion of the globe had ever been seen before,[1] and it is difficult to imagine anything like it ever happening again. After Eusebius, pagan historiography was gradually relegated to the margins of written history in the West and replaced by a tradition of historical thought and writing in which the old gods either found themselves replaced or, in the case of the Jewish god and the Pentateuch, appropriated by Christians and incorporated into their Bible. This was as thoroughgoing an intellectual, as well as historiographic, transformation as can be imagined.

The extraordinary alteration in the horizons of those living through the Christian revolution proved so permeating that, so much the children of that alteration, most people in today's West are unaware of the historical contingencies that so deeply affected Western thinking about the past; they often assume that, consonant with Christian belief, the transformation was foreordained. But like everything else, the Eusebian revolution was the consequence of its singular context. It might not have occurred at all had the Emperor Constantine not decreed that

---

1. Although, of course, an analogous, large-scale, transformation in beliefs was to happen elsewhere with the rise of such other religions as Buddhism and Islam.

Christianity was to be the religion of the empire he ruled; and the revolution probably would not have occurred as it did, and perhaps not with its pervasive effects, had it happened at another time under other historical conditions. Nor was there anything guaranteed about the permanence of the Christian belief system or about its eventual spread throughout the West. Constantine's successor Roman emperors could have tried to return the empire to its earlier beliefs (as one, Julian the Apostate, attempted to do) and denied Christians the legal right to worship their god. Some nation-states have since prohibited the free exercise of religion; witness Spain's expulsion of the Jews and Muslims who refused to convert to Christianity after 1492. Other distinct populations in the Christian West—take the Huguenots in France after Louis XIV's 1685 repeal of the Edict of Nantes, which had protected their religious liberties—have throughout time been stripped of their right to pursue their beliefs in traditional ways or prevented, like the Quakers in early Massachusetts, from worshiping as they wished. Others have been exterminated for their convictions. Moreover, conversion is rarely uniform, and toleration does not necessarily lead to conversion, as the non-Christians now living among Christians throughout Europe and the Americas attest.

Yet despite such islands of nonconformity, Christian historiography's influence is inescapable everywhere in the Western world. Even though other calendars continue to exist, no major holdouts against the Christian dating system introduced by Eusebius and Bede remain, and Christian symbols, myths, literature, and art are the basic furniture of the minds and imagination of most Westerners. Some may resist the thought that history does not unveil a record of progress, and others may not be inspired by teleological hopes of better days to come. But even in resistance, such people are often unaware that what they fight against is the conviction, an intellectual artifact of Eusebian historiography, that the eventual solution to human ills is to be found, if not in Redemption, then, as Marxist historians and those who subscribe to modernization or global systems theory believe, perhaps in history itself. They are captives of the terms in which what they oppose is carried out and of the seismic historical irruption and triumph of the new belief system represented by Christianity into Western culture in the few centuries on either side of Constantine's rule.

Yet it would be wrong to see the transformative revolution worked by early Christian historians as revisionism in the way we understand it today. It was not an alteration in previous ways of viewing the past wrought by historians contending with each other over distinct ways of explaining events. It did not derive from the discovery of fresh evidence or from new interpretive methods. Instead, it came about via a fresh imagining of human origins—that of divine revelation and the life of Jesus—through the decision of a senior cleric of the young Christian community to re-envisage the past in terms consonant with the emperor's newfound religious convictions. No major historical transformation goes for long without gathering to itself a belief system that attempts to legitimize it. Eusebius's *Ecclesiastical History* was of that legitimizing kind.

How is this to be explained? Early Christian historians faced the same challenge to their beliefs that all proponents of new or alternative historical perspectives face, whether they are professional historians or not. They had to convert others to their views and overcome resistance to their beliefs even if sometimes their convictions had to be applied by the sword to resisting cultures. Take, for instance, the fateful Crusades and the murderous religious wars of the seventeenth century among rival Christian belief systems in Europe. But whatever their means, the transformative historiographic tradition that Eusebius and other early Christian historians created out of the Old and New Testaments was above all an intellectual adaptation to irresistible cultural forces taking shape around them. In this respect, the transformation in historical understanding they wrought on the basis of biblical accounts has no equal in Western history. The Christian historiographic revolution stands alone in a category of revisionism all its own.

Yet the term "transformative revisionism" can also be applied to another world-historical belief system and new grand narrative of more recent times—to Marxism. Just as Christian concepts proved themselves compatible with pagan worldviews, just as they absorbed the unitary god and other attributes of the Judaic faith that had long preceded Christianity, so Marxism proved itself compatible with vastly different existing cultural systems and paralleled Christianity in its adaptive capacities. Like Christianity, Marxism—even though not formally a mode of historical analysis—offered a historical interpretation of earthly life and reality, directed attention to hitherto unremarked aspects of human life, and offered to explain historical developments in a new way. Like Christianity with its Crusades, Marxism gained its influence behind the armies and ideologies of Lenin, Stalin, and Mao by force as well as persuasion. Where force was neither available nor appropriate, Marxism, like Christianity, used missionaries—the Communist Party as "the vanguard of the proletariat"—to carry it to those not yet exposed to it. In many cases, Marxist ideas took root by their appeal, their explanatory power, and their congruence with existing conditions. Interpretive schools, doctrinal disputes, and institutional schisms soon proliferated within Marxism as they had within Christianity and other religions. If Marxism did not possess its single Constantine, it had its Stalinist-Leninist and Maoist decision makers who, like Roman emperors and church leaders before them, decreed what the official Communist bible would be and then expected everyone to adopt it on pain of punishment. Like Christianity, Marxism met resistance and failed to penetrate into every social group. Like Christianity, it failed to carry the field universally.

I do not offer such a comparison to establish the coequal historical truth claims of Christianity and Marxism or any other large system of religious or ideological beliefs, nor do I mean to balance off either two thousand years of Christian historiography against less than two hundred years of Marxist ideology or Christianity's providential outlook against Marxist atheism. I make the comparison simply to argue for the similar transformative power of these two revisions of previously held historical convictions. After the intellectual consolidation of each of them in the West, sixteen centuries apart, it was never again possible to understand the past as it had been understood before each of them took root, even if it remained possible to reject much of both of their belief systems. But while one could disbelieve the future Revelation as prophesied in the Bible or the dictatorship of the proletariat as predicted by Marx and Engels, the notion of historical fulfillment and questions about the class structure of societies, whether accepted or rejected, proved difficult to ignore by those who came after the establishment of these two ways of conceiving the world.

Nevertheless, even if these grand belief systems were roughly analogous, even if not equal, in their transformative revisionist strength —each one offering itself as a teleological revisionist historical interpretation of past, present, and future—the differing circumstances of Christianity's and Marxism's origins have always deeply marked the ways in which they have been treated as historical interpretations. Because Christianity had the most venerable claim on the West as an interpretation of the past and future—because Christianity came first in time—Marxism has had to make its way as an alternative to Christianity. Consequently, it has always been seen as a substitute, and often a dangerous one, for Christianity. Thus another rule of revisionist history: priority in time is likely to result in priority of acceptance and then in priority of authority. An initial interpretation, whatever its proven strength, forever imprints its interpretive stamp on subsequent interpretations of a subject. Only over long stretches of time is escape from its influence possible, and such escape is rarely complete.

In the largest sense, three magisterial universalistic schemes have existed in the West: the pagan outlook of Greece and Rome, the Judeo-Christian worldview that broke with paganism, and atheistic Marxism. Yet noting their rough historiographic equivalence is not to make a case for the equivalence of the truth claims among the three. That task is beyond the professional responsibility of historians. Even if one is inclined to dismiss one, two, or all three as explanations of the nature and course of life, their appeal as human explanations of the meaning of existence cannot be gainsaid. All three historical traditions were, and for many remain, interpretations that endeavor to create meaning for living humans. Their existence is a function of human need, not interpretive necessity. Historians' disinclination to use them as interpretive historical systems in no way alters their existence, acceptance, or validity as interpretive systems per se. They exist independent of historians' views of them. The question for students of the past is how, over time, they have influenced interpretations of the known historical past.

∾

Another kind of historical revisionism, smaller in scale than Christianity and Marxism but no less significant for its lasting influence, grows from the contest inaugurated by Thucydides over the purposes and uses of historical thought. I term this variety of history philosophical revisionism because it concerns the purposes and uses of historical inquiry. While not philosophical in the sense that philosophers use the term—not reaching into the very nature of existence, as does ontology, or of knowledge, as does epistemology—this kind of revisionist history comes as close as historical thought can get to considering an age-old question: why do, and should, humans pay attention to their pasts? It is philosophical also in the sense that each side takes its conviction to be axiomatic—a "given"—and, like all axiomatic principles, more or less beyond proof or the felt need of substantiation.

Thucydides' attack on Herodotus was formative in setting up enduring, contrasting approaches to the past. It was a reconceptualization of the very purpose of gaining historical knowledge. In this sense, Thucydides thought the study of political power more important than the study of thought, culture, and society. He sought to derive universal laws and lessons of historical development and leadership from the known past while minimizing the importance of knowledge of other aspects of history. His alternative way of doing history established a permanent philosophical divide within historical thought and writing.

In our era, this disagreement is rarely argued openly among professional historians. When readers take up historical works about public policy, military conflicts, and diplomatic negotiations or biographies of major public figures, they are being exposed to books within the Thucydidean tradition. Social and cultural history is kindred to Herodotus's interests although many historians who study these subjects may be unaware of their ancient genealogy. Occasionally, overt disagreements between partisans of the two variants of doing history break out among historians as they have in recent years over the said-to-be unjustifiable incursions of social and cultural history onto what for much of history's history in the West was a terrain monopolized by political, diplomatic, military, and institutional subjects. But it has typically been those outside academic circles with a political or ideological axe to grind, not academic historians, who have been most likely to weigh in against written history that they believe scants Thucydidean subjects.[2] Conversely, members of groups whose history has long been ignored and who have long been denied access to power and authority often take to insisting on the equal significance of social and cultural history. Yet even when these arguments among historians and others are openly fought— when historians and others debate the "right," the "best," and the "most useful" kind of history—they reflect, as I have tried to show, a tension that seems to be an unavoidable feature of the Western historiographic terrain. It is a feature that arose with the birth of written history; it was not a contest that arose, say, as a result of the Cold War or the rise of feminism. Instead, the debate is deep-rooted in Western historical inquiry.

It would, however, be incorrect to attribute the differences between Herodotus and Thucydides and their followers only to a philosophical divide over the true purposes and most important subjects of historical inquiry. Understanding of the bases of different kinds of history and the arguments that underlie them will remain impoverished if we refuse to acknowledge the varieties of aspiration, intention, and temperament that historians, like everyone else, bring to their work. Differing interests among historians are simply "there" and require no explanation or justification. Those differences are among the features of historical inquiry that lend it the excitement that draws so many people

---

2. This was a frequently heard late-twentieth-century complaint. But even this objection has been difficult to credit, given the large number of books on the history of politics, institutions, and world affairs—and of the subjects that arise immediately from them, such as the histories of slavery, racial and ethnic minorities, women, and civil rights—that continue to pour from the presses. The complaint arose from the undeniable fact that, after decades of inattention, the history of such previously little explored subjects of social and cultural interest as (to cite only a bare few of them) the emotions, sexuality, recreation, and material objects like, yes, pencils and bookshelves, were now gaining their own histories. Naturally, attention to new subjects had to come at the expense, in school and college curricula and among published works of history, of the previous near-monopoly of political subjects. And one could justifiably argue about the proportion of each that should compose a curriculum and reading list. But political history never disappeared; and because of historians' growing conviction that politics cannot be segregated from society and culture, political history is now more richly conceived and more robust than it ever has been.

to it. A single way of thinking historically or a single set of historical interests has never existed and never will. Consequently, tensions within
the community of historians engendered by debates over the respective
merits of sharply distinctive positions on the kinds of historical inquiry
that are most valuable and useful are unlikely ever to be resolved. Instead, there is every reason to believe that the philosophical differences
that have long separated the Herodoteans and Thucydideans will always
affect debates about the purposes of historical thought.

∾

A third variety of revisionist history is conceptual revisionism—a
rethinking of the grounds of any large area or subject of historical
interpretation. This kind of revisionist history tends to be the most
immediately disruptive. I have in mind here the major changes in West-
erner academics' understanding of most of the past by virtue of the
introduction of questions of class, race, ethnicity, gender, sexuality, and
most recently the natural world into what was formerly a comparatively
uniform focus on political history and on the history-making acts of
well-placed males of European origin. In this respect, the second half of
the twentieth century was especially fruitful. Since 1950, scarcely a single
topic of historical inquiry has remained unaffected by the insertion into
it of these and other fresh perspectives on the past. Despite attacks from
critics who bridle at the displacement of previously central subjects of
research and writing by novel ones, the recent reconceptualizations of the
past, when taken together, have amounted to a grand revision of historical
understanding, one that has driven knowledge of the past substantially
ahead. It should go without saying that such understanding has also
deeply affected thinking about current affairs.

A single example from a single general field of historical inquiry,
an example drawn from the nexus of political and social history—the
role of women in society and in the distribution and use of power in the
early American nation—can serve as an illustration of such a reconceptualization. This altered understanding of the realities of women's lives
in the years between the American Revolution and the Civil War arose
in defiance of the long-honored adage of English historian Edward A.
Freeman that "history is past politics, and politics present history." In
the spirit of that conviction, historians had told the history of public

affairs almost exclusively as the story of political parties and institutions, elections and legislative acts, wars and diplomacy. The fresh departure, arising in the 1960s in resolute opposition to this Thucydidean conviction, took inspiration from changes in the surrounding culture that inspired historians to bring all people within view of their professional lenses. Known variously as the "new social history" and "history from the bottom up," this turn in historians' attention revealed the historical significance to all those previously denied it: women, African Americans, Native Americans, the poor and forgotten, eventually gays and lesbians and disabled people—those ignored, scorned, and suppressed in the past. As practitioners of this new kind of history came to outnumber historians of the traditionally studied aspects of the American political world, historians' understanding of the politics of the opening years of the United States became focused more on the social and cultural context of political action and expression than on political thought, policies, and institutions. The result was a sharp intensification of interest in the lives and political roles of slaves as well as freemen, women as well as men, and laborers as well as property owners. In consequence emerged an augmented appreciation of these people's roles in bringing on the Revolution, pushing it in sometimes radical directions, helping create and support the nation's first political parties, defending and attacking slavery, and preparing the conditions for the outbreak of civil war in the 1860s. By the time the twenty-first century opened, it was difficult to think of a single group that had not been shown to have involved itself in the founding of the American nation. These groups gained their historical past when historians as different as Jesse Lemisch, Timothy H. Breen, and Linda K. Kerber brought American sailors, farmers, laborers, enslaved and free blacks, and women into the forefront of Americans who shaped the nation's early political history. Given their scholarship, it was no longer possible to believe that only the educated male gentry had contributed to the process and outcome of revolution and constitution making.

Not only did the inclusion of the entire population of Americans alter the written history of American politics. Political sensibilities came to be seen as inherent in the widest variety of social activity, in some respects to be all-encompassing. Here again, historians were moved by general cultural forces to include under the umbrella of politics people who, by law and custom, possessed no formal role in political affairs as voters and legislators. The traditional assumption had been that campaigning for and holding public office, as well as voting for public officials, were the only acts that bore political significance. But just as historians of political thought and expression had earlier turned their attention to nonelite political expression, historians realized that, by altering their perspective, almost all people at all times could be considered to be caught up in contests over power and political authority.

As a result, little was to be left out of consideration in this fresh approach to political history. It was now possible to see how features of public life like parades, banquets, and ceremonies (such as Fourth of July celebrations) as well as elections; religious observances as well as campaign events; churches as well as legislatures; fiction and works for the theater as well as political broadsides; taverns and inns as well as caucus rooms; and shipboard crews and militia companies as well as the parlors of the polite—all were sites of political reflection, persuasion, protest action, and negotiation. It became clear how the wives (like Dolley Madison) of public officials influenced the actions and thinking of their husbands through salons, soirées, and other social events. Slaves and slavery now moved front and center into the historical picture. Native Americans came to be understood to be major actors in the nation's history. Free blacks, immigrants, and laboring men and women were found to have been active participants in the politics of the cities and towns in which they lived; and irrational, rioting "mob" behavior was reconceived as the intentional collective action of "crowds" whose members rationally sought redress for perceived injustice. All of this added up to a revitalized political history, which absorbed so much within its tent that it came to be referred to as the study of "political culture" and as the "new political history." Now understood as being implicated in all human relationships and as being expressed beyond elections, formal public affairs, and the circles of those claiming to be politicians, political action was reconfigured as a much richer, broadly defined, and intellectually encompassing field of inquiry than the "old political history" of the era of the American Revolution and its aftermath.

Yet there is more to this story. By looking at a single strand of the general retexturing of the nation's early political history—a strand originating in feminism—we can see how the reimagining of history in one area rarely remains within its early channels but instead flows into other areas of historical interest and causes major reinterpretive adjustments to larger swaths of the past. In this case, the successful effort to come up with an interpretive scheme that would explain, first, the historical subjugation of women in early America and, second, their eventual full emergence into the historical record as independent people and agents of change in their own right owed itself to a set of conceptual changes that worked their way into a broader reworking of understanding of all American history. When the scholarly debate about how best to understand women's past began to settle out, it was apparent that histories centered on the acts, thoughts, and achievements of white men alone had been deeply misleading and were no longer tenable. In addition, the introduction of women into the larger history of the United States forced a lasting alteration in the orthodox contents of what historians term the "master narrative" of the American past. But in the context of this book, it turns out that the path to that new narrative did not follow a straight line; instead, it wove its way forward in twists and turns.

The roots of this interpretive development were to be found in "second-wave feminism," so-called for its political and ideological emphases that reached beyond the more limited focus on voting and property rights of the nineteenth and early twentieth century's "first-wave feminism." The new feminism, born after 1945, forced attention onto such issues as family, sexual, and workplace discrimination and abuse; archaic legal rules regarding such widely different issues as divorce, rape, contraception, abortion, and military service; and inequalities in such areas as pay scales, insurance coverage, and mortgage lending. Its motto was "The personal is the political." Its most celebrated and provocative texts were Simone de Beauvoir's 1949 *The Second Sex* and Betty Friedan's *The Feminine Mystique* of 1963. Both books, expressions of broad changes in postwar European and American culture, brought to historians' attention subjects that until then had gone largely ignored in scholarship and had possessed no place in undergraduate education, the preparation of aspiring historians, and general surveys of the past.

For historians, the practical challenge was to decide, first, on what grounds and, second, by what means to introduce women into their scholarship and teaching. Was the goal simply to demonstrate the indisputable fact that women possessed their own pasts and to reveal what those pasts were? Or was it to assess how women's pasts changed the larger historical narratives whose main characters had previously been male and to make room for women as creators and vectors of major changes in human society over the millennia? One could of course easily enough introduce women into previously all-male historical scenes—retelling, for instance, stories of Betsy Ross purportedly sewing the first American flag, vaunting the role of the thousands of Rosies the Riveter in sustaining the national economy during the Second World War, and bearing down on the extraordinary influence over public affairs of such individual women as Sojourner Truth, Jane Addams, and Eleanor Roosevelt. Here, the aim was to compensate and atone for women's previous absence from textbook histories. But that approach hardly advanced in any substantial way the understanding of women's historically subordinate station and their eventual emergence from it. To achieve that aim, two things were needed: new and never-before-pursued research into the historical realities of women's lives and new interpretive concepts.

From the start, feminist theorists and historians differed widely as to how to interpret what they began to discover from the sources, and they are not of one mind today. But as so often happens, some general interpretive tendencies soon made themselves strong enough to organize these scholars' work. Fundamental to them was the conviction, a foundation of second-wave feminism, that history revealed the long stranglehold of patriarchy over human affairs. That argument received its most robust expression in Gerda Lerner's 1986 *The Creation of Patriarchy*. But the concept of patriarchy created immediate difficulties. The trouble with focusing on such an encompassing reality of women's history was that, in addition to being indiscriminate, it conceded what women did not wish to concede—the overwhelming power and authority of men in the past—and it implied that women had possessed few roles and few options to act independently. It was easy enough to agree that women's subordination to men had been the general norm throughout most of human history. But how did patriarchy take hold, and how was it sustained in different societies and at different times? If male power was so encompassing and strong, then what explained women's gaining their freedom from it? In fact, was it really the case that women, through their central location in the family, had historically been encased in psychological lockup within what French theorist Michel Foucault termed a "total institution," or had they always created and possessed at least some autonomy to fashion their own lives within the restrictions imposed on them? Even though these questions aligned with feminism's political and ideological hopes, they were historical questions similar to those posed about slaves' ability to carve out areas of independence within slavery.

The most initially promising approach to explaining the subordination of women to men and their escape from it seemed to lie in the concept of "separate spheres." In the concept's terms, until recent times men and women had occupied distinct, bounded stations in life, women powerful in the domestic realm but without much agency in public affairs, the arena of men's dominion. Evidence for this working assumption was the existence of the venerable law and practices of "couverture," a body of rules that placed control of women's property and their freedom of action under men's "cover"—in the family as well as in the public arena. The law's application required men's assent to the instances in which wives, children, and other dependent females stepped outside their permitted roles; it placed ownership of most women's property in male hands; and it gave wide latitude to male control of sexual and domestic relations. Furthermore, it was argued that the realities of couverture were accompanied and legitimized by a contemporary ideology, what Barbara Welter called "the cult of true womanhood"— the set of practices and often unspoken social and cultural guidelines by which women's status and behavior could be organized and judged. These guidelines acknowledged only the most modest legitimate roles for women, those of taming the supposedly baser instincts of men on the one hand and of nurturing children for citizenship and maintaining republican virtue on the other—the roles of what Linda Kerber, their foremost historian, called "republican motherhood."

But the more historians looked into women's diverse lives, the more the notion of separate male and female spheres, and with it the concept of patriarchy, seemed unsatisfactory. The law and application of couverture, scholars found, were inconsistent; the ideology of "republican motherhood" only set forth an ideal. Neither law nor ideology ever succeeded fully in controlling women's behavior; and in any case by the eighteenth century couverture had proved inconsistent with the emergence of commercial capitalism. Neither law nor ideology was able to withstand the acids of modernity, and both eventually failed to keep women from playing public, eventually political, roles. The more historians examined the American post-Revolutionary past, the more women seemed to be everywhere in public life. Scholars concluded that it made more sense to see that the roles of each sex had been characterized not by their rigidity but, in Carol Lasser's words, by their "fluidity." Women along with men "collaborated in structuring society and politics."

Yet this was not all. Historians also became alert to the fact that men's and women's roles were not only fluid; they also varied extensively by race, ethnicity, class, location, and culture. Furthermore, going beyond the examination of women's roles in society, historians began to follow the lead of Foucault, Jacques Derrida, and Joan Wallach Scott in their "deconstructionist" theorizing of gender as a form of "discourse" that shapes power relationships at all levels and in all sectors of society. Under their influence, historians examined the construction and history of gender—the way in which the definition, performance, and behavior of sexual identity had changed over time. In their view, gender—the sexual identity that individuals take on, alter, and express in different ways at different times and under different circumstances—differs from the biological characteristics of sex that originate in the womb. Here, the history of women coincided with the developing history and theories of sexuality, including those pertaining to same-sex relationships, which, it became clear in the works of such authoritative scholars as John Boswell, could be found as far back as ancient Greece. When the lives of women were also subjected to historical investigation through the insights of gender history and theory, it was apparent that, throughout the past, there had existed a much wider range of "womanhoods" and "manhoods" and of varieties of sexual expression than had earlier been known and acknowledged.

Consequently, historians became convinced that separate sphere norms had cut both ways; they might have constricted women's lives, but they had also emboldened some women who followed those norms. In fact, historians found that in addition to the separate sphere of home being for many women their "natural" world to administer and affect as they might, it had also been a staging ground for women's emergence beyond their domestic roles. Inseparability from their families appeared as much a source of some women's influence as an impediment to it for others. Women—at least middle-class white women—could be found employing the language of domesticity to propel and justify their increasingly public activities, however limited those activities may seem to us now. Equally important, as Caroll Smith-Rosenberg and others employed the newly refreshed concept of separate spheres, the creation of a distinct domain of female love, support, and action was the origin place for the creation of women's protopower and their spread into feminized occupations like teaching and nursing and then beyond those activities. Historians also found that different religious denominations, creeds, and practices could work to confine women or, alternatively, provide them with the spur to seek greater satisfactions and opportunities in life.

The conclusion was inescapable: past mores and views about gender roles and relations had been variable and employed as the case might be by both sexes to promote as well as retard distinct class and political interests. The use of separate spheres ideology could be found, for instance, in the emergence of middle-class women to wide influence as antebellum abolitionists raising their voices in public against moral injustice; activists endeavoring both to promote and retard prohibition and the advance of women's suffrage; women contributing to war efforts at home and standing in for men who had departed to fight; and protesters campaigning to make contraception legally available. In short, research revealed that the law and practice of couverture and such ideologies as that of "true womanhood" were gradually cast aside as women and the market put pressure on standards, expectations, and existing hierarchies of relationships that no longer proved functional in life or acceptable under changing social conditions. Increasingly entering areas of action previously monopolized by men, nineteenth-century American women who took up work in mills and factories and thus came into possession of their own funds could spend or save as they wished. Even remaining unwed could be seen as defiance of dependency, a means of gaining autonomy, and a way of escaping some of what Nancy F. Cott called "the bonds of womanhood." Gaining new freedoms, middle-class women also adapted such previously neutral female domains as fairs and picnics for political ends, joined in petitioning politicians for redress of social ills, wrote schoolbooks filled with moral and civic instruction, and in an era deeply affected by emotional literature and evangelical Protestantism identified themselves with other women—especially slave and working women—who faced steep obstacles in speaking for themselves and escaping their bonds.

One could not, however, conclude that separate spheres had characterized the lives of all women and certainly not those outside the middle class; race and class differences had divided women from each other. But that had not prevented working women from formulating their own lives and "womanhood" as they could and wished—outside the strictures of middle-class spheres and rules. For many women, domesticity had never been a realm distinct from labor, whether free or slave labor; women had often combined work and home, many being forced to do so. It was difficult, too, to ignore the force of separate spheres in the battle for rights and representation—especially among African American women, who struggled to gain respectability during the Jim Crow era. For these women, many of them former slaves, greater, even if limited, control over their own homes and choice of work free of a slave master's interference represented true progress. In all these instances, non-middle-class women were putting the opportunities embodied in their restricted domains of action to work for their own benefit. The realities of separate spheres had liberated as well as confined them. Thus it came about that, through empirical research, historians continued to find new uses for the concept of separate spheres. While "true womanhood"—a distinct definition of women's role—had in many instances proved to be a prison for some wives, mothers, and unmarried women, evidence showed that achieving it had also been an aspiration of other women and families, especially those trying to rise into the middle class. In many cases, the relative haven of the domestic world had served for many women as a welcome, chosen refuge from the fearful world of commerce and industry. That is, "true womanhood" and "separate spheres" could be chosen realms.

The challenge for scholars of women's past was to acknowledge the brute fact of women's long historical suppression while allowing for women's own choices, endeavors, and successes, from within often harshly binding limits, in creating their own histories. It also required an acknowledgment that women's situations could be improved as well as limited by men's actions and could reciprocally alter those of men. So useful, in fact, has been the revised understanding of women's creation and manipulation of various theaters of action in the past that the concept of separate spheres is now applied to all human history. Historians now understand the past as a history of always-changing relationships between interdependent men and women rather than a history of women's stable and abject subordination to men. The relations between the sexes in the long modern era are now understood as having always been to some degree negotiable, unstable, and very much affected by the agency of women themselves. In Linda Kerber's words, historians now seek to show "how women's allegedly 'separate sphere' was affected by what men did, and how activities defined by women in their own sphere influenced and even set constraints and limitations on what men might choose to do—how, in short, that sphere was socially constructed both *for* and *by* women." Rather than hemming women in, as was first believed, it is now understood that separate spheres provided many women the freedom to create and advance their own interests and lives.

What conclusion are we to draw from this complex history of the idea of separate spheres? Surely one of them is that conceptual revisions of former interpretive schemes cannot be expected to enjoy stable resting places; all concepts can be put to uses for which they were not originally intended. The series of separate spheres reconceptualizations is also illustrative of the often complex path by which a long-held consensus about a distinct part of the past comes under scrutiny and a fresh consensus is built, itself then to become open to reevaluation and subject to criticism, reexamination, and restatement. In this case, one conceptual scheme—that of separate spheres—replaced that of the all-encompassing, but for that very reason indiscriminate, concept of patriarchy before the concept of separate spheres was itself attacked as being invalid, only then to be resurrected as historians realized that separate spheres had in fact provided the locales in which women's confidence, authority, influence, and participation in society were in many cases born, nourished, and fulfilled. From viewing women as victims of the ideology of domesticity, historians came instead to believe that women had used this ideology for their own purposes—to gain influence, education, satisfaction, and freedom from male domination. Separate spheres thinking, in Nancy Cott's words, had been "the basis for a sub-culture among women that formed a source of strength and identity and afforded supportive sisterly relations"—an interpretation that accorded to women and the ideology of separate spheres an influence independent of male and general social norms. Such an interpretive trajectory is but a single example of how a conceptual revision can come into being, then be cast into the shadows, subsequently to reemerge a second time to recover a solid portion of the acceptance it originally enjoyed. Such complex conceptual tangles have occurred frequently in the history of historical thought. They compose much of the continuing struggles to understand the past.

∾

These kinds of revisionist history do not exhaust the varieties that one can distinguish from others. Two more varieties, closely linked, arise directly from the evidentiary sources that are the foundation of historical inquiry. They are evidence-based revisionism and method-driven revisionism. Each of them is an alteration to previous interpretive approaches—the first due to the discovery of new historical sources, the second through the application of new analytical methods to already known evidence. Both can engender significant developments in historical knowledge.

The first of these varieties of historical argument—evidence-based revisionism, a variant arising from the discovery of major new historical sources—is in many respects the Holy Grail for most historians, who cherish the hope of one day discovering evidence of the past, be it manuscript documents, rare printed works, or physical artifacts, never before known and whose discovery substantially alters what is already thought. Often such discoveries confirm what historians already know.

Yet sometimes when new materials are unearthed, as they were in the late 1940s in the celebrated instance of the Dead Sea Scrolls, entire traditions of thought and belief can be transformed and new realms of inquiry opened. In the case of the Dead Sea Scrolls, their discovery deeply affected previous understanding of biblical and ancient history. Sometimes the opening of new evidence can be less lasting but equally consequential. Such has been the case, for example, with the gradual, continuing release of the tapes of the White House conversations of Richard M. Nixon. As they have been made public, those tapes have clarified and confirmed what was already understood about the former president's paranoia, obsessions, and misdeeds and have helped fill out the history of the Nixon administration. Along the same lines is the new evidence contained in newly opened Soviet archives after the dissolution of the Soviet Union, evidence that has forced major revisions in Soviet and Cold War history. And as was the case with Charles Beard's exploitation of never-before-used treasury records, sometimes it requires only fresh use of long-known evidence to inaugurate a major reanalysis of significant historical developments.

Equally consequential is the application of new means of analysis to long-known evidence to create fresh historical understanding—method-driven revisionism. The authority possessed by this kind of alteration to formerly accepted views grows from the application of research techniques developed outside the discipline of history to evidence historians have previously examined in other ways, methods that grant new significance to old sources and allow new meaning to be drawn from them. A widely debated instance of method-driven innovation in interpretation was the application of statistical and econometric methods to existing evidence about slavery—especially about the changing cost of slaves on the domestic slave-sale market and the changing prices for land being opened or resold in the South before 1860. As I indicated in Chapter 1, when methods developed by statisticians and economists were brought to bear on such cost data lying long unexamined in archives, fresh vistas opened onto the profitability of slavery in the antebellum American South and thus of the "rationality" of slaveholders' battle to preserve the peculiar institution.

Another major instance of the method-driven reevaluation of

existing evidence that has led to a revision of previous historical understanding involves the relationship between Thomas Jefferson and his
domestic slave Sally Hemings (who also happened to be the daughter of
his deceased wife's father and thus Jefferson's sister-in-law). It was clear
as soon as the modern controversy over their relationship commenced
in the 1970s that whatever turned out to be the historical consensus
about the controversy would have an impact on understanding the history of black-white relationships throughout American history. After
all, this issue concerned the author of the Declaration of Independence
and touched on the claims and values of the man considered to be the
creator of the nation's self-image and the father of American democracy. Historians' findings about the intimate personal bonds between
Jefferson and Hemings were bound to be freighted with heavy cultural
significance. Moreover, questions never directly addressed earlier by
historians—Was Jefferson's relationship with his slave more than
contractual? Was it sexual, perhaps even affectionate? Did Hemings
exert emotional leverage over her owner? Was Jefferson a hypocrite?—
reflected a general, broader transformation in historical thought and
perspective that gained fresh strength in the 1960s, one that, as it did in
the study of politics generally, moved the spotlight of history from the
governing, financial, industrial, largely male elite toward people long
ignored by historians. From this fresh interest emerged a new variety of
biography as well as new studies of the private behavior of entire populations of men and women.

Almost every evolving line of historical inquiry seemed to converge on Jefferson—the new history of race relations, of private lives,
of gender, and of the South. Historians were also influenced by newly
available methodologies to undertake probes of evidence long inert in
archives, just as they had regarding the profitability of slavery. To many
of them, there was much appeal in applying to their own scholarly interests techniques developed in other fields. These methods offered them
the chance to learn from existing evidence more than available older
methods had so far allowed.

Here, two distinct developments originating outside the discipline
of history were congruent with scholars' growing interest in people's
private lives and in people long ignored. The first was psychology. Even

though psychological theorizing lacked firm methods and findings that could be replicated, it offered promising lines of inquiry into the hidden realities of people's mental and private existence. What could the previously hidden lives of people reveal about their public positions and writings, and vice versa? What might the contradictions between major historical figures' public pronouncements and private behavior bring to light about entire cultures and national character? How might the application to historical questions of psychological theory, however speculative, begin to reveal some of the concealed, unspoken, even un-recognized realities of the past?

DNA analysis, a technique dependent on innovations in technol-ogy as well as genetic science, was the second method developed outside historical circles that held promise of yielding new historical knowledge. Here, the approaches of a new science offered hope of new under-standing when applied to genealogical and related evidence previously beyond the reach of historical analysis. It could, for example, illuminate the origins of large populations of people, help map their migrations, explain the spread of plants, animals, and diseases, and chart changes in the environment. In this case, the possibility of applying DNA science to resolving the long-running dispute over the paternity of some slaves at Monticello was too good to ignore. It was not long before historians sought to put this new science to historical use.

While sexual exploitation of their slaves by white owners was well known and widespread and while mixed-race people were to be found throughout the American population, sexual relations between the races were long considered illicit, in the North as well as the South. As a result, rumored, even widely reported, intimate black-white re-lationships within the households of leading southern figures were rarely publicly acknowledged, and the widely accepted code of silence by which such relationships were protected gave denial of such rumors within slaveholding society the authority of demonstrated truth. On rare occasions, white society accepted the existence of an open, if un-legalized, marriage between a white man and a black woman, as it did in the case of Jefferson's friend Thomas Bell (who lived in a common-law marriage with Sally Hemings's mother, Elizabeth). But the numbers of such acknowledged relationships were small and never enough to pose a

challenge to unwritten law; they were, at least among the gentry, simply
tolerated exceptions.

From the 1790s, rumors existed of such a relationship between
Thomas Jefferson, not yet president of the United States, and his slave
Sally Hemings. The rumors would probably have remained a local
matter in Virginia had not Vice President Jefferson, emerging with
James Madison at the head of the young Democratic-Republican
Party, entered into battle with President John Adams over the White
House in 1800. During the run-up to the presidential election that
year, Jefferson employed one James T. Callender, a Scottish democrat,
journalist, pamphleteer, and opportunist then resident in Philadelphia,
to attack Adams. For his accusations against the president, the Adams
administration brought Callender to trial under the Sedition Act, and
he was found guilty, fined, and imprisoned. When Jefferson gained the
presidency in 1801, he pardoned Callender but would not agree to the
latter's request to be appointed postmaster of Richmond, Virginia. In
retaliation, Callender switched political sides and began attacking the
president. First, he made public the evidence, unknown until then, that
Jefferson had been behind Callender's attack on Adams. Then in 1802,
after visiting the vicinity of Monticello and no doubt talking with those
who knew more about Jefferson than most others, he made bold to
publicly accuse Jefferson of having fathered children with "Black Sally."

Not surprisingly, for the following century and a half such a charge
gained little running room. It might be repeated among those who had
learned of it during Jefferson's presidency and might later be whispered
here and there, but almost always privately and rarely unsalaciously.
In that day, north and south, it was difficult to credit a rumor that
the author of the Declaration of Independence, third president of the
United States, and champion of democracy had engaged, even though
long widowed, in such an interracial liaison and surely not in one that
resulted in children. The South had its own special reasons to suppress
all scandal-mongering about a southern slaveholding president: if valid,
such charges contravened southern insistence that the color line was
never breached, at least among gentlemen and gentlewomen of property
and standing. Once slavery had ended with the Civil War, no doubt precisely because slavery had ended, neither northern nor southern society

was going to make room for the acknowledgment or acceptance of yet another previously ignored fundamental reality in relations between blacks and whites. Interracial affectionate and sexual relationships of any kind would for decades remain socially offensive and, in many jurisdictions, illegal.

As is so often the case, historians long followed prevailing postbellum views.[3] By the middle of the twentieth century, the "Jefferson Establishment"—an informal group of scholars whose major figures were Dumas Malone (author of an esteemed six-volume biography of Jefferson), Julian P. Boyd (founding editor of the extraordinary multivolume edition of *The Papers of Thomas Jefferson*), and Merrill D. Peterson (Jefferson biographer and historian of his image in the world)—maintained and patrolled the boundaries of what had become a kind of orthodoxy in the historiography of the world-historical Virginia figure. Admitting to Jefferson's flaws and errors, they nevertheless downplayed or dismissed evidence, not then authoritatively developed, that Jefferson owned the children whom he might have fathered with his own bondservant. Could one imagine a man of Jefferson's greatness involving himself in an enduring, nonmarital, perhaps loving relationship with an African American slave? Could that scamp Callender be believed? To such historians, whose authority over Jefferson historiography kept other historians at bay, these questions answered themselves. If any scholars had been curious enough to look deeply into the rumors in any depth, they left no evidence of having done so. When they did mention Callender's accusations in their works, they did so only to dismiss them as being without evidentiary support and, given the overwhelming idolization of the third president, beyond the bounds of plausibility. As much in the grip of common opinion as nonhistorians, they adopted a kind of informal agreed-on *omertà* to cover with the taint of preposterousness the age-old whispers of the Jefferson-Hemings link.

---

3. The concept of "path dependency" is relevant here. A sociological term, it usually refers to decisions made and courses followed because of previous and existing circumstances, actions, and thinking. No less than others, historians fall into such rutted paths of assumption and thought that eventually become interpretive conventions. It is the role of fresh research and thinking, like the research and thinking I review here, to jolt historians out of their well-worn tracks.

In hindsight, given the changes in American society that accelerated after 1950—changes especially in race relations and in women's place in American society—it seems inevitable that Callender's ancient charges and historians' dismissal of them would eventually be subjected to new scrutiny, and such scrutiny was not long in appearing. Rumors of Jefferson's paternity of Hemings's children had long circulated in the African American community. In 1954, *Ebony* magazine resuscitated Callender's 150-year-old charge by invoking the recollections of aging black Americans who claimed their ancestry from Jefferson. The publication's anonymous author clearly had in mind the first creditable such claim, the published 1873 memoir of Madison Hemings, one of Sally Hemings's children. Yet as long had been the case, white historians dismissed Madison Hemings's testimony as so much hearsay and, in any case, not creditable inasmuch as it was the testimony of a black man.

It was historian Winthrop D. Jordan, more than a generation younger than members of the Jefferson Establishment, who became the first widely read scholar to note, albeit glancingly, in his masterly 1968 work *White Over Black: American Attitudes Toward the Negro, 1550–1812*, that all five of Hemings's children had been born within nine months of Jefferson's return to Monticello from travels elsewhere. Even Jordan's authority, however, failed to lead others to investigate further, and the issue continued to smolder without gaining greater scholarly attention. That changed in 1974 when Fawn M. Brodie became the first historian to confront directly and at length the possibility that Jefferson had in fact fathered Sally Hemings's offspring.

In the context of revisionist history, it is relevant to note here that Brodie's strong challenge to the continuing efforts of the Jefferson Establishment to contain and delegitimize enduring rumors of Jefferson's maintenance of a concubine at Monticello was mounted by someone who differed from Jefferson's academic defenders in four critical respects. Brodie was female; she was deeply conversant with Freudian psychology; like Jordan she was younger than most of Jefferson's protectors; and she was not from the South. Even if these factors did not determine her critical stance, they put her potentially at odds with the existing community of authority represented by older, male historians of the early republic who were then taken to be the most reliable voices about the Squire of Monticello's life. Here again is an example of the way in which factors external to the gathering and evaluation of evidence—factors that are perspectival—can influence any effort to interpret the past. Brodie brought new questions, a new intellectual outlook, and a new openness to evaluating the evidence that had long lain unexamined in surviving records. While it turns out that she did not and could not proceed as far as her successors would, she provided the intellectual accelerant that would forever change Jefferson scholarship.

One of the earliest women to gain tenure as a professor of history at a major research university (UCLA), Brodie had read widely in psychoanalytic theory and had undergone psychoanalysis. In her earlier biographies of such widely different figures as Mormonism's founder Joseph Smith, antislavery radical Thaddeus Stevens, and explorer Richard Burton, Brodie had ventured into psychobiography—a then-young variety of life history often derided, like Sigmund Freud's theories themselves, for lacking an underpinning in evidence that could be verified. A historian might speculate about the mental state or psychological troubles of a particular person or the irrational actions of some crowds, but, as critics pointed out, it was not possible to summon clinical evidence or autopsy results in confirmation of such speculation. Yet despite attacks on the validity of the application of psychology to the interpretation of individual lives and group behavior and the continuing reluctance of most professional historians to venture down this path of inquiry, the claims for psychobiography were not without promise, especially in opening up new lines of inquiry. Might not the findings of psychology, deftly and responsibly employed, allow some fresh insight into aspects of personality previously overlooked or revealed indirectly by existing evidence, especially insight into a person's inner and private life usually ignored in biographies of major public figures? Freud had applied his own theories to the lives of Moses and Leonardo da Vinci. And by the time Brodie tried her hand at the genre, the noted psychologist Erik Erikson had written widely acclaimed biographies of Martin Luther and Mohandas Gandhi.

One of the earliest historians to adopt Erikson's approach, in her *Thomas Jefferson: An Intimate History*, Brodie concentrated on Jefferson's largely unknown private existence instead of on his better-known public life. Some of her emphases—such as Jefferson's lifelong experience with crippling migraine headaches—were unlikely to cause critical commotion. But in dealing with Jefferson's relations with his household slaves, she stepped into a political, cultural, and historiographic minefield. She confirmed Jordan's earlier brief sketch that all of Sally Hemings's children were recorded as having been born roughly nine months after Jefferson had returned to Monticello from trips elsewhere. A firm, avowed admirer of Jefferson, Brodie also entered psychological speculation into the historical record as she tried to link Jefferson's tortured speculations on race, his tangled relationship with his own slaves, and his debilitating migraines. She thus opened up an entire, new frontier of historical research and historiographic debate (to say nothing of public controversy). Some critics accused her of having substituted psychological surmise for historical fact. As fierce paladins of the third president pointed out, a strong candidate for the role of Hemings's lover was Jefferson's nephew Peter Carr, who seemed to be at or near Monticello whenever Jefferson was there. Since Carr could not be ruled out, his name was brought forth as rendering Brodie's reading of the evidence too flimsy to credit, and many critics subjected the novel application of psychological theory to Jefferson's biography to heavy assault.[4] Standing alone, Brodie's speculations failed to convince many people of the validity of her arguments. Yet after a century and a half of historians' unwillingness to touch the issue, she had raised it to fresh significance among professional scholars and provided some cover to others who might venture further along the path she had blazed.

Given the absence of additional evidence or new ways to approach the question of Jefferson's hidden slave family after Brodie intervened,

---

4. I did not escape their wrath. After I wrote a favorable public review of Brodie's book, a fellow historian much senior to me summoned me to his office and threatened to take his differences with me public. I explained to him my conviction that such a spat would not make life any easier for him than for me. I also could not avoid pointing out, with as much of a twinkle in my eye as I could summon, that, were the year of our conversation 1804, I might have grounds for summoning him to an "interview," if not at Weehawken then somewhere else, and, being younger than he, I would likely have a better aim and quicker draw. He responded that he would think over his threat. He never made good on it, and, fortunately, our previously warm collegial relations resumed.

the controversy quieted for more than two decades, participants in it unable to move much beyond the lines of argument that Brodie had laid down. That ended with the 1997 publication of Annette Gordon-Reed's *Thomas Jefferson and Sally Hemings: An American Controversy*. A historian trained in the law, Gordon-Reed revealed once again how permeable to external approaches historical thought always is: she brought an attorney's approach to bear on the evidence. Applying evidentiary methods normal in courtrooms to historical facts (such as those requiring the equal treatment of hearsay evidence on both sides in a legal dispute), she showed how historians had accepted whites' claims about Jefferson's life while dismissing those of African Americans, thereby breaking a fixed rule of trial testimony. Insisting that the recollections of blacks be treated equally with those of whites, she also ventured more deeply than others had into the oral recollections of Hemings's children and of those who had known Jefferson and his descendants. Given Gordon-Reed's punishing criticism of previous historians' discriminatory approach to long-held beliefs in the black community, as well as of their resistance to the examination of claimed facts—neither of which would have been allowed in a court trial—she shifted the consensus among scholars to the view that Jefferson and Hemings had clearly shared an intimate relationship.

Neither Brodie's nor Gordon-Reed's arguments could carry the day without firm scientific confirmation. This came with the 1998 publication, in the authoritative science journal *Nature*, of a study that concluded, through the analysis of DNA from a claimed descendant of Jefferson and Hemings, that Jefferson was indisputably the father of Hemings's last son Eston Hemings and probably of his siblings, too. Equally important, it put to rest any doubt that Peter Carr had been Sally Hemings's lover: no match existed between Jefferson's DNA and that of Carr's descendants. So powerful were these findings, and so authoritative Gordon-Reed's earlier arguments, that the exhibits and guidance offered at Jefferson's celebrated home, Monticello, were altered to reflect them.

Some people, including a few professional historians (all of them, significantly, of an older generation than Gordon-Reed), refuse to accept the authority of this most recent professional consensus. Yet rare is now the practicing historian who doubts that Jefferson was the father of children by his slave concubine. Instead, because of the application of legal and scientific methods external to the discipline of history, the burden of demonstrating otherwise has shifted to those who continue to doubt the strength of the new consensus.

∾

In this rough, informal typology of revisionism, there must in the end be a place for what can only be termed normal revisionism—adjustments to previously held approaches to or interpretations of historical subjects that alter understanding of them. Rare is the written history, rare especially among works written by professional historians, that does not add something, even if not something earthshaking, controversial, or even challenging in a major way, to the stock of historical understanding that has gone before it. Even the third or fourth narrative of a Civil War battle is likely to provide some new details to the published record, some new emphasis drawn from long available information, some new argument that needs to be subjected to the tests of evaluation and criticism. This normal kind of revisionist history may not substantially force a change in existing accounts; it may not set a new course for all future consideration of the same subject. But it is revisionist history nonetheless. While no one writing a history of the Civil War will be held to account for not consulting the work in which this new perspective on this battle is put forth, prudence and wisdom are likely to lead most serious historians to consult it if only to make sure that they have missed nothing significant about the fighting.

In many respects the most fundamental step in historical inquiry, the one that must open any investigation of the past once a historical question has been asked, is the examination of the documentation of events. Once historians ask whether a document is genuine, whether its author can be confirmed to have witnessed what the document relates, whether others confirm what the author alleges—once historians evaluate their evidence, the task at the very heart of their work—all bets are off, and all stated facts stand open to substantiation, qualification, or outright rejection in the light of other known evidence. While usually not actuated by the inspired forensic intentions of someone like Lorenzo Valla, intent on exposing the fraudulence of the *Donation of Constan-*

tine, this kind of basic historical detective work casts an unblinking eye on the claims of an event's participants, onlookers, and memoirists—on all the immediate documentation about that event (witness reports, recollections, reportage, photographs, and the like) that is known to exist. Frequently as a result, interpretations built on previously available evidence must undergo alteration. Such has been the fate of histories written by contemporaries since the origin of historical inquiry.

Take, for instance, *The History of the Rebellion and Civil Wars in England* (first published in 1702), the great, engaged, royalist account of the early years of the English Civil War of the 1640s, written by its author in exile. That author, Edward Hyde, the first earl of Clarendon, served in Parliament and was a member of King Charles I's Privy Council before the king's execution. Possessed of on-the-spot knowledge of public affairs in the 1640s, he wrote his account of the Civil War in the late part of that decade. While not the only first-person account of the era's events, as a memoir of what Clarendon had been party to the work has long been taken to be a classic of its kind—its immediate, vivid characterizations being of the quality and dependability that only a participant and contemporary could capture. Not surprisingly, however, as more has been learned about the tumultuous history of seventeenth-century British history, of the Stuart monarchy, of Oliver Cromwell's interregnum, and of the restoration of the monarchy in 1660, and since later students of the English Civil War have felt no need to vindicate the king's party as Clarendon did, much of his account has been superseded. But even though many of its claims and arguments have been found wanting—even, that is, as his history has been broadly revised through considered scholarship and a waning of old political commitments—the demonstrably accurate aspects of Clarendon's I-was-there reporting, his point of view and convictions, and his portraits of the day's leading figures remain inherent in all successive histories of the same subject. While modern histories of the events of the 1640s encompass many more dimensions of the Civil War and thus better satisfy the historian's commitment to balance and detachment than did Clarendon, newer histories lack the immediacy that every memoir of lived history like Clarendon's can convey.

When we come closer to our own era, efforts to substantiate or to revise on-the-spot reportage and memoirs in the light of other evidence have become the conventional first steps in every historian's work. Take, as another example, the 1965 account by historian Arthur M. Schlesinger, Jr., of the abbreviated administration of John F. Kennedy, *A Thousand Days: John F. Kennedy in the White House*. A special assistant to Kennedy, Schlesinger served in the executive mansion for the administration's duration as a kind of court historian, one who was expected to write the history of Kennedy's presidency while working to maintain its documentary record. Schlesinger, however, was involved in more than note-taking and event recording; he also participated in substantive discussions and occasionally helped devise policy. And while no one should ever have assumed that Schlesinger's account was unbiased, there was also never any doubt that, because his up-close report of Kennedy's presidency carried with it the authority of verisimilitude, it could not be ignored. Moreover, the first account to appear after the president's assassination, it would assume a large place in the historiography of the era. But with the addition of other accounts, the opening of the Kennedy administration's full archives, and the work of other professional scholars, it has become apparent that Schlesinger's account is incomplete and partial: it captures only part of the Kennedy administration and the president's life during it, and, as might be expected, it is parti pris. Schlesinger could not have known all that was going on around him, especially in those parts of the administration and in those dimensions of policy making in which he was not involved. And he did not report, if he knew of them, the less attractive aspects of the Kennedy White House, such as the president's dalliances with women not his wife. As a result, no historian would today rely on Schlesinger's account without checking every assertion against other available evidence, nor would any historian take Schlesinger's coverage of the administration as complete. Yet neither would any historian ignore what Schlesinger wrote as an early draft of that history. This is the normal course of historical inquiry.

Few, however, believe that normal revisionist history—whether the critical appraisals of participants' accounts or additions to previously written professional histories of an event—is what champions and critics have in mind when they refer to revisionist history. And most of the time they do not have this variety of revisionism in mind. Additive history constitutes the lowest common denominator of revisionist history, the kind of history so predominant since the birth of professional historical studies in the nineteenth century as to merge seamlessly into what constitutes what most historians first come to think of as history to begin with—the narrative telling of events. But it is revisionist history nonetheless because it supplements and thus alters, even in modest ways, what has been known or understood previously. Take a hypothetical Civil War battle, the example that I use to illustrate many matters. Its newest historian has examined a cache of never-before-examined letters buried in the collection of a local southern historical society, letters that were written home by a Confederate soldier. Those letters reveal that, contrary to after-battle reports long studied by historians, this soldier had written to his family that his battalion had never received the orders to attack enemy lines that had been sent from his commander's headquarters because the orders' courier had been captured. On account of the soldier's newly found assertion, the reason usually cited for this particular Confederate battle loss—superior Union tactics and marksmanship—now has to be seen as probably incorrect; instead, the Grays surrendered the battlefield due to the absence of command directions, not lesser competence.

What, however, are the consequences for general knowledge of the Civil War of this addition to the historical record? Probably modest, but not entirely insignificant, ones. With this new perspective on a single battle, we have removed one weight from the scale of Confederate lack of military skill and added one to the measure of Union good luck. While such an addition to knowledge is unlikely to cause a commotion among academic scholars of Civil War battles or to be noticed in the pages of major newspapers and magazines, it may catch the eye of those, such as people responsible for local commemorations or battle reenactments, who have other stakes in the emergence of this interpretive nuance. It may also cause researchers to look for yet more evidence about the battle, which might lead to additional, perhaps even more consequential, alterations in understanding of the larger war. No one would object to that.

∾

It should be clear by now that historians accept the incompleteness of all understanding of the past. The past's details are too numerous, the evidence about it too fragmentary, and the variety of minds seeking to know about it too varied to allow anyone to write finis to historical speculation. Most historians therefore try to absorb what they can from the widest variety of historical interpretations while at the same time maintaining a critical distance on what those interpretations contain. On the basis of honed knowledge, they are free to accept or reject all interpretations and all revisions to what they have known and thought. Relatedly, they can and always do wish for evidence that adds to the knowledge they possess. But historians also know that every fresh view of any subject of the past, whether or not they accept that view, constitutes an effort to get closer to always-wished-for, if inherently unobtainable, complete knowledge of what occurred in times previous to their own. In this sense, historians aim for the same goal even if they disagree about how to get there and about what they have additionally learned once they do.

This fact makes it essential to emphasize again, as I noted when discussing the historiography of the American Civil War in Chapter 1, that rarely does a new approach to a discrete historical subject render already existing approaches entirely valueless. A particular line of inquiry may be displaced by another but never eradicated entirely. What has already been written about a subject can never be removed from its further consideration. What is out of date in one era may take on fresh significance in another, just as a new interpretation may only temporarily interrupt a line of argument that springs back to life even stronger for being challenged. Often, a line of argument will appear in an era when it is not consonant with its cultural or intellectual circumstances and consequently prove unable to gain traction in its own time, only to gain full development in a later one.

A notable example of such discordance between significance and "fit" is seen in the fate of social and cultural history in the two centuries after 1750. The histories of Voltaire and Gibbon, grounded, in the manner of Herodotus, in the cultural and social history of their subjects; of Thomas Babington Macaulay, who exploited such sources as songs and ephemeral broadsides in his mid-nineteenth-century *The History of England;* and of Macauley's nephew George Macaulay Trevelyan (who famously termed his *English Social History* "a history of the people with the politics left out") all pointed in a new direction that might have re-directed some attention away from the political and military subjects that had been the standard fare of historiography since Thucydides. But the era of late-eighteenth-century wars and revolutions proved inhospitable to any major departure in the way history had been written for more than a millennium. So, not surprisingly, when early in the nineteenth century professional academic history emerged along with modern universities in the German states under the leadership of Leopold von Ranke, it was thoroughly traditional in its emphasis on political, institutional, and military subjects. The result was an end, for more than another hundred years, to the historiographic initiatives of Voltaire, Gibbon, Macaulay, and Jules Michelet, the last of whom took the whole human canvas of his native France for his subject. When later historians like Karl Lamprecht, Henri Pirenne, and Jacob Burckhardt tried to revive social, economic, and cultural history (under the term *Kulturgeschichte*) and create an interest in comparative history at the end of the nineteenth century, their works did not find favor with the likes of Max Weber (a student of Leopold von Ranke) and Friedrich Meinecke (a student of intellectual historian Wilhelm Dilthey) on the grounds that this reawak-ened kind of Herodotean history was inattentive to politics and political thought. As a result, Lamprecht's, Pirenne's, and Burckhardt's initiatives gave way before the traditional authority of Rankean political history, and their students had difficulty gaining coveted professional positions. Social history remained in the shadows until it finally caught on with the French *Annales* school in the 1920s and 1930s and then flowered else-where on the Continent and in the Anglophone world.

The scorn that greeted Lamprecht's innovations and the depre-ciation of his students' work is not the only example of historians' dis-missing the work of others whose scholarship would eventually prove valuable in understanding the past. François Furet, the distinguished historian of France, used to tell the story of standing for his *agrégation* exam, a trial required of all those seeking entry into the company of advanced teachers and scholars in France. It was 1954, and one of his examiners was the great French historian Fernand Braudel, who asked Furet what the subject of his scholarship was to be. "The French Revo-lution," was Furet's reply. "But don't we know all that already?" asked

Braudel. Here was mature certainty speaking to aspiring youth. Braudel was confident that the scholarly debates that had long roiled the historiography of the French Revolution had been settled by Marxist-based social and economic histories, as well as by the work of *Annales* historians like himself, and that he could thus effectively know the final resting place of the historiography of the Revolution. Yet by the time Furet died in 1997, as if in taunt of Braudel he and many other historians had made it impossible to ignore the French Revolution and the role of ideas and culture behind it. Traditional, Marxist, and older *Annales* explanations of the Revolutionary turmoil could no longer hold the field to themselves. So much for Braudel's certainties.

As these tales suggest, all who seek knowledge of the past will do well to accept the likelihood of the simultaneous existence of different, possibly clashing, views of the past as well as the incompleteness of all efforts at historical interpretation. They will look on all histories as provisional. Most professional historians are inured to such uncertainty and ambiguity. They know that what they think and write will be subjected to debate and evaluation, sometimes to harsh criticism, occasionally to outright rejection. They know that all historians possess the option to disagree with other historians. They may smart from attacks, admit to error, revise their views, or reject criticism; but, once launched like the histories of Voltaire, Gibbon, Michelet, Burckhardt, Lamprecht, and Pirenne, different ways to view the past will always be available to future historians to consider. In our day, the coexistence of large, robust fields of political/diplomatic/institutional (Thucydidean) and social/cultural/intellectual (Herodotean) history shows that no single way to do history, no single line of inquiry, need permanently elbow any other off the field. Both can advance side by side, desirably in conversation with each other, so as to bring about adjustments, revisions, and enlargements in each. In this way, historical understanding is constantly enriched.

For Further Reading, Chapter 4

The classic presentation of the "cult of true womanhood" is Barbara Welter, "The Cult of True Womanhood, 1820–1860," *American Quarterly* 18 (1966): 151–174. On the complex history and use of the concept of separate women's spheres, three essential works are Nancy F. Cott, *The Bonds of Womanhood: "Woman's Sphere" in New England, 1780–1835*, 2nd ed. (New Haven: Yale University Press, 1997); Linda K. Kerber, "Separate Spheres, Female Worlds, Women's Place: The Rhetoric of Women's History," *Journal of American History* 75 (1988): 9–39; and Anne Firor Scott, *The Southern Lady: From Pedestal to Politics, 1830–1930* (Chicago: University of Chicago Press, 1970). See also Carol Lasser, "Beyond Separate Spheres: The Power of Public Opinion," *Journal of the Early Republic* 21 (2001): 115–123, and two essays accompanying Lasser's: Mary C. Kelley, "Beyond the Boundaries," ibid., 73–78, and Julie Roy Jeffrey, "Permeable Boundaries: Abolitionist Women and Separate Spheres," ibid., 79–93. Joan Wallach Scott's classic essay, "Gender: A Useful Category of Analysis," can be found in Scott, *Gender and the Politics of History* (New York: Columbia University Press, 1988), 28–50. A collection of essays that reveals the breadth of modern thinking about the history of women, gender, and sexuality is Scott, ed., *Feminism and History* (New York: Oxford University Press, 1996). See also Carroll Smith-Rosenberg, "The Female World of Love and Ritual: Relations Between Women in Nineteenth-Century America," *Signs* 1 (1975): 1–29. The starting point for the history of same-sex relationships is John Boswell, *Christianity, Social Tolerance, and Homosexuality: Gay People in Western Europe from the Beginning of the Christian Era to the Fourteenth Century* (Chicago: University of Chicago Press, 1980).

An addition to the major works about the relationship between Thomas Jefferson and Sally Hemings mentioned in the text is Annette Gordon-Reed, *The Hemingses of Monticello: An American Family* (New York: Norton, 2008), which integrates the Hemings family into Jefferson's life as if the debate over the man's paternity of his slave's children is a settled question, which to most historians it is. A wide-ranging collection of essays on the controversy is Jan Ellen Lewis and Peter S. Onuf, eds., *Sally Hemings and Thomas Jefferson: History, Memory, and Civic Culture* (Charlottesville: University Press of Virginia, 1999). See also the essays in "Forum: Thomas Jefferson and Sally Hemings Redux," *William and Mary Quarterly*, 3rd ser., 57 (2000): 121–210. For a minority report of holdouts, not all of them historians, see M. Andrew Holowchak, *Framing a Legend: Exposing the Distorted History of Thomas Jefferson and*

Sally Hemings (Amherst, NY: Prometheus, 2013). A full history of the debate over the Jefferson-Hemings relationship before Gordon-Reed's 1997 book is Scot A. French and Edward L. Ayers, "The Strange Career of Thomas Jefferson: Race and Slavery in American Memory, 1943–1993," in Peter S. Onuf, ed., *Jeffersonian Legacies* (Charlottesville: University Press of Virginia, 1993), 418–456. The genetic evidence of Jefferson's paternity of children by Hemings is found in Eugene A. Foster et al., "Jefferson Fathered Slave's Last Child," *Nature* 396 (November 5, 1998): 27–28. On James Callender, see Michael Durey, *With the Hammer of Truth: James Thomson Callender and America's Early National Heroes* (Charlottesville: University Press of Virginia, 1990).

FIVE

Some Fruits of Revisionist History

A s I have tried to make clear, altered historical interpretations
have had major impacts and captured the interest of people
well beyond the boundaries of the community of professional historians. Some debates confined normally to the
universe of scholars break out of intellectual and academic circles to
affect public discussion and, occasionally, politics. Sometimes a clash
of views commencing in the larger society works in reverse: it ends up
influencing the community of historians in a kind of contrapuntal exchange of arguments, such an interpretive sally from outside historians'
circles resulting in spirited responses from historians and then a general
melee of reciprocal attack and counterattack.

Perhaps most significant, controversies over the meaning of past
events can have a major impact on the very way in which a nation—in
fact, any community—defines itself and how its citizens or residents
understand their political, social, and cultural origins and roles. Accordingly, one should never assume that the kinds of interpretive differences and conflicts that I have outlined in previous chapters are mere
academic trifles—scholarly conflicts of concern only to researchers
and of no consequence to public affairs. Nor should we think that even
intra-academic conflicts can be fenced off from the rest of the world.
Experience has repeatedly shown that the contents of written histories

can coincide with public events so as to bring historians' specialized works sharply into focus and give them contemporary resonance, sometimes to explosive effect. We need look no further than to Eusebius's *Ecclesiastical History* and Lorenzo Valla's exposure of the *Donation of Constantine* for examples of the impact that revisionist histories have had on the Western world. All works of history, but especially those of major revisionist import, can become matters of intense civic concern and have major public and cultural consequences.

Yet the civic implications of historical works mark out only one dimension of the function that deepened historical knowledge plays in the larger universe of human affairs. Every interpretation of the past can also affect understanding of the present; and the ways people lay claim to the past, whether interpreted by historians or by others, can directly affect current events—sometimes for good, sometimes for ill. The search for understanding of the past always reflects the needs of living people. Broadly conceived, historical understanding is like a gyroscope: it provides people with a kind of essential orientation and stability as they move through their lives even as those very lives and the contexts in which they take shape change.

In ideal cases, altered historical knowledge, like additional human experience, aids individuals, their communities, and their nations to adjust their understanding of themselves as time passes. Because distinct understandings of the past can play this critical orienting role, any revisions to individuals' or groups' customary way of viewing the past can arouse strong emotion and bitter debate—within large populations of people as well as between individuals. Consequently, when clashes over the past leak from one sector into another—from academic circles into public affairs and vice versa—as the examples that follow in this chapter show, they can generate everything from general unease to deep fissures within human communities.

Since the nineteenth century, with the emergence of the formal intellectual discipline of history within universities, these divisions have often commenced in the different situations of academic historians and members of the general public. Professional historians characteristically seek fresh knowledge of the past and regularly weigh the arguments of authoritative scholarly works that push a subject into new territory. The very sociology of their work—the insistent search for new knowledge, the intense interest of small groups of specialist scholars searching for additional understanding of the subject in which they are invested, and professional competitiveness—puts a premium on verification of evidence as well as strength and plausibility of argument. Disputes are normal among professional historians; they accept the fact that known evidence can support more than a single way of looking at the past, and they have long accepted the fact that argument often leads to further progress in understanding as well as to a narrowing of interpretive differences. Although historians' arguments frequently carry ideological and political significance, a large proportion of academic debate takes place without rancor and with an acknowledgment among scholars that, despite their many differences, they learn from each other. Some consider themselves, even without using the term, as occupying what the sixteenth-century jurist-historian François Baudouin called "the office of historian," as people with responsibilities both to the past (of capturing and understanding its integrity) and to the present (of keeping the past alive in service to contemporary life).

By comparison, those who are not professional historians are likely to seek a different set of satisfactions from the history they learn formally in school and college and absorb informally within their families and communities—confirmation of their views, recognition of and consolation for past wrongs, deeper understanding of current circumstances, and the sheer pleasure of gaining insight into other times, places, and circumstances through stories well told. In addition, given the way that historical information is presented in schools and validated by communities of people, it carries with it strong elements of patriotism and certainty. People who absorb historical knowledge only during their schooling or from the groups they belong to are likely to put less stock than scholars do in academic historical understanding, and they usually demand less in the way of verification and substantiation when they read works that carry personal meaning for them. They also usually care less than scholars for a work's positioning in the larger literature of its subject. They are not likely be drawn to the argumentation and required substantiation of fact that is woven deeply into academics' professional canons; they may consider challenges to traditional views illegitimate; and they can be resistant to holding more than a single interpretation of the past in view as they try to make sense of earlier times. Yet members of the general reading public are frequently no less sensitive than academics to the contemporary significance of historical arguments and no less engaged in the larger stakes that may be involved in the controversies historical knowledge can stir up—stakes that can alter a nation's place in the world as well as affect its internal politics.

Significant differences of conviction between academic historians and members of the general public also arise from the fact that the latter's debates do not take place within a community of similarly situated people who follow certain agreed-on approaches to research and debate and adhere to long-existing protocols of conduct. Public controversy is less fettered and less rule-bound than academic disputation. The public's involvement in historical debates thus sometimes results in no-holds-barred public battles over the meaning of the past, battles that can be both more protracted and more freewheeling than those between academics. No fence surrounds disputants, no boundaries to behavior or argument exist, and no one can predict where an argument will go.

That proved to be the case in respect to the two historical controversies that are the subjects of what follows. The first of these battles—over the meaning of the French Revolution—has roiled the French nation for more than 225 years. The dispute illustrates the ways in which historical controversy becomes part of a national community's cultural and intellectual makeup and self-identification, how it intersects with politics, and how, in effect, it allows different segments of a national population to adjust their thinking to changing understandings of a shared past. The second controversy—over how to display and interpret the fuselage of the *Enola Gay* on the National Mall in the mid-1990s—shows how differing interpretations of the past can draw scholars and members of the American public into an ideological and historical free-for-all.

However different in scale and historical significance each of these controversies proved, both grew from deeply held positions in different, and different kinds of, political, social, and professional camps, each one believing that on the outcome of the controversy hung major political, cultural, and civic consequences. The contests originated in, and were in turn swept up by, the political and ideological battles of the eras in which they took place and can be said to have originated with both Right and Left, each of which held two beliefs that are always at the center of controversies over the meaning of the past. The first of these convictions was that history was on their side. The second held that on each side's prospective victory hung major consequences for the nation-state. In both instances, neither the Right nor the Left was satisfied with the outcome.

In fact, debates over history's lessons and meanings do not always end in victories. Nor do challenges to accepted interpretations arise only from one end of the political spectrum. Challenges to interpretive orthodoxies and to momentarily ascendant schools of interpretations can emerge from anywhere at any time because of changing social and cultural circumstances. Revisionist history cohabits with no particular party, nor can contestants over the past ever be certain that the outcome of a particular historical dispute is one that will endure.

∾

The first example I choose to illustrate the potential consequences that debates over the past can entail concerns one of the central issues of political science: the creation of a nation-state—in this case the birth of modern France and the spread of the idea of French citizenship among the French people.

The setting of this dispute is France's distinctive, intellectualized culture, in which disputes over theory and ideology are the common currency of public conversation and where adherence to ideas possesses a singular cultural force. In no other nation is pride in its worldwide intellectual influence a larger component of its people's self-image. Consequently, bitter disputes over the past are not features of the French academic world alone. They play out in public in often urgent debates about common schooling, social policy, religion, and international affairs. Many of these disputes can be traced back to the divisions created by the French Revolution, whose fissures—social and cultural as well as political and ideological—have remained close to the surface of French life ever since. By the reckonings of some observers, disputes separating royalists and republicans within France dating back to the 1790s were still to be seen in responses to the 1968 tumults in the streets of Paris.

Others see today's tensions between French Catholics and the champions of secularism and *laïcité* as reverberations of the bitter contests that separated clerical and nonclerical partisans in the Revolutionary Era. There exists a no more concrete manifestation of the enduring strength in contemporary French memory of the Revolution than the decision of inhabitants of the Vendée region on the French west coast, an area torn by savage civil war violence in the 1790s, to sit out the 1989 bicentennial celebration of the Revolution.[1] As a result of such a living presence in France of its revolutionary past, debates about the causes and legacy of the Revolution seem never to lose their pertinence to current affairs. Accordingly, what historians of the French Revolution argue about can still engender widespread repercussions, just as changes in French politics can deeply affect the ways in which French historians, joined by historians of the Revolution in other countries, present their nation's revolutionary past.

The continuing presentness, as well as the length and complexity, of the French Revolution has made it difficult enough, in many respects impossible, to arrive at consensus views about its causes and consequences. Complicating matters further is the fact that, in the centuries since the Revolution commenced, so numerous and varied have been the writings about it that it is sometimes hard to see the forest of the Revolution for the trees of its literature. It would serve no purpose here to summarize the entire body of interpretive historical works about the Revolution. What instead invites emphasis is the function of this literature in helping to define the nature of France to the French legatees of their Revolution. The constant additions to, and revitalization of, existing interpretive approaches to the Revolution have invested this literature with a special salience in the country of its origins.

Moreover, in a long-running series of conceptual revisions, the Revolution's events are always being refracted through some specific ideological or cultural lens. This is not unusual. We know that once any

1. This was not entirely surprising. In 1793, the Vendée was ravaged by bloody violence that took at least 250,000 lives, more than six times the number killed throughout the rest of France by institutionalized execution via the guillotine and by other means in the better known Terror of 1793–1794. Historical memory and its consequences, like those that still haunt the Vendée, are difficult to eradicate, both from human lives and from historiography.

event occurs, it becomes part of the memory legacy of everything that follows it; and once those who have lived through it have passed from the scene, the lives, thinking, and circumstances of those who follow take over the determination of how surviving evidence of the event is portrayed and understood. Culture produces memory, and memory engenders culture. Yet as has been particularly the case with so vast a historical phenomenon as the French Revolution, what others think and write about it afterward inevitably intervenes between what is thought by professional historians to have happened and what nonhistorian members of successive generations believe to have happened.

The impulse to get the Revolution straight is also embodied in the additional fact that while the French Revolution created modern France, the historiographic battles over the French Revolution were, from the start of the Revolution itself, a factor in the formation of the modern French nation-state and of the French people. It is difficult to imagine a more weighty function for works of history than their contribution to the creation of a nation and the consolidation of the political and institutional apparatus by which it is governed. What successive generations of French interpreters have written about the Revolution are not mere pieces of historical literature; they are elements in the structure of modern French nationhood and citizenship.

As well they might be. Wherever they occur, nation-creating revolutions, especially when attended with widespread violence—the guillotining of the king, queen, and thousands of others under the Terror, the massacres in the Vendée, wars with other nations starting in 1792—are rarely surpassed in a people's consciousness of its beginnings as a single, modern community. Americans know that well. The events of 1776 that yielded the Declaration of Independence, the successful defense of American independence in war, and the consolidation of the American Revolution under the Constitution make up in American thinking a single moment of birth under the leadership of the "Founding Fathers." The great Revolution in France that followed—one that, even more than its American variety, changed the course of history and affected life as far off as Moscow, Egypt, and the infant United States—was not likely to be seen within France as historically any less significant. And while France was torn apart and its early republican governments succeeded by imperial France under Napoleon Bonaparte, both of those regimes tore Europe apart, too. Little wonder that the causes and consequences of this great upheaval continue to resound in political, as well as intellectual, contests.

While debate over the significance of the rupture of history represented by the Revolution began the day the Bastille fell, it is customary to open every analysis of the long controversy over it, at least in the Anglophone world, with an account of the celebrated ideological battle between Edmund Burke and Thomas Paine. Formidable writers, both were spectators to events taking place across the Channel inside Britain's historic enemy. One abominated what he learned; the other cheered on the possibility of change in a transformed France. Neither was a historian.

Burke, a political figure as well as thinker, struck first in 1790 with his *Reflections on the Revolution in France,* a short work now considered a founding document of modern conservatism. He sought to answer the arguments of moral philosopher Richard Price, who likened the tumult in France to the Glorious Revolution of 1688 in England. Both of them, Price contended, had spread "enlightenment ideas" universally throughout the world. By contrast, Burke accepted the Revolution of 1688 for having incorporated into the English state the best of the previous regime, not broken with it, as he thought the French had done. Burke was also horrified by the early violence in revolution-torn France (even though he wrote *Reflections* before the outbreak of the institutionalized killings, the Jacobin Terror and the regicide of Louis XVI, for which the Revolution remains most widely known). He viewed the Revolution and its violence as threatening social and political order wherever its influence were to be felt. Its supporters, he wrote, assumed the power to "subvert and destroy, but none to construct." The Revolution was an "irreparable calamity to . . . mankind." A foe of the Revolution's abstract claims to freedom and equality, Burke came to the defense of monarchy and property, spoke for the accumulated wisdom of experience and time, made the case for gradual over precipitous change, and accurately predicted the eventual corruption of the revolution in military dictatorship.

Paine, a political activist as well as thinker and writer, struck back at Burke in his longer, equally controversial work, *The Rights of Man,*

which appeared in two parts starting in 1791. Lauding the French Revolution for ending the despotism of hereditary monarchy ("tyranny"
and "despotism" he termed it), Paine saw in it the birth of a new era of
human freedom and, more seditiously, a spur to greater equality in Britain and to the reform of British government. Paine's text became a cause
célèbre on both sides of the Atlantic and helped lead to the emergence of
two-party politics in the United States. The long battle over the meaning
and value of the French Revolution was on.

Yet as much as the writings of these two great antagonists set the
template (at least in Britain and the United States) for every succeeding argument about every succeeding revolution, their contents were
not historical arguments, nor were their authors' aims historical in
nature. Like other early French works about the Revolution by Joseph
de Maistre, Germaine de Staël, Benjamin Constant, Augustin Barruel,
and François-René de Chateaubriand—none of them avowed historians
—they had political more than historical aims. The books that were
to constitute the formal origins of the historiography of the French
Revolution—that is, of explicitly historical works written by historians
—had to await a full generation to make their appearance. When they
did, as with American Civil War histories, the first French works of
French Revolution historiography emerged not from academic circles
but rather from the pens of skilled amateur historians when sufficient
evidence on which to base historical claims and arguments about the
great revolutionary conflict initially became available. It is not without
significance that the members of this founding school of revolutionary
historiography were liberals comfortable with the Revolution's general
aspirations.

The principal figures of this first wave of French historians of the
Revolution were François Mignet and Adolphe Thiers, near contempo-
raries from southern France, both trained as lawyers in the city of Aix-en-
Provence, who had opened their careers as journalists opposing the
Bourbon Restoration of 1814. When in 1830 Charles X was overthrown
by another branch of the Bourbons and a constitutional kingship, the
July Monarchy of Louis Philippe I, installed in its stead, Thiers and
Mignet supported the prospective liberalization of French authority,
and both served under the new regime. The histories they subsequently

wrote reflected their conviction that historical argument could buttress the young, liberal, bourgeois state. In this sense, they are considered the founders of the liberal interpretation of the French Revolution. From its beginning, the historiography of the Revolution was to be in service to politics.

The views of Mignet and Thiers created the interpretive scheme of the Revolution against which all succeeding works on it have had to contend—the theme, a classic example of whig history, that the story of history has to do with progress toward freedom, whose realization, in French terms, will manifest itself in the political triumph of the bourgeois Third Estate. Mignet's and Thiers's involvement in politics also presaged the place that history and historians would frequently play in French public life. Thiers would eventually become one of France's leading parliamentarians and, after Napoleon III had been deposed and the Second French Empire had collapsed in 1870, the president of France under the Third Republic who helped bloodily suppress the Paris Commune of 1871. These men were not armchair historians.

Mignet and Thiers saw their works on the Revolution published at almost the same time, roughly thirty-five years after the fall of the Bastille. In 1824 Mignet produced *L'Histoire de la révolution française*. In it, he exhibited the traits of what would eventually come to characterize the historian over the storyteller: the determination to analyze as well as to narrate events and to try to assess the significance of his chosen subject. At the very opening of his book, he stated his favorable view of the Revolution: "It substituted law in the place of arbitrary will, equality in that of privilege; delivered men from the distinctions of classes, the land from the barriers of provinces, trade from the shackles of corporations and fellowships, agriculture from feudal subjection and oppression of tithes, property from the impediment of entails, and brought everything to the condition of one state, one system of law, one people." Mignet could not know it, but those emphatic last two words heralded a theme of Revolutionary historiography that characterized it for much of the following two centuries. It was a theme that gave to the politically charged debate over the causes, consequences, and meaning of the Revolution a specific, French resonance. History was thenceforth to aid in the construction of French nationhood and citizenship. The composition and definition of *le peuple français* now fell to historians as well as to politicians and philosophers.

Mignet's book was also noteworthy for being an early version of what would become a full-blown body of works treating the French Revolution as a bourgeois revolution. Adopting this interpretation, Mignet condemned the Ancien Régime, cheered the establishment of the rule of law and the spread of greater social and political equality under the Revolution, and denounced the excesses of the Terror. While historians today consider the causes of the Revolution that he cited as insufficient in number and range, his was the first stab at an assessment of its origins. He also introduced into his explanatory scheme, one that foretold future historians' interests, such general factors as human passions and people's reliance on symbolism and civic religion to find meaning in the events of the revolutionary era. No friend of the masses, Mignet dismissed the Parisian *sans-culottes* as a mob; yet he also showed an awareness of the role of awakening class divisions in giving the Revolution the character it possessed. In this way, too, his history was a harbinger of things to come.

Of these two early historians of the Revolution, Thiers became the better known. His *L'Histoire de la révolution française,* published in the 1820s, filled ten volumes; his following *L'Histoire du consulat et de l'empire,* which appeared between 1845 and 1862, totaled twenty. His prodigious output provided contemporaries with information about the Revolution that had never before been generally known and laid a solid basis for debates about such major dimensions of the Revolution as the Jacobin Terror, the Napoleonic Empire, and the Bourbon Restoration that have rarely abated. Like Mignet, Thiers viewed the Revolution as an overall benefit to France and welcomed the emergence to greater national power of a liberal, republican French bourgeoisie. But while liberal in a middle-class sense, Thiers like Mignet had no sympathy with the plebeian working masses, whose desires for greater freedom and security had been awakened to world-historical consequences in the 1790s and were stirring again when the two men wrote.

The historians who followed these pioneers of Revolutionary history did not hold the same reservations as the two men did about the mass of the French people. In fact, Mignet's and Thiers's principal successors—especially Thomas Carlyle and Jules Michelet—elevated the *menu peuple,* the common people, above the sober liberal middle classes by picturing them as the moving force behind the removal of the shackles of the Ancien Régime. Usually seen as "Romantic" historians for their sweeping celebrations of the power of popular protest and action, in the context of this book Carlyle and Michelet should be viewed as the first to interpret the Revolution in terms that differed from those of Mignet and Thiers. This distinction entitles them to be called the first revisionist historians of the French Revolution. More significant, in contrast to the liberal historical interpreters of the Revolution they were offering another origin story of the modern French nation—an origin story whose heroes were the laboring masses.

Because Carlyle's *The French Revolution* stands as close to the novels of Walter Scott and Charles Dickens's *A Tale of Two Cities* as it does to Thiers's histories, it is often denied its place in historical literature and is seen instead as a kind of fiction. But there are no solid grounds for denying this Scottish belletrist credit for helping inaugurate an enduringly significant line of historical interpretation. Until Carlyle—whose grandiose, cynical, anecdotal 1837 book is a notable example of conceptual revisionism—wrote about the Revolution, a kind of calm, liberal approach to the phases and nature of the upheaval had been the norm. With Carlyle, picturesque, passionate hyperbole took over. Here, for example, is his description of the attack on the Bastille: "For four hours now has the World-Bedlam roared: call it the World-Chimaera, blowing fire!" On the flight of the king to Varennes: "How great is a calm couchant People! On the morrow, men will say to one another: 'We have no king, but we slept sound enough.'"

When it came to his love of the people, if not his florid excess, Carlyle was surpassed by Jules Michelet, an academic man of letters who combined prodigious research with literary brilliance. For him, the indefinable spirit of *le peuple*—the mostly unknown individuals who had rarely broken into historical accounts before—was at the very center of French history. Nowhere was his compassionate approach to the past more conspicuous than in his 1847 *The History of the French Revolution.* Michelet seemed to take the vast revolutionary event personally—"Not one of the great actors of the Revolution left me cold. I was one of them." Like Carlyle, Michelet was vague about whom he included in *le peuple*. Were they the substantial bourgeoisie of the Third Estate, the urban *sans-culottes* of the working class, or the farmers of rural France? Yet his partialities were never in doubt. The Revolution had been one great fraternal event that brought the people together as nothing before in world history. For Michelet, the Jacobin Terror and the bourgeois oligarchic Directory that ended it had sold out the original experiment in popular democracy. Accordingly, Michelet had nothing but contempt for the bourgeoisie and its *salons:* "I never left them without finding my heart shrunk and chilled." For the people he had only "the tender remembrance of precious souls that I have known in the most humble conditions. . . . The people have in themselves a sacred poetry. . . . I, who have sprung from them . . . I come to establish against all mankind the personality of the people. . . . One people! one country! one France!" Here was Mignet's "one people" appearing as representative of a unitary nation.

The distinctive rhetoric of so many mid-nineteenth-century histories of the French Revolution, like those of Carlyle and Michelet, cannot be passed over as so much overwrought Romantic expressiveness. While their language and its mystical overtones may be foreign to the presentation of history as we now read it, in many respects their unbuttoned style was integral to their revisionist interpretive aim. Changes in interpretation summoned changes in style. Carlyle and Michelet had to adapt, and in some respects create for their purposes, a new language of historical writing, a historian's variant of the language of Romanticism, through which to express their new approaches to the Revolution. The words they invoked to convey their sentiments were entirely in keeping with the emotional and interpretive thrust of the view of the Revolution they offered their readers; they were also the kinds of words compatible with the style of contemporary French novelists like Victor Hugo. Moreover, especially in the works of Michelet, a skilled excavator of little-examined sources, the discovery of the role of the people, which earlier historians had overlooked, joined itself to his distinctive style to highlight, if not exalt, the acts of common men and women and create an emotional bond between historian and reader that in its time seemed genuine and winning.

In many respects, it was Carlyle's and Michelet's lack of clarity and the capacious expanse of their views that rendered their works, especially Michelet's, so popular. It did no harm that, in Michelet's case, those works, including his twenty-four-volume *Histoire de France* and a work conspicuously titled *Le Peuple,* were so numerous. Michelet greatly enlarged the proportion of the people of his native France who could be seen as actors in their own history. And Michelet, like Mignet earlier, in many respects paved the way for the future class interpretations of the Revolution.

But reading tea leaves for insight into the future would have led you astray. Confirming the proposition that no single historical interpretation ever monopolizes the interpretive terrain, a strong counterattack on Michelet's and Carlyle's histories eventually appeared. Echoing Burke's earlier conservative assault on the Revolution and all that it represented, some historians began to take sharp issue with Carlyle's and Michelet's popular historiographic championing of the French people. Two of the most prominent among them were not, in the strictest sense, historians. But each, in different ways, gave voice to a line of thinking that laid down an enduring challenge to positive views of the world-shaking events that followed the storming of the Bastille.

The first of these was the great political thinker Alexis de Tocqueville. Though writing thirty years after Mignet and Thiers, Tocqueville held views of the Revolution that fit more comfortably with those of this early generation of historians than with those of his own time like Michelet, who were more liberally disposed toward the French people. However complicated his political views, Tocqueville shared with Mignet an analytical approach to the Revolution, a knowledge of its archives, and his predecessors' liberalism. The concrete political engagements that brought him into public office as foreign secretary during the Second Republic can also be likened to Thiers's. Like him, Tocqueville had trained as a lawyer.

But unlike the others, Tocqueville, the descendent of Norman aristocracy whose parents had barely escaped the guillotine, laid more emphasis on the Ancien Régime that preceded the Revolution than on the Revolution itself. (This is no doubt due to the fact that he intended to write a second volume, one on the Revolution, but did not live to complete it.) He emphasized the similarities and continuities between the two eras while acknowledging that the Revolution had opened a new period of historical ideology and action. Distinctive among nineteenth-century historians of the Revolution, he argued that the true revolution of the previous century had been the subversion of the Ancien Régime by monarchical despotism—that is, that the real French Revolution consisted in the French state's gathering all political power to itself before 1789. Yet his great 1856 work, *The Ancien Régime and the Revolution,* did not, at least in the short term, inaugurate any major new line of inquiry or interpretation; and it did not contribute to the emergence to consciousness of the French people as independent historical actors as Carlyle and Michelet pictured them. In fact, while in the deepest sense a liberal who understood the significance of the advent of representative government and believed that the enlargement of the popular will and the march of equality and democracy were irresistible forces, Tocqueville was horrified by much of the Revolution's aspects. It created, he wrote, "a far stronger and more absolute government than the one the Revolution overthrew . . . yet talked of popular sovereignty . . . while stripping the nation of every vestige of self-government, of constitutional guarantees, and of liberty of thought, speech and of the press." Tocqueville's interpretation made clear that the more radical, popular histories of the post-1789 years would never have the field to themselves.

In his unwillingness to celebrate *le peuple français,* Tocqueville was joined by Hippolyte Taine, a narrator of stories, not an analyst or systematic thinker like Tocqueville. Taine was more litterateur than historian, more critic than researcher, more interested in the psychological and sociological origins of events than in their political significance, and a reactionary rather than a Tocquevillian liberal conservative. His principal contribution to historical letters was his five-volume *The Origins of Contemporary France,* which appeared between 1875 and 1893. Despite its title, it had to do principally with the Revolution. In contrast to Michelet, Taine exhibited a deep fear of an aroused people. As an early rightist opponent of French events after 1870—the end of Napoleon III's Second Empire; the creation of the Third French Republic, which was establishing itself out of the chaos of the Franco-Prussian War of 1870–1871; and the Paris Commune of 1871, whose Communards destroyed much of Paris before their defeat—he believed in hierarchy, stability, authority, and legitimacy, scarcely the qualities that characterized the revolutionary regime of which he wrote.

Taine reserved his wrath for conspiratorial Jacobins, depicted the masses who fell in behind the Revolution as a disreputable rabble, condemned the centralization of power under Revolution and Empire, and denounced what he saw as the abstract intellectualism of the Enlightenment *philosophes* on whom he placed much blame for the tumult of the post-1789 era. The triggering force of Revolutionary France, he wrote in a style reminiscent of Carlyle, was not the king but the people—"that is to say the mob of a hundred, a thousand, a hundred thousand beings gathered together haphazardly, on an impulse, who, with . . . howling and misshapen Liberty sits at the threshold of the Revolution like Milton's two specters at the gates of hell." If France were to develop as a modern European nation, Taine implied, it could not do so as a popular republic. As was often to prove the case in the historiography of France, Taine hauled history in to help direct the course of the nation's political development. Yet ironically, in doing so he only put greater focus on common French people as political agents and as fit subjects for historical treatment. Here was reactionary historiography contributing to a focus on the very people who had been woven into the historical record by Taine's liberal predecessors. By failing to shift historiographic attention away from the people—in fact, by accepting the nation-building role for historical interpretation inaugurated by Mignet, Thiers, Carlyle, and Michelet—Taine contributed to historiography's authority in forming a new understanding of French history, one that proved unable to slow the continuing appearance of progressive interpretations of the Revolution. Moreover, Taine's brand of interpretation, which in effect traced itself back to the earliest counterrevolutionaries of the post-1789 years and looked forward to the dangers of twentieth-century populist, totalitarian rulership, was to prove incapable of gaining a foothold within the large field of historical arguments that came to be considered worthy of consideration by serious historians. The difficulty that such an interpretation as Taine's faced became starkly clear on the appointment of the first person to hold an academic chair in the history of the French Revolution.

American readers, accustomed to their nation's diversity and to the wide geographic and institutional dispersion of centers of American intellectual and cultural life, may overlook the authority that Parisian centers of learning, most of them state institutions, have always played in French intellectual and cultural life. French tradition makes the creation and dissemination of knowledge a state function. So when a thinker or scholar of a particular interpretive bent takes up an academic chair at the University of Paris and becomes associated not only with that ancient institution but also with the city's other *grandes écoles*— the institutions in which so many of the nation's leading intellectuals hold appointments and so many of its leading public figures have been prepared—it is assumed that the imprimatur of government falls on its holder, and the incumbent's views are often conceded a kind of preferred standing over those of others. Such was the case with the appointment, on the 1889 centennial of the fall of the Bastille, of Alphonse Aulard as the first holder of the chair in the history of the French Revolution at the University of Paris (known popularly as the Sorbonne).

Aulard's rise to prominence owed much to his role as a kind of unofficial spokesman for the Third Republic and his determination that his history of the Revolution, like that soon to come in the United States from the likes of James Harvey Robinson, be "useful" history. But it grew as well from his central role in the development of the formal discipline of history within French universities. Like von Ranke before him in Germany, Aulard led the creation of professional academic methods and standards in France, a development by this time becoming a general phenomenon on both sides of the Atlantic. Occupying a professorial position in a university at the top of the hierarchy of French academic institutions and one devoted to France's greatest modern convulsion, he possessed immense authority. This assured that his interpretive position was more likely than others to become a kind of orthodoxy among French academics and be difficult to dislodge.

In *The French Revolution: A Political History, 1789–1804*, a four-volume work that appeared in 1901, Aulard explicitly disavowed interpretive partisanship. But he could not hide his partiality for the bourgeois, anticlerical republicanism that emerged from the Terror—and thus his implied partiality for the Third Republic of 1871; nor could he

suppress his sympathy for Georges Danton over more radical Maximi-
lien Robespierre and for the proletarian impulses of the *sans-culottes*.[2]
These preferences put him in league with most of his predecessors and
implicitly with earlier historians who had showed partiality toward popular democratic politics. It kept open the door to successors who would
be farther to the left than he. It also deepened an interpretive tendency
that kept the views of, say, Taine in the shadows. But where Aulard had
his greatest influence was in his Thucydidean focus on the politics of
revolution and in his lack of interest in its social, cultural, intellectual,
and even psychological roots. As elsewhere, this created a formidable
barrier to the future emergence of other kinds of history and can be seen
as retarding the growth of a broader approach to the historical problem
of the Revolution.

That was not, however, the end of it. There was to be one more
phase of Revolutionary historiography centering on the mass of the French
people before this entire increasingly orthodox approach to the French
Revolution, reaching back as far as Paine, finally exhausted itself and gave
way to something new. That phase was Marxist in nature. It moved the
historiography of the Revolution sharply leftward, a shift that lasted for
almost a century. As I have noted, socialistic elements, especially a keen
sensitivity to the demands of the people (however they might be defined), had for decades been part of this historiography. The introduction into histories of the French Revolution of the leitmotif of conflict
between members of different social and economic classes within the
French population did not arrive out of the blue. What was novel in the
Marxist approach was the comparatively rigid structure of class interpretation it threw over the events of the Revolutionary Era, its claims to
"scientific" certainty, and the related implication that the events of the
day were somehow inevitable.

Karl Marx himself had been deeply interested in the French
Revolution and referred to it frequently in his writings, but he never
addressed it directly at length. This was in sharp contrast to the focus
of his 1852 work, *The Eighteenth Brumaire of Louis Napoleon,* which

2. One's preference between the two figures has long stood as a sign of a historian's politics.

focused on the 1851 coup d'état of "Prince-President" Louis Napoleon (who became Napoleon III under the co-called Second Empire). Marx's principal contribution to the historiography of the French Revolution, as to every other subject he and his ideological partner Friedrich Engels touched, was the notion of class. For example, as they wrote in *The German Ideology*, "When the bourgeoisie overthrew the power of the aristocracy [during the Revolution], it thereby made it possible for many proletarians to rise above the proletariat, but only insofar as they became bourgeois." Accordingly, Marx saw the events that followed the storming of the Bastille in class terms—as the work principally of members of the Third Estate, who as members of the bourgeoisie were agents of revolution who guided and controlled the proletariat. To orthodox Marxists, the Revolution resulted in the destruction of the hierarchical, feudalistic Ancien Régime and in its replacement by a bourgeois capitalistic system of government and economy. Yet, they argued, even if the Revolution had been a bourgeois revolution, other classes participated in it—first the nobility, whose demands led to the king's summoning of the Estates General in 1787, then second and more important the urban proletariat, the *sans-culottes* of Paris, who stormed the Bastille and were central to the Terror. How historians writing in Marx's shadow would work out the details of his class interpretation—how, for instance, they would treat the Terror and the emergence of Bonaparte—would fill many books and occasion many disputes in the decades to come.

It is a safe assumption that major new historical circumstances in a nation or society are likely to engender adjustments to existing historical views. Such might have been predicted for late-nineteenth- and early-twentieth-century Europe, as revolutions and wars continued to roil France and other countries and as industrial and commercial capitalism increased its hold. Two major nations—Germany and Italy—took form from previously independent, lesser political jurisdictions, and the Bolsheviks ousted the Romanovs in Russia. Marxism became the expression of the search both for an explanation of what was occurring in the contemporary world and for the search for solutions to the problems that such vast changes brought in their train. Not surprisingly, the next stage in interpretations of the French Revolution bore a sharply Marxist form.

In France, Marxism at first had a temperate cast. Rather than being set forth as a hard "scientific" explanation of past events, it was wielded in the form of humanitarian, democratic socialism—the search for greater government responsibility for the people's welfare. And as had happened before, the first full-blown socialist interpretation of the French Revolution came from the pen of a public figure rather than from that of a professional historian. He was Jean Jaurès, the founder of the French Socialist Party, who emerged from the study of philosophy to become, through service in the Chamber of Deputies, one of France's great parliamentarians and liberal forces. His *Socialist History of the French Revolution,* which began to appear in 1901, revealed Jaurès, who had mastered the writing of Karl Marx, to be a thoroughgoing socialist interpreter of revolutionary events. In volumes that emphasized the social and economic factors that caused and sustained the Revolution, he, like Marx and Engels before him, laid emphasis on the central role of the bourgeoisie, whose rise to power was "the fundamental significance of the Revolution." Taking his cues from earlier historians who had celebrated the role of the *sans-culottes,* he reserved a prominent place in his work for the Parisian working class—for "the militant virtues of these oppressed proletarians who, for a century, have often paid with their lives for an ideal dimly perceived." He tried to show "to the people—to the workers and peasants—how the stature of the proletariat grew with the Revolution and how it took shape in the heat of events." While no doubt others would have come along to introduce Marxist themes into the historiography of the Revolution, even if not the kind of moderate humane Marxism that was Jaurès's,[3] it mattered much that this great nationalist was the vehicle of Marxism's formal introduction into Revolutionary historiography, for his success in applying a Marxist analysis to this subject of the historical past lent to other socialist approaches to the subject an authority and durability that they might otherwise not have enjoyed.

But there was to be yet another step in the process of placing middle-class and laboring French people at the center of the history of

3. Jaurès joined with Émile Zola and others in defending Alfred Dreyfus against anti-Semitic attacks in the 1890s, and he was an ardent opponent of France's entry into World War I until he was assassinated for his resistance to it.

the Revolution. That came with the introduction of hard Marxist class theory into the historiography of the subject. Its earliest French expositor was Aulard's student Albert Mathiez, whose influential works announced Marxism's arrival at legitimacy in this subject of historical inquiry. Mathiez came to hold and advance a sharply different view of the Revolution's violence than did his teacher. The Bolshevik Revolution of 1917 having intervened between the publication of Aulard's *French Revolution* and Mathiez's identically titled work, it spurred a reconfiguration of thought as well of politics. Mathiez saw the Revolution as the victory of the proletariat and for the militant radicalism of the *sans-culottes*. In addition, the workers' triumph during the Terror, however short-lived that triumph was, could be seen as the harbinger of what was taking place in post-tsarist Russia in the years in which Mathiez wrote his three-volume work, published between 1922 and 1927. Here in the Soviet Union was what a true class-based assault on an age-old regime looked like; here was the living legacy, Mathiez thought, of what had started in the streets of Paris in 1789.

Nothing better illustrated Mathiez's embrace of the Bolsheviks' October Revolution than his acceptance of the violence of the Terror and his celebration of the radical, dictatorial leadership of Robespierre. For Mathiez, Robespierre was the democratic representative of an aroused working class. Mathiez argued, moreover, that in the Terror, the most radical phase of the Revolution, could be glimpsed the dawn of a transformation in social relations as well as in politics and the state. But how then was one to explain the Terror's failure—the failure of the *sans-culottes*—to maintain the proletarians' hold on power? Mathiez charged that to the bourgeoisie, whose counterstrike of Thermidor— the reaction against Robespierre that ushered in the more moderate Directory—put an end to the hopes of the radical Revolution and thus of new possibilities open to the *menu peuple*.

Mathiez's embrace of orthodox Marxism was most clearly evident in his application of the concept of class struggle—the contest between the middle and working classes for power—to his depiction of the Revolution. And nothing better illustrated his break with the older, socialist interpretations of Jaurès and Aulard than his dismissal of the comparatively moderate rule of Danton during the Revolution and his conviction that no revolution could succeed without the violence of Robespierre's Terror. In Mathiez's historiographic scheme, the French people, as members of the middle and working classes, had at last come fully into their own as the leading protagonists of the Revolution and thus, by implication, of subsequent French history. Mathiez's position was to be strongly challenged only when France had emerged from World War II and fresh ways to view the Revolution had become possible.

Mathiez's successor in the Sorbonne chair that he and Aulard had held was another Marxist, the widely admired Georges Lefebvre, known initially in France for his massive thesis on the Revolutionary peasantry. Lefebvre's occupancy of France's premier position in the history of the French Revolution made clear that Marxist interpretations of the subject had now become an orthodoxy of their own, one that had replaced the earlier liberal-republican consensus that had inaugurated historical studies of the Revolution. Lefebvre was also thoroughly up to date in the emerging twentieth-century techniques that came to define academic history, especially in the statistical analyses of evidence and the use of documentation of the lives of the widest variety of groups and individuals—characteristics of what, in others' application, would become hallmarks of the *Annales* school. In his hands, especially in his 1939 work, *1789*, and his two-volume *The History of the French Revolution* (published in the 1950s), the rural and urban masses of France took center stage. Only through attention to the food shortages and rising prices they faced before the Revolution, Lefebvre argued, could the outbreak of Revolutionary violence be understood. Yet what made his works so appealing was his flexible use of orthodox Marxist concepts. Yes, socioeconomic classes were clearly definable actors in history; but different classes—the aristocracy, the bourgeoisie, urban workers, and rural peasants—were in the political ascendancy at different times in the years of the French Revolution; and each one, in Lefebvre's rendering, initiated its own uprising.

Lefebvre's student and successor in the same Sorbonne chair, Albert Soboul, followed roughly the same course of interpretation, albeit with enough added emphasis on class struggle that he was celebrated at his 1982 death by members of the Communist Party, in which he had long held membership. Soboul's appointment as the third of the Marxist dynasty in the same professorial chair suggested that the socialist approach to the French Revolution, one inaugurated by Jean Jaurès, had begun to run out of fresh ways to understand the role of the workers and peasants of the eighteenth century. Also by Soboul's time, there should have been no doubt that the true subject of these long debates over the causes, consequences, and broader meaning of the French Revolution had to do with more than the events of the twenty-five years succeeding the fall of the Bastille. These debates reflected the realities of French politics and culture after the defeat of Nazism: the always widening definition of the French people (which did not incorporate women as voting citizens until 1945); the strong leftward drift in much of the French academic world, which accepted active radicals into leading professorial positions; the still raw historical memories not only of the Revolution but of the ruins of World War I and France's collaborationist role in World War II; Cold War tensions both inside and outside France; and long-running battles over such issues as social welfare policies and farmers' and workers' rights. The age-old question as to whether the Revolution had been a Good Thing for France could still not be put to rest.

Yet the historiography of the French Revolution had done more than simply mirror contemporary French life. A long line of socialist historians had helped raise rural peasants, urban workers, small shopkeepers, and women out of the historical shadows and endowed them with roles as individuals and class collectivities that had not been visible before. These scholars showed convincingly how the role of spontaneous groups as well as of clearly defined classes could be seen as integral to the history of the Revolution—and, by implication, to all history. They brought to the front the role of "crowds" (a softer term than "mobs") in advancing and representing the Revolution, especially in French cities. They exhumed the Revolutionary Era actualities of French life in a wide variety of communities as they dug into the lives of individual French people. And led by such historians as Jacques Godechot and the American scholar Robert R. Palmer, they placed the Revolution in the larger genealogy of Atlantic and Western revolutions.

Not surprisingly, however, a reaction to Marxist orthodoxy eventually set in. The reaction's leading figure was François Furet. Like Soboul, Furet had been a member of the post-1945 Communist Party;

but unlike Soboul he renounced his membership in it and led the history of the French Revolution away from its Marxist path onto a new one. The greatest irony of this historiographic passage from Marxism to a kind of determined neutrality, one that made Furet's new dispensation "conservative" in comparison to what preceded it, was that the kinds of interpretations that he and those associated with him advanced came quickly to be known as "revisionist"—as if a long line of historians had not already been challenging, adding to, and altering existing interpretations of the Revolution. Nothing better illustrates the fact that examples of historical revisionism and the use of the term itself can be found across the ideological spectrum and that the terminology of "revisionism" can justifiably be applied to interpretive schemes regardless of their political implications. In this case, revisions to what had become a leftist orthodoxy in French academic circles can be credited to originally Marxist historians who gathered converts from what, in comparative terms, was the Right.

This turn away from Marxist interpretations of the French Revolution did not appear overnight. Well before the 1960s, French Marxist historians had begun to quarrel among themselves. In arguing, for example, that the *sans-culottes* were not proletarians, Soboul had been bitterly attacked by other Marxists. More significant, in the United States and Great Britain, whose historians of the Revolution were not so strongly harnessed to Marxist approaches but whose works were gaining increased respect within France, cracks were opening in the long-lived leftist conception of the Revolution. This was so even though some historians in the latter two countries, foremost among them the British historian Christopher Hill, continued to write many resolutely Marxist works about the great event. The detailed research of the American scholar George V. Taylor, for instance, called into question the way in which Marxists had defined and interpreted late-eighteenth-century French social and economic classes and refused to accept their depiction of eighteenth-century classes as clearly defined or rigidly demarcated in society and politics. British historian Alfred Cobban effectively attacked the French Marxist orthodoxy about the Revolution—a "religious belief" and a "secular religion" he called it—for its claims to scientific certainty and for its emphasis on social and economic causes rather than a broader range. It had been "distorted by all the overtones," he wrote, "of nineteenth-century social thought and present-day social conditions."

But it was Furet's two-volume 1965 work *The French Revolution,* written with Denis Richet, that signaled the beginning of the end of the dominion of the long-held consensus Marxist approach to the great conflict in France. By presenting the Revolution through the eyes of disenthralled Marxists who wrote after the costs of Stalinist totalitarianism had long become clear, the book earned Furet and Richet the enmity of Furet's former Party comrades. Yet it is his 1978 book, *Interpreting the French Revolution,* that is considered Furet's great achievement. In that work, he broke with the decades-long encrustations of Marxist materialist interpretations and, as had Tocqueville before him, took the Revolution as the last major event of the Ancien Régime as much as the origin of modern France.

Furet's most impressive interpretive thrust was to argue that socially, economically, and administratively, the France of 1820 was not as different from the France of 1780 as other historians had assumed; contrary to so much previous interpretation, he argued, the Revolution was not a grand rupture of French history, nor did it decisively create a new national identity. This led Furet to ask why, then, so many contemporaries—and historians after them—had convinced themselves that the Revolution had made such a vast difference to the Gallic nation. His response? The "real" Revolution had occurred in the realm of culture, as evidenced by changes in such markers as discourse, language, and symbols. In keeping with trends on both sides of the Atlantic, Furet broadened the notion of "politics" to one of "political culture" and shifted attention to language and contemporaries' use of such concepts as liberty and democracy. That is, he stressed how the Revolution was represented in words, and he turned historians' emphases back to political ideas and the role of Enlightenment thought in the late eighteenth century. In this respect, his criticism was understood to be aimed as much at the *Annales* school, its methods, and its focus on social and cultural history as on earlier historians of the Revolution and the Marxist school. Social interpretations of the Revolution, he implied, had little more to yield—at least for now. Perhaps as significant, Furet arraigned the unceasing historiographic conflict over the Revolution—

the never-ending French historians' battles over the causes and meaning of France's birth as a modern nation. As he asseverated in 1978, "The French Revolution is over." Furet meant by this pronunciamento that historians ought to find fresh ways to interpret the Revolution by freeing themselves from the political and ideological disputes that had permeated the historiography of the Revolution since 1789.

We should probably expect any line of interpretation that exists for more than 150 years, as did the socialist-Marxist interpretation of the French Revolution, eventually to run dry of significant further contributions. A set of arguments begins over the years to yield fewer fresh insights. As in the case of scientific paradigms, as Thomas S. Kuhn reminded us, anomalous and freshly discovered evidence, as well as events that still beg understanding but cannot easily be incorporated into existing theoretical models, begin to weaken old interpretations' explanatory powers. Some new vantage of attack, some untried line of interpretation can now gain a foothold among researchers and scholars. This is what began to happen toward the close of the twentieth century.

Yet if Furet's multifaceted attack on older interpretations announced the smash-up of the conventions of two centuries of argument over the Revolution, it did not put an end to historians' efforts to go yet deeper into the complex phenomenon that started in Paris in 1789 and was brought to its effective end at Waterloo in 1815. Instead, there resulted a crumbling in any generally accepted view about it. Today, no central interpretive tendency of the subject exists. For instance, Keith Michael Baker has followed Furet into the study of political culture, but with a distinctive emphasis—a "linguistic turn"—on the political language of the Revolution's major radical figures. Reflecting the concerns of our own time, Lynn Hunt has introduced into current historiography the study of the Revolution's claim to leadership in the championship of universal human rights, itself a subject that nests comfortably with an even more general historical interest in transnational history. And as is the case in so many sectors of historical thought, scholars are now examining the Revolution in its global perspective—not only how it affected the larger world but how it has been understood outside France and Europe.

Perhaps the greatest and most influential departure from previous approaches to the Revolution has been the introduction of gender into the subject. Historians, principally women historians, have made others recognize that the Revolution was antifemale. In attempting and claiming to sweep away centuries of traditional social organization and political rule, the Revolution built itself on claims that it was constructed on "rational" grounds rather than on the Ancien Régime's less defensible ones. In doing so, historical interpretations that fell in with that assumption ensured that narratives of the Revolution would appear in all-male garb; after all, only an all-male polity could be "rational," and only males could qualify as political agents, as voters and office holders—that is, as part of *le peuple*. Once historians began to see the Revolution through the lens of gender—from the perspective of the social construction of gender roles, not of their supposedly "natural" reality—the Revolution took on an entirely different cast. If it were seen as a male event for males only, then France had been left in many ways as traditional as it always had been—a view that, in another context, Furet had advanced in his work on political culture. Here, the works of Dominique Godineau, Joan B. Landes, Lynn Hunt, and Joan Wallach Scott were central in forcing attention onto the exclusion of women— female "people"—from the Revolution's beneficiaries as well as onto such realities as the "eroticizaton" of patriotism, as in, for example, the emergence of Marianne as the symbolic embodiment of republican France, her imagine serving as a way of binding males to the new French state. Understanding of what constituted the French people had once again been greatly broadened.

Accordingly, with richly conceived new historical scholarship on the Revolution continuing to emerge, a new, firm resting place for understanding the Revolution is unlikely to come into being. That in itself constitutes a major change of historical emphasis. The role of non-French historians as leading scholars of the subject has surely played its part, for they were never as likely to assume the Revolution's central place in French history as were the French themselves. Events that followed the Revolution, including three major internal French political revolutions (those of 1830, 1848, and 1871) and three major wars (those of 1870–1871, 1914–1917, and 1940–1945) also reduced the commanding stature of the Revolution as "the" great event in the nation's modern history. And no longer does France's revolution stand alone as a major world-historical event, those of Russia and China having intervened to signal other great moments in human history. But what matters most is that historians of the Revolution had for more than two hundred years succeeded through their scholarship in bolstering efforts to define the idea of the French people and to undergird efforts to create an enduring French republic and broaden the people's participation in it as citizens. By the final quarter of the twentieth century, that historical task—not a common one for historians to undertake—had been more or less accomplished.[4] The extended historiographic project of conceptual revisionism had helped all French people understand their historical role in their nation's modern growth and to accept the responsibility of people of all classes for what had happened in France during that great series of past events. By having done so, this line of interpretation had exhausted itself.

In concluding this brief sketch of the changing interpretations of the French Revolution, it is difficult to avoid wondering whether the historical literature about it followed changes already under way in French society or, by contrast, helped secure those changes as they were occurring. Do changes in scholarly views of a subject merely reflect present history or do they contribute to it? Any dispassionate reflection leads to the inescapable conclusion that scholarly interpretations serve both as reflections of and contributions to contemporary life. To view two centuries of arguments over the causes and significance of the French Revolution as nothing more than ideological or scholarly debates is to miss entirely the function of those debates in orienting the French people to their present as well as to their past. It should therefore be gratifying to readers of history, as well as to those who create historical knowledge professionally, that in learning and arguing about the past they inevitably engage themselves in the life of their own days. No history is merely revisionist. All history, being revisionist, is embodied in

---

4. At least for the native Gallic French. The definition of the "French people," just like that of the "American people," continues to undergo change as France absorbs non-French immigrants.

all people's lifelong endeavor to understand their lives—their lives as they are as well as they used to be.

∾

If the historical debates about the French Revolution lend weight to the proposition that historical interpretations can develop so as to affect, while mirroring, the direction in which an entire society develops, the example of the fray over the way to interpret the American use of atomic weaponry on Japan reveals a different function for historical thought. In this case, interpretive differences arising in different sectors of society —between academic, mostly left-of-center historians and the larger public, especially conservatives and military veterans—opened fissures in American society and exacerbated, rather than softened, those divisions. But as also bears emphasis, the battle over interpretive revisions to earlier postwar orthodoxies about the use of nuclear armament has ended in the first quarter of the twenty-first century, as it did regarding the French Revolution, with the orthodox side of the balance sheet being strengthened and, albeit in altered terms, readopted by historians—at least for the moment. Again, the "conservative" rather than the "liberal," the "Right" rather than the "Left," view of a part of the past has become settled professional opinion.

The first historical interpretation of the bombings supported the views of many contemporaries. It was put forth publicly and most authoritatively by the very figure who knew most about the secret discussions that had led to the bombs' use: Secretary of War Henry L. Stimson, chief wartime adviser on this matter to President Harry S. Truman and someone well aware, as he put it in 1947, that the decision to employ the bombs "blasted the web of history and, like the discovery of fire, severed past from present." One would now say that the decision in which Stimson participated was overdetermined—that is, brought about by the confluence of many considerations, no single one of which would have carried the day alone but all of which irresistibly converged to lead to Truman's order for the bombs' use. Yet however the decision was arrived at, no historian can ignore the parallel reality that from the start of the secret deliberations that led to the development and employment of the bombs, many people, scientists chief among them, fought against their use. Thus the very birth of this set of events was accompanied by many of the same disputes—scientific, technological, military, political, and moral—that broke out publicly fifty years later after simmering for decades.

Among the considerations that led Truman, Stimson, and others to decide in favor of the bombs' use, there was the strong desire, first of all, to end the war as quickly as possible. That determination coincided with the desire to minimize the prospective cost in casualties to the United States and its allies if an invasion of Japan's home islands were required to bring about Japan's defeat and surrender, the recent battle for Okinawa having proved the high cost of fighting against entrenched Japanese forces. Moreover, despite growing opposition in Japan to the war's continuation, Japanese officials were failing to pass word to the United States that they might concede the war if the emperor were allowed to retain his throne—no doubt failing to do so because the Allies were remaining firm in their call for surrender without conditions. Also, American planners were not confident that continued aerial bombing and the tightening of the full U.S. naval blockade would force the island nation, already effectively defeated, to surrender or that Japanese forces elsewhere in Asia would lay down their arms. Since the use, already under way, of incendiary bombs on Japanese cities was showing no apparent effect on Japan's determination to fight, perhaps one or two knockout bombs would break Japanese will, obviate an invasion that everyone feared for its likely costs, and bring about unconditional surrender. The administration also was wary of Soviet motives in promising to enter the war in Asia; with the European theater now at peace, American policy makers wanted to shorten the interval of any Soviet military action and reduce Soviet claims to have standing in a surrender settlement. Additionally, American officials were hopeful that evidence of the bombs' destructiveness might serve as a warning to the Soviets against any prospective future claims in Europe.

All of this said, questions about the technical dependability of the initial American bombs made inexpedient in policy makers' view a public demonstration of one of them even after the successful July 1945 secret test explosion at Alamogordo, New Mexico. Furthermore, a warning issued to Japan not long after by the Potsdam Conference about the unstated consequences of Japan's further refusal to surrender had not moved the island government to treat with its enemies. Then there was this nagging political issue: with the American public souring on an extension of the war and troop shortages making themselves felt, could the administration avoid use of a war-ending weapon, however horrifying its destructive force might prove to be, when its existence was bound to become known? The political costs of a failure to use the bombs risked being too damaging to the Truman administration. Here, then, were the contents of the orthodox justification for the bombs' use against which every future criticism about their employment and every challenge to their morality would have to be directed. To be faithful to known, recorded historical facts, the commemoration of the fiftieth anniversary of the flight of the *Enola Gay* would have to take into account these justifications a half century earlier for, as well as the arguments against, the bombs' use.

Thus arose the political donnybrook of 1994–1995. If any public controversy confirms the difficulty of gaining acceptance of a fresh view of the past when a large group of participants in the events under debate remain alive, it is the bitter contest over displaying the fuselage of the *Enola Gay,* the B-29 bomber that dropped the first of two atomic weapons on Japan, in the Smithsonian Institution's National Air and Space Museum and the museum's proposed interpretation of the war-ending atomic bombings of Hiroshima and Nagasaki in 1945. Yet the influence in that political battle of surviving civilian and military participants and of others who lived through World War II cannot alone explain the acrimony of the controversy or its outcome. In this case, context overcame particulars in such a way as to defeat the public presentation of anything but the orthodox view of the significance of the two bombs. And while the controversy's outcome could give full comfort to neither party in the fight, both can be said to have achieved something of value for Americans generally.

Planning for the commemoration began calmly enough. The general view of the Second World War as the "Good War" was deeply rooted in Americans' consciousness. As the fiftieth anniversary of the bombing of the two Japanese cities approached, no one raised objections to marking the occasion at some national institution, and the

National Air and Space Museum on the National Mall in Washington seemed the natural location for the birthday exhibit. Built to house the artifacts and relate the history of flight in the United States, from its 1976 opening in the midst of the Cold War the museum was widely taken to be an expression of a broad desire to celebrate the nation's technology, its aeronautic achievements, its prowess in space exploration, and its airborne military might. Not surprisingly, it quickly became one of the most-visited museums in the United States and, as others have called it, a kind of temple to air power. Its constituencies—none more so than the aerospace industry and the military's air arms—were available for mobilizing should the contents of the museum or any conventional interpretations of them in any way seem to be traduced. By the 1990s, the museum had taken on attributes of a showplace as well as a shrine; all was to be uplift, progress, and success—the realization of soaring imagination. The indisputable fact that airborne flight and weaponry had led to errors, disasters, carnage, and horror—caused by and experienced by people everywhere, not just Americans—was easily overlooked in the museum's louder hymn to achievement. As if the absence of any "interpretation" could be a perspective somehow devoid of a point of view, any avowed "interpretation" of the nation's aeronautic past whatsoever was not easily going to find a snug home in an institution that so many thought of as a site for the display of "objective facts."

In the interval between the museum's opening and the fiftieth anniversary of the bombing of Japan, the museum's curatorial staff had begun to expand the institution's educational function alongside its exhibiting activities. This changing approach to curatorship—adding explanatory material to exhibits as a supplement to an older approach that employed a comparatively mute presentation of objects—was entirely in consonance with advances in museology internationally. Museums of all sorts—those that exhibited fine art as well as historical and other objects—were placing increasing emphasis on explaining the origins and significance of the works they displayed and presenting what was unknown and disputed about them alongside what was known and established. This approach left visitors and viewers free to apply their own thinking and sensibilities to what they saw and learned. While it might occasionally run afoul of the wishes of donors (like the corporate interests and the U.S. Air Force, the latter responsible for the gift of so many of the aircraft and rockets displayed on the Mall), by and large this shift in museum presentations had proceeded smoothly. The proposed exhibit about the atomic bombs, one that would include the *Enola Gay,* was planned to follow this approach.

In the spirit of new curatorial practices, the museum's staff members turned to the latest scholarly understanding of the closing days of the Second World War. Here, in the early 1990s, they found as much complexity and disagreement as clarity and consensus. Questions surrounding the overwhelming use of airborne weaponry—first the area bombing of cities and countryside with conventional ordnance, then the use of incendiary city bombing, finally the use of atomic weapons— had to do with its necessity and humanity: one could ask whether the war would not have ended roughly as it did through the destruction of enemy cities by the use of saturation bombing on Dresden, Hamburg, and other German sites. Instead of surprising the Japanese with the A-bombs, might the United States not have continued the firebombing of Japanese cities that, well before the Hiroshima and Nagasaki explosions, had laid so many of them waste? Might the United States have avoided the use of atomic weaponry by risking an open demonstration of the bombs' power in the American Southwest so as to bring about Japan's quick surrender without their direct use? How were claims that the two bombs had prevented one million American casualties during an invasion of the Japanese mainland to be assessed? And what role did anti-Asian racial prejudice and revenge for the 1941 attack on Pearl Harbor play in Truman's decision to order the bombs' use? These were the same questions, among many others, that contemporaries in the 1940s had asked; they were not questions new to the 1990s or to historians and the museum's curators. Answers to them had been already advanced by policy makers and scholars. To old military and diplomatic hands as well as professional historians, these issues, most of them filled with moral freight, had long been familiar.

Even during the bombs' development and before the full impact of their employment could be assessed, some scientists at work on the Manhattan Project that produced the American weapons had expressed deep disquiet about the morality of using the bombs. In the flush of victory in the 1940s and 1950s, many Americans—among them *Time*'s founder Henry R. Luce, senior journalists Hanson W. Baldwin and David Lawrence, historian of World War I Harry Elmer Barnes, Admiral William D. Leahy, even John Foster Dulles, George C. Marshall, and Dwight D. Eisenhower—had openly questioned and criticized the use of the bombs to bring about the surrender of Japan. The official U.S. Strategic Bombing Survey had gone so far in 1947 as to conclude that "certainly prior to 31 December 1945, and in all probability prior to 1 November 1945, Japan would have surrendered even if the atomic bombs had not been dropped, even if Russia had not entered the war, and even if no invasion had been planned or contemplated." Others attacked the application of the doctrine of unconditional surrender—the insistence that Japan capitulate without being granted American concessions—for having strengthened the case for the use of the bombs to bring Japan to its knees; without insistence on Japan's condition-less capitulation, they argued, that nation would have given in without continued and intensified bombing. Others interpreted the bombs' use as a weapon not of warfare but in the emerging Cold War contest with the Soviet Union and thus irrelevant to the conclusion of the Pacific war. Some pointed to evidence of deep anti-Asian prejudice as a factor that freed American decision makers from inhibitions they might have felt if faced with pressure to drop atomic bombs on European territory; after all, even the Nazis had spared Paris.

As early as 1945 the implied criticisms embodied in such questioning earned them the label of "left-wing revisions"; no one had to await the 1990s for that tag to be applied to the work of any historian who questioned the American bombings of 1945. But it was John Hersey's 1946 literary sensation *Hiroshima* that had the greatest impact in forcing fresh questions into public debate. Neither polemical nor argumentative, the author, a wartime correspondent in the Pacific, simply conveyed to his readers the unimaginable horrors, expressed in their own words, witnessed by six survivors of the bombing of the first Japanese city to be attacked by a nuclear weapon. Broad-based antinuclear sentiment in the United States was born with Hersey's book, not with scholarship or ideology, less than two years after the war had ended.

As American and other official archives were gradually opened to examination in later years, as the memoirs of participants in the planning and execution of the bombings of Japan appeared, and as the Cold War intensified and doubts about its origins and prosecution mounted, professional historians took up the questions that contemporaries in the 1940s had posed. The first works to bring academic research on the bombs into view began to appear in the early 1960s, just as tensions over growing American involvement in another war in Asia began to make themselves felt, tensions that were now superimposed on Cold War anxieties. First came Herbert Feis's 1961 *Japan Subdued: The Atomic Bomb and the End of World War II*, which argued that the grounds of Truman's decision to employ the bombs were more complex and nuanced than had been previously believed. But it was Gar Alperovitz's 1965 *Atomic Diplomacy: Hiroshima and Potsdam; The Use of the Atomic Bomb and the American Confrontation with Soviet Power* that put a larger variety of issues under fresh analysis and initiated the enduring scholarly debate that proved critical when it came time to mark the passage of a half century's time since Hiroshima. Alperovitz's dissection of the decision to employ atomic weapons raised many of the questions earlier put forth by nonhistorians—questions of strategy, diplomacy, politics, and race. But for the first time, his answers were those of a scholar working from archives. He found questionable the use of the two bombs (especially the second one) and the insistence on unconditional surrender when Japan was signaling its willingness to end the war short of the annihilation of more of its cities and the threat to Japanese civilization itself. Could it not be said, Alperovitz asked, that the United States had put the bombs to use gratuitously—not to bring Japan to its knees but rather to signal to the Soviet Union its possession of massive weaponry and to thwart further Soviet advances in Europe?

Other historians soon added their own investigations to these initial scholarly works. By examining the sources of casualty estimates, some questioned the oft-raised, deeply political argument that the bombs had prevented one million American lives from being lost in the event that the United States had invaded the Japanese archipelago. These scholars argued, as many continue to do, that a firm, authoritative, and credible estimate of avoided American and Japanese deaths (the latter always essential to a full accounting) was probably impossible to come by. In addition, using freshly opened archives from the Truman administration, other historians showed that political pressures played a large role in Truman's decision. Evidence mounted that the president, the Manhattan Project's director Major General Leslie R. Groves, and others in government were acutely sensitive to the prospective political fallout were it discovered that the United States had failed to use the potentially war-ending weapons in its possession. This argument was strengthened when it was revealed that Harvard President James B. Conant, one of Truman's science advisers, had pushed for a city-destroying use of the bomb instead of a demonstration explosion in order to enhance the chances of American postwar control of atomic energy, a concern widely shared among nuclear physicists. "It was," Conant wrote, "the only way to awaken the world to the necessity of abolishing war altogether." Such evidence threw fresh doubt on long-questioned claims that the use of nuclear weapons had been made on military grounds alone.

The nation's growing recognition, during the civil rights movement, of racial discrimination in its midst also made historians sensitive to evidence of strong midcentury racism toward Asians. John W. Dower, a historian of Japan, and military historian Ronald H. Spector, a veteran of the war in Vietnam, bore down on evidence of the role of racial prejudice in the decision to use the bombs. They pointed out that, even acknowledging Americans' desire to make Japan pay for its well-known racism against other peoples, the depth of their vengefulness for Japan's 1941 attack on Pearl Harbor was difficult to explain as mere enmity for Japan's military actions. Even revenge for such Japanese atrocities as the Bataan Death March did not seem adequate explanation for the bombs' use. Other historians cited evidence that military leaders and policy makers had brushed aside many other relevant considerations in their haste to end the war. If the celebratory tale of heroic acts and clear moral justification were to survive by the time of the planned *Enola Gay* exhibit, that tale would face heavy going from scholars who were insisting that known facts greatly complicated the picture.

Not that the arguments of such historians were themselves not called into question by other historians. Scholars were by no means in agreement among themselves. By far the most sensitive of all the contested issues concerned the preservation of American lives. Even if the oft-used estimate that one million American lives had been saved by the bombs' use was not susceptible to firm confirmation, there could be no question, some scholars argued, that tens of thousands of veterans and their families had avoided the tragedies of death and injury. This sentiment was aptly captured by the title of an essay by scholar and World War II veteran Paul Fussell: "Thank God for the Atom Bomb." No triumphalist words could have been better chosen to sum up rejection of the broadening library of historians' interpretations of the bombing of Hiroshima and Nagasaki.

These debates among professional historians about the closing phases of World War II took place largely out of view of most Americans and were confined principally to academic circles. They might have remained there had not the project to rescue the *Enola Gay* from its quiet resting place, restore it, and exhibit it as the centerpiece of the fiftieth-anniversary exhibit on the Mall gathered steam both within and outside museum precincts. Put on display would be one of the most potent emotion-laden icons of American military might, no less freighted with meaning than Charles A. Lindbergh's *Spirit of St. Louis* or the nation's earliest satellites already on view there. But museum officials knew that any exhibit about the bombs would open in the midst of mounting cultural battles. Increasingly, art and other displays—such as those of Robert Mapplethorpe's explicit photographs of male nudes and a 1991 exhibit of the art of the American frontier—had already been subjected to bitter criticism. Two successive conservative chairpersons of the National Endowment for the Humanities had attacked the political views of the practitioners of the very humanities disciplines of which the officials were custodians—as if the two federal figures themselves had no political inclinations. One could have guessed that the temper of the larger population was not likely to tolerate a balanced debate over the commemoration of one of the signal events of the modern era.

In planning their exhibit, museum officials also knew that earlier attempts to house and display the *Enola Gay* had failed; the plane had lain disassembled for years. Even within the exhibit's advisory committees were veterans who scoffed at the heroism of the *Enola Gay*'s crew and who considered any endeavor to display a weapon of "genocide" (as one called it) to be foolhardy. But little did museum staff members fully anticipate the domestic uproar caused by the exhibit's plans when those plans became known. They anticipated that the chief danger to the exhibit would come from the Japanese and Japanese-Americans. In doing so they overlooked the prospective snares involved in trying to induce the exhibit's future visitors to consider its many possible meanings. As it proved, the times and circumstances in which the museum acted were ones in which political and cultural currents interacted with unusual force.

By the mid-1990s, Americans were no longer uniform in their conviction that the United States was innocent of the evils so long charged against others. This was so even after the crumbling of the Berlin Wall in 1989, the nation's quick and overwhelming victory in Operation Desert Storm that ended the First Gulf War in early 1991, and the dissolution of the Soviet Union a few months later. But it was the loss of Vietnam that most deeply shadowed planning for the *Enola Gay* exhibit. Bitterness over that war's loss and the expenditure of more than fifty-eight thousand American lives for what was widely argued to be no good purpose revealed itself in the protectiveness of veterans' associations and the active military services about any hint of criticism of their members' military courage and sacrifice. Where such memorials as those at Pearl Harbor had earlier gone up with little fuss, the vexed history of efforts to create the Holocaust Museum and the memorial to the men and women lost in the Vietnam War—a memorial eventually considered by many to be a classic of its genre—suggested the obstacles beginning to face all memorialization projects, obstacles visible again since then in battles over Civil War monuments. By the mid-1990s, in the midst of strong efforts to bring into focus African Americans', women's, minorities', and other groups' historical contributions to American life, the public became increasingly divided about what and who should be recalled with public monuments and plaques, who should make and fund those decisions, and how they should be interpreted. How were celebration and sober assessment to be presented in a balanced fashion in the midst of what came to be called the "history wars"?

In a context fraught with such political, ideological, and scholarly division, planning for the *Enola Gay*'s display could not, as it proved, proceed tranquilly, nor, in the event, could the National Air and Space Museum mount the exhibit it originally envisaged. There seemed no successful way to get around a discussion of Truman's motives in ordering the bombs' release or of the bombs' necessity; yet without some recognition of the cost the Japanese had paid for the American bombs, to many the exhibit would be empty and without moral grounding. What proved more of an obstacle was opposition to any hint that such questions could be raised within the exhibit space; the American Legion and the Air Force Association, the latter an organization of active and veteran air force members strongly supported by the aerospace industry, stood ready to see to that. Neither welcomed any unorthodox views, and surely neither would welcome them from outside. As often happens in such cases, people not acquainted with long-fought professional debates were angered that anyone could raise questions about the wisdom of dropping the bombs—as if those questions were new. Membership organizations roused their followers to protest. The U.S. Senate passed a resolution calling the use of atomic bombs "merciful" in recognition of American lives saved. The chief historian of the air force went so far as to term the bombings "morally unambiguous." Once such opposition to the exhibit's plans became known, the fight spread to members of Congress, whose votes could jeopardize the Smithsonian's overall funding if it did not give in to the growing opposition.

On a collision course with powerful interest groups, the Air and Space Museum's staff surrendered to its critics. A full account of the museum's own missteps, such as a failure to anticipate the political sensitivities involved in questioning any aspect of the rightness of the bombs' use, as well as the divisions within its ranks, need not be repeated here. In the event, a drastically scaled-down exhibit replaced what had originally been planned as a comprehensive examination of then-current historical understanding, one that might have raised the many complex historical and moral issues that had surfaced since 1945. Instead of a fully restored *Enola Gay,* only the fuselage hung above its spectators. In place of an invitation to viewers to consider the complex issues surrounding the use of the bomb the plane had dropped, visitors were treated to a bare-bones history of the development of the nation's B-29 fleet and of the *Enola Gay*'s restoration. Information replaced knowledge, declarative statement stood in for inquiry, and something close to an interpretation-less presentation of facts faced the visiting public. The exhibit went on to be among the most visited in the history of the Air and Space Museum—whether because of its subject or because of the controversy surrounding it no one could tell.

Not surprisingly, this denatured exhibit sustained wounding criticism from the other direction—from scholars who charged the Air and Space Museum with capitulating to political forces and surrendering the high ground of museum professionalism and scholarly detachment to patriotic tub-thumping. As John Dower wrote, "As the fiasco of the *Enola Gay* exhibition at the Smithsonian Institution showed, American recollections of the war reveal a powerful emotional and ideological impulse to strip the historical record of all ambiguity, all contradiction, all moral complexity, and simply wrap it in the flag." This is all the more striking, Dower pointed out, when compared with the more measured, complex, and enduring feelings of the Japanese, who, despite their government's refusal to own up to much of its responsibility for the horrors it inflicted on other peoples in the 1930s and 1940s, possess a much more rounded attitude toward their country's acts than those who prevented the presentation of such ambiguities on the Mall.

But should we be surprised at the tug-of-war between memory and history within any citizenry? Edward T. Linenthal, a leading interpreter of this affair, argues that there is no escaping "the inevitable tension between a commemorative voice—'I was there, I know because I saw and felt what happened'—and a historical one that speaks of complicated motives and of actions and consequences often hardly considered at the moment of the event itself . . . between a reverently held story and its later reappraisal." At this critical intersection between the recalled and examined past, between the brain's recording and its later reworking of lived experience, between individual and community needs for a shared narrative understanding of life, and between scholarly and political examinations of known evidence, there opens a terrain on which disagreement and difference will always contend. For historians, the challenge is to adapt to the intrusion into their work of public need and cultural and political currents, as well as to accept the fact that some historical questions—like the morality of the bombings, whether Japan would have surrendered short of the bombs' use, and the number of likely casualties on both sides after an American invasion—are unamenable to definitive resolution. But in fairness to all parties, nonhistorians, from whom less circumspection and reflection are to be anticipated, should also be asked to exhibit some of the same, reciprocal regard for historians' convictions and uncertainties as they insist historians extend to their own.

If nothing else, the bitter episode of the *Enola Gay* exhibit shows that while historical knowledge can in many instances lead to justice and the healing of wounds, it can also embitter and divide. Arguing about the past holds the risk of severe political and cultural turmoil no less than conflicts over civil liberties and peoples' rights. In these never-ending debates over the realities of the past, neither a direct nor an inverse relationship between fresh historical thought and public reaction can easily be demonstrated, any more than the emergence of public battles over the past can be predicted or easily controlled. All of which is to say that historical study reflects the interest of the individual historians who pursue it while often arousing members of the public in unforeseen ways. In these cases, neither camp is likely to yield easily to the claims of the other.

Yet if the battle over the *Enola Gay* is to provide any useful knowledge, we must ask what is to be made of an outcome that most historians consider to have been a debacle for the presentation of history in museums—what historian (and former chief of Air Force history) Richard H. Kohn has termed "one of the worst tragedies to befall the public presentation of history in the United States in this generation"—while their public opponents view the exhibit as having been an unalloyed triumph. The answer to that question seems no easier to come by now than it was in the 1990s. History has always served as a weapon of ideological warfare. Yet with the passage of years and in the context of the long history of contests over the past, a more balanced assessment than could be reached in 1995 is possible now.

There can be no doubt that the work of scholars and the debates among them had by 1995 led to major advances in knowledge and understanding about the decision to employ nuclear weapons over Japan. That result could not have been achieved fifty years earlier. To be sure, the evidence that gradually became available after 1945 was not always creditable to American policy makers (to say nothing of those of Japan). At the time, there had never been a full canvass of the deep and complex moral questions that the use of nuclear weapons posed to those with knowledge of what was at stake. Fear of the political as well as actual costs of delaying the use of the bombs or forgoing their use altogether strongly affected the decision among senior military officers, as well as the president and his advisers, to employ them. Concerns about Soviet actions in Asia as well as Europe—a factor that, in the end, proved un-amenable to influence when the USSR declared war on Japan after the bombs had fallen and before Japan had capitulated—may have been excessive. But American policy makers had every reason to wish the war to end as soon as possible without further loss of American and Japanese lives; in itself, that wish had heavy moral components. In ad-dition, time was of the essence if American and Japanese lives were to be saved, despite only the mistiest estimate and hastiest calculation of their numbers—numbers still in dispute as they are likely to remain. It is also hard to believe that Soviet maneuverings in eastern Asia would have been any fewer had the Soviet Union not entered the Pacific war at the last moment. Similar are the difficulties faced by the counterfactual conclusion that the nuclear arms race would have been avoided if the United States had not employed the new weapons at its disposal.

Yet contrary to some strong intimations otherwise, there never was anything out of keeping with the conventional practices of historical inquiry and the demanding standards of scholarly inquiry when histo-rians of the bombs took up the issues they did. Even if in some quarters many people questioned the legitimacy of raising moral, military, and political concerns about the decision to employ the bombs and attacked those who did so, the pursuit of inquiry into those issues could not have been suppressed. After all, anyone looking closely at scholarly discus-sions of these issues would have found that historians differed among themselves as to the significance of their evidentiary discoveries and the conclusions to be drawn from them. Furthermore, all their findings, arguments, and differences were aired in publicly available scholarly books and journals, sometimes more widely in newspaper reportage

and magazine articles, and freely available to anyone who sought access
to them. Since these historians welcomed their works' availability to the
general public, they should not have been surprised when their moral
qualms were rejected by many members of it. Historians' responsibilities, which they fully met, were to explain and, where necessary, to
defend their findings and arguments; they could not control how their
findings and arguments would be received and should have known
that they could not. By the same token, opponents of the exhibit as it
was originally planned should have borne in mind that a political victory would not easily constitute a win in scholarly circles; historians of
the bombs would remain the authorities in the arena of endeavor in
which they pursued their scholarly inquiries even if their own consensus about the causes of the weaponry's use were to change—as it has
continued to do.

In assessing a historical controversy as supercharged as this one,
it has to be borne in mind that the claims of these two groups—of historians and of members of the public—have no easy equivalency. The
claims are not coequal in their nature, nor are they of the same strength
in all contexts, especially when they are removed from what scholars
call their "communities of discourse." Each set of arguments takes on
its significance and develops its following within a distinct intellectual,
social, and cultural domain; the groups assume their views of the past
in separate realms that rarely interact. Occasionally, the outlooks of
both communities overlap—fortunately often without the results that
disfigured the *Enola Gay* exhibit. Sometimes their commitments to gain
knowledge and understanding mutually reinforce and sustain each
other—a phenomenon well known among history "buffs" and historical
reenactors. But although the members of one group sometimes influence those of the other—scholars, for instance, being alerted to new
lines of inquiry by questions on the minds of nonscholars, members
of the public learning from the work of professional historians—their
quests for understanding typically run along parallel, not intersecting,
courses. In seeking knowledge, they often have distinct aims in mind—
scholars usually looking to present new knowledge and viewpoints
about the past, nonscholars seeking confirmation of long-held views

or inspiration from what they learn.[5] Such aims are altogether natural and appropriate to each group, so that while neither can be assured of carrying the day in political and intellectual debates, the legitimacy of the pursuit of understanding by both, even when that pursuit differs in purpose, is never in doubt—at least in an open, liberal democracy.

Yet as can be learned from the *Enola Gay* free-for-all, bringing these two sets of expectations, aims, and approaches to the past into contact with each other often provides tinder for misunderstanding and, sometimes, bad faith. When such a circumstance presents itself, the two worlds clash for authority and precedence, and they position themselves against each other even when, were the contest to be framed in different terms, some sort of mutually acceptable arrangement might be worked out. More important to bear in mind in the context of this book is that even when, set in battle ranks against each other, one side achieves a victory of sorts over the other in a public arena, as did the Air Force Association over historians and curators of the *Enola Gay* exhibit, there is no certainty that one side will gain permanent advantage over its opponent. Gains and losses may indeed be booked, as such things are, in what amounts to a political accounting. But, as in annual financial reports, the gains and losses recorded after a battle comes to an end vary with the season and in their significance.

Historical knowledge and opinion enjoy different purchases within different populations. In contests over revisions to historical understanding, this means that in an open society, each community of interest is free to adhere to whatever version of the past suits its needs and interests. It does not mean that all views will be accepted by scholars, and it does not mean that any view will be safe against criticism, ridicule, or outright rejection. But in its own domain, a widely held view

5. Scholars are no more immune from "confirmation bias"—the tendency to find in existing evidence what they hope to find or to see and hear what they wish to see and hear— than are others. They are, however, professionally subject to peer criticism when suspected of such bias, and their professional canons keep pressure on them to monitor their own inclinations. Needless to say, they do not always try with enough zeal to subject themselves to such self-correction. Yet even in bias there can be illumination, especially when a particular argument is driven to its extremities, just as there may be in the analogous tactics of prosecutors and defense attorneys in legal cases. Truth does not always emerge nor understanding grow from prudence, balance, and understatement alone.

of the past is likely to remain secure from external influence and change as long as its adherents do not change their views or until the circumstances that help support those views are altered. To the extent that that is so, no combatants in a historical dispute can be sure of its outcome or of their own relative strength during its continuation. That outcome and their strength will always remain contingent on the realities of the eras in which any battle over the past takes place.

One must also keep in mind the sociological, psychological, and professional realities that sustain the members of each group. Veterans and their supporters—indeed, any group of people whose sense of self-worth depends on the maintenance of a strongly held worldview—have powerful grounds, as well as an understandable psychological need, to believe that what they have done has been worthy and that the costs they have borne have been for some purpose larger than themselves. Solidarity and cohesion in the face of danger being so constitutive a part of veterans' collective identity, people of the military arms do not easily break ranks with one another. That inclination is not likely to be set aside in deference to the advance of knowledge, nor will veterans bend to what they see as a questioning of patriotic truths to which they have devoted themselves and for which they may have risked their lives.

Ideally and by comparison, historians have a professional commitment, in their efforts to create accurate accounts of the past, to ignore public opinion to the best of their ability and instead to follow evidence and thinking where they lead. While seeing themselves as part of a larger community of practitioners, they place a lesser value on cohesiveness than on fidelity to fact and independence of judgment. Though they can often appear to be oppositional, nothing in their standards of conduct calls them to be the adversaries of orthodoxy in any of its forms. Instead, they think of themselves as committed to the critical evaluation of evidence and of existing interpretations of the past. That they frequently find themselves in the position of questioning what may be conventional beliefs or common understanding is of no great satisfaction to them. It is simply a constituent element of who they are as professionals. Many of them may of course have political or other axes to grind, but the canons of their craft unavoidably subject their findings and arguments to the unbound evaluation of their professional peers. Even under criticism, they rarely give in easily to others' expectations. Their compass is set to what they think of as the pursuit of accurate knowledge of what happened in the past, and little will deter the best of them from that aim. Consequently, when a consensus view of some historical topic takes hold, it is not for lack of challenge to it. Nor is there any assurance that the consensus will hold indefinitely. As in life itself, provisionality remains the hallmark of historical interpretation.

These realities and commitments do not, however, protect historians from disappointments, some of them bitter. From the perspective of 1995, professional history about the use of nuclear weapons over Japan, once exposed to view, suffered a stinging public defeat; instead of moving forward, public historical understanding seemed to most historians to have suffered a heavy blow. Yet, as ought to have been predicted, historical scholarship and thinking about the end of the Second World War continued unabated after historians' late-century setback. Military and veterans groups may have demonstrated their muscle with Congress and succeeded in preventing a full, open exploration of sensitive historical and political subjects; yet once their own objections to the planned exhibit went public, they failed to prevent the controversy from igniting wider interest and thus gaining a somewhat greater purchase on popular consciousness. And it is difficult to see how, in this or in any other case, it could have been otherwise. As in all historical disputes, where permanent victories and permanent defeats are rare, in this particular one no end to the controversy has come into sight.

An observer of the 1995 *Enola Gay* affray might have ventured the guess that as they passed from the scene, the influence of those who fought to preserve a clearly defined memory of their achievements during the Second World War would wane. As it did, perhaps the views of those critics whose interpretations of the bombings had been struck from the *Enola Gay* exhibit would then gain greater acceptance. Yet no one should ever expect historiography, any more than history itself, to move in predictable ways. The greatest irony of the *Enola Gay* episode is that, despite the efforts made by so many historian-critics of the bombing to prevail in this dispute, they have not carried the day—not even in historians' circles. The reason for their failure to do so has little to do with the eruption of public condemnation in 1994. Instead, it has resulted from continuing interpretive conflict among academic historians themselves. And for the moment at least, one set of academic historians has bested the other.

At the opening of the third decade of the twenty-first century, most historians of World War II and its climax on the Japanese archipelago have come to a consensus that, all things considered, the use of nuclear bombs on two Japanese cities was legitimate, justified, and unavoidable. That is to say, the position taken by the Air Force Association and the many critics of the original plans to exhibit and interpret the *Enola Gay* on the Mall has in its principal claims been, for the moment at least, vindicated by the work and conclusions of professional historians. This in no way means that the debate over the bombs' employment has ended or ever will, nor does it render useless and unnecessary any effort to keep alive the difficult moral issues associated with their development and use. Neither does the fact that the most knowledgeable and authoritative historians of the bombs' use have come to this conclusion make it inappropriate once again to try to exhibit the *Enola Gay* in such a way and in such a location that all of the issues surrounding its historic flight can be considered by members of the public—first as historical issues, then as moral ones. For the fact of the matter is that by the early twenty-first century, revisionist historians' interpretations have been cast aside in favor of those of a more orthodox bent. This in no way removes the moral issues from the equation. It rather insists that once all the historical issues have been identified, they must be argued and resolved on historical grounds and that the historical issues are precisely that—issues to be debated and altered by historians as new evidence appears and new professional perspectives are advanced. Then, as in this case, once all factors pressing in on contemporaries in 1945 and all of the facts they knew or accepted are identified and their own assessments and decisions understood, the debate over the bombs' moral costs may commence. Moral arguments without firm professional grounding will not otherwise withstand the scrutiny of time.

We ought to ask ourselves whether it is ever historians' part *as historians* to go beyond determining what happened in the past and why it did so. Is it their role *as historians* to function as moral arbiters of what people in the past did? From its outset among the ancients, historical study has always served, inescapably one has to conclude, as a kind of moral science in which the knowledge and meanings that historians create and diffuse are freighted with moral significance. Yet that significance is always in dispute; and historians, like other humans, never come to agreement about the meanings, either for those deceased or living, that historical knowledge holds. As citizens, too, historians have never found a way fully to sterilize their scholarly discoveries and conclusions from the moral and civic issues that the past always raises. Nor should it be wished that they do so. But is it scholars' function to decide whether the bombs brought victory to the Allies and peace to the world or whether they raised the specter of destruction to a new level and made fear of annihilation a constant in humans' lives? Historians are expert at discovering and analyzing past realities; they are not employed to decide political questions or determine strategy. To criticize them for their hard-won scholarly views is to criticize them for the tasks they have set themselves since the days of Herodotus and Thucydides.

Also, it is not as if the Japanese have been immune from cultural wars such as those that engulfed American historians in the mid-1990s. They, too, have debated their role in initiating the war and prosecuting it with harrowing brutality; in subjecting China, Korea, and much of southeast Asia to inhumane occupation; in their halting and lukewarm acknowledgment (contrary to Germany's official acts) of their nation's complicity in the devastation of the war in the Pacific; in their felt sense of being victims of both conventional and atomic bombings even if the Japanese were the war's perpetrators; in continuing to venerate their wartime leaders; and in resisting revision of textbooks that sidestep all these issues. That is, the Japanese have proven neither much better nor much worse at settling their differences over these matters than have Americans. Neither war guilt nor the effort to escape war guilt knows national or cultural boundaries.

Seen from the perspective of twenty-five years, it is easy to view the reaction to the planned exhibit in the National Air and Space Museum as the displacement onto this exhibit of anger stemming from other sources—the treatment of veterans after their return from the Vietnam War, doubts about the continuing superiority of American air might, and widespread uneasiness over changes in American society and culture brought on by unprecedented claims for recognition and equal treatment advanced by women, African Americans, gays, and lesbians. But while displacement may be a useful diagnostic concept in psychology, it does little to help us determine the strength of the arguments of the exhibit's opponents. Who is to decide whether memory or history, celebration or criticism, should gain the upper hand? The *Enola Gay* exhibit's opponents might well have been pleased by their success in preventing what they considered to be an overly critical "leftist," "anti-American" view of the role of atomic weaponry in the last stage of World War II from being shown in the capital, but they could not be sure that some other institution might not mount a critical view of the bombs, even without the iconic airplane as its centerpiece.[6]

Historians understandably have reason to feel aggrieved when others ignore or oppose the findings, knowledge, and understanding that they devote their careers to creating. But their historical perspective ought to give them, of all people, a larger view of their defeats in the arena of public acceptance and opinion—if "defeat" it can justifiably be termed. Such a wide view ought to be one consequence of their own justifiable desire as members of a professional community to see historical knowledge carried beyond the confines of the scholarly world. Ironically, to the degree that, in the early twenty-first century, that goal is much further on the way to being realized by historians than it was a quarter century ago, it now comes up against the costs of its realization—the unforeseeable, sometimes negative, ideological, and ill-spirited responses on the part of members of the public to their work.

Yet none of this ought to suggest by contrast that the forces that

6. Eventually that happened. When a smaller exhibit embodying some of the contents and reflecting some of the intentions of the originally planned Smithsonian exhibit on the Mall was later mounted at the American University Museum in Washington, little was made of it in the press or by military and veterans groups. This suggests that the principal problem for members of these groups was that the original exhibit was to be on display in a national museum, where it would appear as representing a federal interpretation of events in 1945. Then in 2003, the entire *Enola Gay*, not just its fuselage, went on exhibit, with scant text, at the Smithsonian's Udvar-Hazy Facility near Dulles International Airport in Virginia. One wonders whether, if the entire *Enola Gay* could have been accommodated in 1995 at a nonfederal facility and accompanied by the interpretive scheme originally envisaged by Smithsonian curators, the exhibit might not have gone off as planned and without widespread outcry.

brought down the original plans for the *Enola Gay* exhibit have permanently carried the day. Public moods shift; participants in memorialized events die; texts and artifacts lose their potency; new meanings emerge from old. Who knows but that, at the centennial anniversary of the end of World War II in 2045, the fully reassembled aircraft that carried the bomb dropped on Hiroshima will be able to be displayed on the National Mall without significant public outcry? The odds against accurately calling the final victory in this lively contest one way or the other are high and likely to remain so for decades. In an open society, this is to be expected. It is also to be treasured.

∾

The sketches of the two historical controversies that I have offered here reveal the inherent plasticity of historical understanding and suggest that the full resolution of disputes about the past are difficult to come by and perhaps impossible permanently to achieve. Each of these arguments represented a dispute without certain end; each has resisted dispositive settlement. Such ambiguous resolution is latent when serious, sensitive disputes break out of their confines among professional historians and enter public debate, as all historical controversies always verge on doing in an open society—the very kind of society the controversies enliven and strengthen. In trying to illustrate the range of arguments about the past that bear fruit not simply in public controversy but also in historical knowledge, I could just as well have reviewed long-standing debates about whether the New Deal or World War II ended the Great Depression in the United States (a matter of importance whenever political contests over economic "pump priming," public work expenditures, and tax rates come into play); whether the Holocaust was a German or a wider phenomenon (when efforts are made to attribute responsibility for genocide, racism, and other forms of discrimination); whether we should think of women's historically subordinate condition as a result of their occupying a separate social sphere forced on them by law and culture or as the result of the social construction of gender (how best to further the advancement of women's rights); or whether American forces in Vietnam were on the way to achieving victory for the United States at the very moment they withdrew (a question that can enter the picture when political figures contend over military preparedness, military budgets, diplomatic strategy, and national will). By implication, my earlier discussion of the historiography of the Civil War can be used to make the same point—that no historical issues whose disputed contents interact with contemporary concerns are without felt consequences for the lived lives and understanding of those who engage in such controversies. Never are these kinds of issues likely to gain a stable resting place or to be settled to everyone's satisfaction.

Moreover, provisionality has proved to be a constant of contemporary historiography not simply because of the political stakes involved. Destabilization is always in the wind because of the introduction of fresh perspectives that may have little to do directly with contemporary concerns. Take for instance the recent reconfiguration of American colonial and later history within its larger Atlantic context. That reorientation has brought France, Spain, and other European countries, the lands of Africa and Latin America, and African Americans and North and Latin American native peoples into the picture of historical change while removing Great Britain and its American colonies from the center of attention of historians. Analogously, the world's current globalization has made it advisable for historians to examine the ways in which all cultures and polities may have been affected by changes far beyond their borders. The creation of and advances in such fields as bioarcheology, paleogenomics, dendrochronology, proteomics, meteorology, linguistics, and genetics (to name but a few) have given historians new tools to interpret vast changes in human migration, habitation, agriculture, and health that were beyond the reach of their understanding only a few decades ago. Consequently, we have learned how native populations of the Western Hemisphere affected their environments long before the arrival of Europeans and have greatly deepened our knowledge of the emergence of distinct tribes, languages, and cultures in the Americas.

Thus to see the fast-held positioning of opposing sides in many controversies, the sometimes bitterly contested pursuit of such disputes, and debates about unorthodox perspectives on venerable historical subjects as yielding no gains whatsoever is seriously to misconstrue the reality and significance of scholarly arguments. It is like dismissing different interpretations of symphonies, different stagings of theatrical works, and different artistic depictions of the same event as so much unnecessary repetition—as if all conductors, all directors, all artists are not free to offer their own versions of reality and thus try to add to understanding of it. Interpretive battles about the past clarify issues. They offer the chance to anyone observing them to reconsider previous convictions. They provoke scholars and others to further research and thought. And as I have repeatedly emphasized throughout this book, they lay down additions to the rich interpretive subsoil that has already built up under the subjects they concern, additions that consequently lie in reserve to nourish further thought through time without end.

All revisions to historical interpretations add to the possible ways of understanding the past—even if it comes to be agreed that some of them lack sufficient validity, authority, and plausibility. Interpretations leave a record just as the past itself does. Once written and published, they become part of the past in which they take up residence, and that past becomes part of the inheritance of successor historians who try in their own way to understand the times before their own. That is to say, revisions become part of our history, part of the evidence as to how humans of a specific place and time looked at the past they had inherited. Like pentimento in art, where each application of paint leaves evidence of what has been earlier applied to a canvas, every historical interpretation embodies traces of other interpretations that came before it.[7] All

7. Warranted here is an aside on the appropriation and integration in many works of history of other historians' approaches, questions, and arguments. Historians are not exempt from the human inclination to borrow from others, to use others' innovations for fresh purposes. Their professional responsibility in such cases is to acknowledge and cite those other historians in footnotes and bibliographies, as I have done in this book. In this respect, they are no less open—in some respects they are more open—than other professional practitioners. Are we not used to film writers and directors scavenging previous films for motifs, plots, inside jokes, and scenes? (Just look, for instance, at *Sunset Boulevard.*) Works of literature incorporate older tales to make new works. (Shakespeare's *Romeo and Juliet* comes immediately to mind.) We find in works of art the sly self-portraits of artists as well as painted references to earlier masterpieces and popular imagery. (A notorious example of appropriation is Andy Warhol's series of paintings of Campbell's Soup cans.) Composers take phrases and harmonies from others' compositions to make entirely new works. (Mozart borrowed for *Don Giovanni,* and Brahms paid homage to Beethoven's *Ninth Symphony* in his own *First Symphony.*) Identical musical sequences are transformed in different hands. (The same five-note motif leads off Zez Confrey's "Stumbling" of 1922, Irving Berlin's "Always" of 1926, and Richard Whiting's "Louise" of 1929.) We should therefore not expect historians to renounce

historical arguments linger in the subsequent literature of a subject; secure against erasure, they become inherent in all future argument. They bear witness to what earlier was thought to have happened in the past even if they are no longer considered to be valid interpretations. In this sense, the historical understanding of the French Revolution lost nothing during successive transformations in it, nor did understanding of the end of World War II suffer permanently by being the subject of an ideological and intellectual imbroglio on the Mall. Each gained by being repeatedly and combatively argued out. And thus it always is: no further consideration of a historical subject can ignore the points of view revealed in previous disputes about it. Just as accepted interpretations can lose their salience under new circumstances, interpretations that at one moment are felt to be unacceptable can take on plausibility under fresh conditions.

How and why historical inquiry undergoes continuing renewal is itself a subject of historical thought; historiography is the way in which historians understand the history of their own thinking. And if it can by now go without saying that no historical controversy exists in a cultural or ideological vacuum, it is equally the case that no historical subject can be beyond interpretation; none can reach the certain, final end of its development. To hope, as members of the Air Force Association hoped, to mount an exhibit that was factual but interpretation-less is to hope for something that is not possible; even the mere facts declared in an exhibit's labels carry meaning and imply choices among facts available for statement there. No "pure," permanent universally accepted vantage point on the past can exist because no historical event, such as a debate about how to present the history of World War II's conclusion, can exist without context. No one who writes history or thinks historically occupies a location outside society, culture, and time. There is no unmovable, contextless Archimedean point from which to see the past

---

what has proved a source of inspiration and ideas to other thinkers and artists. They learn from one another; they borrow from one another to create new lines of argument; and they acknowledge one another's influence. They are not without respect for other historians even when attacking them, when using the same evidence to make different arguments, or when appropriating arguments advanced by others for purposes that those other historians never intended.

unaffected by the viewer's own history. To believe that such a point exists is no different from believing that humans can live without oxygen. Even the claimed absence of interpretation is an interpretive stance.

Consequently, battles over interpretations reveal the different contexts in which its contestants live and understand their lives; those battles expose the fault lines in human hopes and perceptions. Given their labors to get knowledge of the past straight, to narrow interpretive differences, and to arrive at some sort of consensus, even a temporary one, about some aspect of earlier times, scholars understandably believe that their versions of the past possess authority and credibility. But on what grounds is such a claim to be understood? In an open society, all views have the right to exist, a right (at least in the United States) limited under law only in exceptional circumstances and for exceptional reasons. There is no official body to which scholars or members of the public can appeal either for determinative protection of their views or triumph over the views of others. No Supreme Court of History exists to decide what constitutes the authoritative One Way in which each subject is to be viewed. Conflicts over the meaning of the past must be fought repeatedly in public, and decisions as to the relative merits of different interpretations must be left to time and chance—as well as to almost inevitable revision.

Thus historical inquiry is, as it has been from its inception in ancient Greece, always provisional, partial, and perspectival; its results are always subject to addition, challenge, and alteration. Historical knowledge is ineradicably incomplete and uncertain. This book's final chapter adds yet more weight to that assertion—while holding firmly to the conviction that historical investigation, despite its inherent limitations, leads inexorably to the enrichment of human understanding and life.

For Further Reading, Chapter 5

As I have already indicated, the sheer size of the literature about the French Revolution will daunt anyone who ventures to examine it. I do not try to encompass or review all of it here. As elsewhere in this book, I urge readers to consult the various works I name in the text itself.

While all students of the French Revolution will have their own favorite one-volume overviews of that vast phenomenon, mine are Peter McPhee, *Liberty or Death: The French Revolution* (New Haven: Yale University Press, 2016), and Jeremy D. Popkin, *A New World Begins: The History of the French Revolution* (New York: Basic, 2019). François Furet's confident assertion that "the French Revolution is over" is the title of the first essay in *Interpreting the French Revolution,* trans. Elborg Forster (Cambridge: Cambridge University Press, 1981). An example of the debate that Furet's approach to the Revolution has stirred up, even among those who are sympathetic to his general concerns, is Lynn Hunt's hard-hitting, recondite review of *Interpreting the French Revolution* in *History and Theory* 20 (1981): 313–323. Among the best surveys of the current eclecticism of French Revolution scholarship and thinking, a fairly comprehensive if polemical one, is Furet and Mona Ozouf's *Critical Dictionary of the French Revolution* (Cambridge: Harvard University Press, 1989). Its final section—a set of essays on the major (mostly French) historians of the Revolution—is especially useful as a guide to the Revolution's historiography. Another lucid review of this complex body of scholarship is Sarah Maza, "Politics, Culture, and the French Revolution," *Journal of Modern History* 61 (1989): 704–723.

Selected important works by the historians named in the text include the following: Albert Soboul, *The Sans-Culottes: The Popular Movement and Representative Government, 1793–1794* (Princeton: Princeton University Press, 1972); Robert R. Palmer, *The Age of the Democratic Revolution: A Political History of Europe and America, 1760–1800,* 2 vols. (Princeton: Princeton University Press, 1959, 1964); Jacques Godechot, *France and the Atlantic Revolution of the Eighteenth Century, 1770–1799* (New York: Free Press, 1965); George V. Taylor, "Neocapitalist Wealth and the Origins of the French Revolution," *American Historical Review* 72 (1967): 469–496; Alfred Cobban, *In Search of Humanity: The Role of the Enlightenment in Modern History* (London: Jonathan Cape, 1954); Richard Cobb, *The Police and the People: French Popular Protest, 1789–1820* (Oxford: Clarendon, 1970); Dominique Godineau, *The Women of Paris and Their French Revolution* (Oakland: University of California Press, 1998); Joan B. Landes, *Visualizing the Nation: Gender, Representation, and Revolution in Eighteenth-Century France* (Ithaca, NY: Cornell University Press, 2001); Joan Wallach Scott, *Paradoxes to*

Offer: French Feminists and the Rights of Man: A History (Cambridge: Harvard University Press, 1997); Lynn Hunt, *The Family Romance of the French Revolution* (Berkeley: University of California Press, 1992); and Hunt, *Inventing Human Rights: A History* (New York: Norton, 2007).

Useful surveys of recent interpretive trends are Gary Kates, ed., *The French Revolution: Recent Debates and New Controversies,* 2nd ed. (New York: Routledge, 1998); William Doyle, *Origins of the French Revolution,* 3rd ed. (New York: Oxford University Press, 1999), especially its first three chapters; Ronald Schechter, ed., *The French Revolution: The Essential Readings* (Malden, MA; Blackwell, 2001); Paul R. Hanson, *Contesting the French Revolution* (Malden, MA: Wiley-Blackwell, 2009); and Thomas E. Kaiser and Dale K. Van Kley, eds., *From Deficit to Deluge: The Origins of the French Revolution* (Stanford: Stanford University Press, 2011). Also relevant is David A. Bell, *Shadows of Revolution: Reflections on France, Past and Present* (New York: Oxford University Press, 2016), especially part III, chap. 7, "A Very Different French Revolution." A general survey of two centuries' worth of interpretations of the Revolution is Peter Davies, *The Debate on the Revolution* (Manchester, UK: Manchester University Press, 2006), whose distinct value lies in its excerpts from the works, discussed here, of many historians of the Revolution, whose style and approach can conveniently be sampled in its pages.

The original, orthodox justification for the use of atomic bombs over Japan is covered in Louis Morton's authoritative essay, "The Decision to Use the Atomic Bomb," in Kent Robert Greenfield et al., *Command Decisions* (Washington, DC: Office of the Chief of Military History, 1960), 493–518. That version has been modified and expanded by succeeding scholarship but never altered in its basic details. On the *Enola Gay* controversy itself, the essential book, consisting of essays by many historians, is Edward T. Linenthal and Tom Engelhardt, eds., *History Wars: The Enola Gay and Other Battles for the American Past* (New York: Metropolitan, 1996). Pertinent select works by other scholars include John W. Dower, *Embracing Defeat: Japan in the Wake of World War II* (New York: Norton, 1999); Ronald H. Spector, *Eagle Against the Sun: The American War with Japan* (New York: Free Press, 1984); Martin J. Sherwin, *A World Destroyed: The Atom Bomb and the Grand Alliance* (New York: Random House, 1975); Michael S. Sherry, *The Rise of American Air Power: The Creation of Armageddon* (New Haven: Yale University Press, 1989); Paul S. Boyer, *By the Bomb's Early Light: American Thought and Culture at the Dawn of the Atomic Age,* 2nd ed. (Chapel Hill: University of North Carolina Press, 1994; and James S. Hershberg, *James B. Conant: Harvard to Hiroshima and the Making of the Nuclear Age* (Stanford: Stanford University Press, 1995). Paul Fussell's controversial essay "Thank God for the Atom Bomb" can be found in his book of essays of that title (New York: Summit, 1988). An insider's view of the *Enola Gay* controversy, this one by the director of the National Air and Space Museum at the time, is Martin Harwit, *An Exhibit Denied: Lobbying the History of Enola Gay* (New York: Copernicus, 1996). Two related works about the Smithsonian Institution more generally are Steven C. Dubin, *Displays of Power: Controversy in the American Museum from the Enola Gay to Sensation* (New York: New York University Press, 1999), and Robert C. Post, *Who Owns America's Past? The Smithsonian and the Problem of History* (Baltimore: Johns Hopkins University Press, 2013).

The best current evaluation of Truman's decision to use the bombs is J. Samuel Walker, *Prompt and Utter Destruction: Truman and the Use of Atomic Bombs Against Japan,* 3rd ed. (Chapel Hill: University of North Carolina Press, 2016). It should however be supplemented by the compressed, subtle analysis of the decision by Barton J. Bernstein, "The Atomic Bombings Reconsidered," *Foreign Affairs* 74 (Jan.–Feb. 1995): 135–152, as well as by Bernstein's many other essays, reference to which can be found in the other books and articles cited here. More recent surveys of the historiography of the debate over the decision to employ the bombs over Japan include Walker's "Recent Literature on Truman's Atomic Bomb Decision: A Search for Middle Ground," *Diplomatic History* 29 (2005): 311–334, and Michael Kort, "The Historiography of Hiroshima: The Rise and Fall of Revisionism," *New England Journal of History* 64 (2007): 31–48. Robert P. Newman, *Enola Gay and the Court of History* (New York: Peter Lang, 2004), is a tart attack on those who have argued that the Hiroshima and Nagasaki bombs were unnecessary. Other more recent works that emphasize emerging American war-weariness in 1945 and the difficulties that American armed forces were facing in resupplying and redeploying their troops from Europe and replacing destroyed matériel in the Pacific Theater include

Waldo Heinrichs and Marc Gallicchio, *Implacable Foes: War in the Pacific, 1944–1945* (New York: Oxford University Press, 2017). A balanced assessment of Truman's decision to use the bombs, one that comes in on the side of necessity while reviewing all relevant secondary literature and arguments, is William D. Miscamble, *The Most Controversial Decision: Truman, the Atomic Bombs, and the Defeat of Japan* (New York: Cambridge University Press, 2011). A notable treatment of the subject is the balanced, critical examination by Max Hastings, *Retribution: The Battle for Japan, 1944–45* (New York: Knopf, 2008), chap. 19, which, along with Walker's *Prompt and Utter Destruction,* presents the current consensus counterweight to "revisionist" interpretations. A general review of the closing months of the war in the Pacific is Gerhard L. Weinberg, *A World at Arms: A Global History of World War II,* 2nd ed. (Cambridge and New York: Cambridge University Press, 2005), chap. 16.

SIX

History and Objectivity

No review of the realities of revisionist history is complete without attention to historians' long-held hope of achieving objective history—a hope that has gradually succumbed to the conviction among most historians that no such achievement is possible. The leading historian of the ideal of objectivity among historians once called it an "enormously charged emotional issue." Yet thirty years later, historians are likely to respond to that characterization with perplexity. For few historians today are troubled by the problematic nature of the ideal of historical objectivity, few bother to grapple with its bearing on their work, and few introduce their students to the epistemological and other theoretical intricacies that questions of objectivity raise for their pursuit of historical knowledge. It is no longer an issue that concerns them.

Consequently, many who read what follows will be mystified by its inclusion and inclined to dismiss it precisely on the grounds that it is of no consequence to the normal endeavors of practicing historians and their readers and thus irrelevant to the subject of this book. Yet the provisionality of all historical interpretation is bound up with some of the established realities of human thought in general and of historical thought in particular. These realities require some final reflections in any consideration of revisionist history.

In considering them, it is essential to recognize that the entire discipline of history is undertheorized in comparison with many of its kindred disciplines in the humanities and social sciences; in this regard, one thinks especially of literary studies. History's undertheorization stems from the strong empirical imperatives of historical scholarship. The analysis of the surviving evidence of the past is where historians are trained to commence their work, and their practices include many means to check the strength of evidence and increase the power of the interpretations they build on it. Questions about the origins, intentions, veracity, and bias of evidence become reflexive to professional historians even though they are rarely exposed or attracted to the more formal theoretical issues that lie behind those practices. These conventional evidence-checking techniques include comparing different, and different kinds of, evidence; balancing conflicting accounts; assessing the authority and reliability of firsthand reportage and long-after-the-fact recollections; and correcting for memory defects and lapses. All such long-followed practices give them confidence that their practiced skills effectively bring the past reasonably accurately to life. Still other conventions of their professional world, such as the review by professional peers of their work before it is published and the postpublication reviews that their scholarship receives, provide historians strong grounds for thinking that the footings of their labors can withstand assault.

Yet historians' confidence in how they pursue their work does not dispose of the matter of their endeavors' theoretical validity. To face that question, they have to confront the hard problem of western historiography—the objectivity question. It lies at the heart of all modern historical practice and of all the dimensions of historical interpretation that previous chapters have covered. The question is this: can any history be "objective" history, objective in the sense of being the story and explanation of precisely what happened—incontestable, universally accepted, value-free, authoritative, and final? This is no new question over which historians have argued just in recent years; it has been asked for at least two centuries. From the dawn of modern university-based historical studies in the nineteenth century, scholars have debated whether history is a "science" whose findings have a dependable certainty valid for all times, or a form of literary, storytelling "art" whose presentation

is ineluctably limited by the times, circumstances, hopes, beliefs, dispositions, and gifts of the people who write it.[1] Can there be any history,
historians ask themselves, that is impartial, detached, without a point
of view, and not distorted by historians' own times—free, that is, of its
author's own conscious, as well as unconscious, biases? If not, does this
mean that every different history of every different subject is worthy of
the same respect—or disrespect—as every other? If so, are we left only
with insoluble relativistic confusion as to what is good history and what
bad, what happened and what did not?

After Leopold von Ranke set up the antinomy between historical
science and art by arguing that it was the duty of historians to discover
and present the past "as it essentially happened," the struggle to capture
and reveal the past as it actually took place became most historians'
governing aim. It turned into what has been called their "founding
myth," an aspiration to which most historians still adhere while having
become disenthralled by the difficulty of ever achieving the goal. Even if
historians strive to be as true to existing evidence as they can be—using
all known resources about a subject, being faithful to the known facts,
giving all sides of a question a fair hearing, and making clear (to the
degree they are conscious of them) their own bents of mind—who is
to know and who is to tell whether what they write is the best history
of their subjects? Evaluations will differ, sometimes widely, about a history's quality and validity. Even when a consensus about the value of a
specific work comes into being, how are dissenting views about it to be
accommodated?

As if these complexities are not enough, our understanding of the
science of memory and of the philosophy, language, and logic of historical inquiry have all advanced far in the last century. Because logicians,

1. This tension—whether history is an art or science—has played itself out in the academic
world in a debate over whether history is part of the humanities or the social sciences. Depending on individual historians' intentions and the nature of the subjects they pursue, it can
be one or the other, sometimes both at the same time. College and university administrators
sometimes tie themselves in knots trying to determine in which organizational and admin-
istrative division to place history, and historians are themselves not of one mind about the
matter. The difficulty of coming to a firm decision ought to be seen as part of the richness of
historical inquiry, not of its limitations.

philosophers, scientists, and theorists of knowledge are themselves not of one view about reality, certainty, and truth, twentieth-century thinkers have sowed widely influential doubts about whether there is or ever can be valid objective truth claims in any domain of thought. Consequently, if such complexities and disagreements exist, what are we to make of the authority, dependability, and accuracy of what is offered as history, whether or not it is said to be revisionist by those who write and assess it? If all history is to some extent incomplete, perspectival, provisional, and influenced by historians' temperaments and circumstances, how can any history be considered truthful, accurate, and dependable?

To make matters more complicated still, these questions and the assumptions behind them have, like everything else, their own pasts. The history of the ideal of objectivity, as well as of the growing opposition to it, is an innovation in historical time. Like everything else, both have arisen out of distinct historical circumstances, have been subjected to harsh criticism, and, like every other known kind of thought, have been put to uses not envisaged by their original proponents. Yet the assumptions behind such questions and assertions necessarily fall prey to their very philosophical foundations. For if every postulate—in our case, every rendering of the historical past—is taken to be the reflection of partiality, language, and culture, then on what grounds can we have confidence in the "truth" and "objectivity" even of statements about truth and objectivity? Thus, like all historical interpretations—in this case an effort to make sense of revisionist history—my own views must contend with the fact that what I have written is itself only provisional. The question then immediately arises as to in what spirit and with what attitude can readers of this book confront the deep conundrums of historical knowledge, especially those relevant to an understanding of changing views of the past? This is the question with which I conclude. It is also the question whose answer can be taken to be something like the credo of a historian living and practicing in the twenty-first century.

∾

All consideration of whether it is possible even to approach the goal of objective knowledge of the past must be grounded first of all in a brute fact—the ineradicable distance between history-as-it-happened and history-as-it-is-written. As historian David Lowenthal has observed of the difficulty of recapturing the actualities of the "foreign country" that falls behind us in time, "No account can recover the past as it was, because the past was not an account; it was a set of events and situations." That is, because even if you try to capture the past in words, photographs, films, or paintings, you can do no more than capture the evidence, memory, or after-the-fact imagining of it. The past—an actuality—is the events themselves. That past, like nature, is indifferent; it simply takes place. By contrast, written history is purposeful. Books about the past and monuments and memorials to it are the results of thought and intention, artifacts of the times in which those books and memorials are created, as well as the products of the people who write, create, and erect them; they are artifacts neither of all times nor of all people.

Lowenthal goes on to observe that "as the past no longer exists, no account can ever be checked against it, but only against other accounts of that past; we judge its veracity by its correspondence with other reports, not with the events themselves. . . . The historian does not even select from the totality of what has happened (*res gestae*), but from other accounts of what happened (*historia rerum gestarum*); in this respect, so-called primary sources come no closer to the reality of the past than derivative chronicles do." That is to say, an event is never independent of its being seen, experienced, believed, and interpreted. Neuroscientists and psychologists back up Lowenthal's assertions, their findings, as I indicate in what follows, showing that much of the past is lost simply for not being perceived or, if perceived, often misperceived. In addition, the full, distinct elements of any single event, even if those elements may not be infinite in number, are probably beyond human identification and counting; and each time new ingredients and aspects of it are discovered, the event itself changes in people's thinking about it. The subjectivity and contextuality of all efforts to understand that event also render impossible a complete, agreed-on, interpretively indisputable account of it. Even if, in the rare instance, all of an event's elements are exhaustively identified and recorded, unanimous agreement about what those elements mean is unlikely to be reached. From these realities arises the revisionist probability inherent in all historical thought: our accounts of what happened in the past are as contingent on time, culture, society, and thought—that is, on the context of the historians who present those accounts as plausible, if not full, reports of the past—as they are contingent on those past events themselves. All historical interpretations are temporary community agreements about a part of the past—the results of a reciprocal exchange between events and their interpreters.

Lowenthal's axiomatic propositions also entail an implied corollary that separates historical scholarship sharply from scientific experimentation: nothing of the past can be replicated. We are left only with reports about past events and post-facto approximations and interpretations of them; no reenactment, however skilled and accurate, can bring them back. Moreover, so complex is any event, so often contingent on the most apparently insignificant, quite possibly unrecorded, act or accident, that the omission of that part of an event from an account or reenactment of it may sharply alter both, just as it might have deeply affected the event itself. To this reality must be added the fact that, save when newly discovered evidence can prove other evidence partial or inaccurate, historical propositions beyond brute facts—for instance, the assertion that "World War II saved the New Deal"—cannot usually be falsified, potential falsifiability being an element of scientific pursuits that most scientists consider to be fundamental to their work. By contrast, historical claims can only be argued with and rarely definitively proven to be false (or, for that matter, unquestionably valid).

Such fundamental realities present insuperable obstacles to the achievement of objectivity just as they do to complete knowledge of a subject. But those obstacles were not in view when the assumptions that most people bring to what they write and read of the past were laid down starting in the eighteenth-century Enlightenment. These norms, implicit as long ago as the ancient confidence that The Truth could be found, emerged in the modern era from growing skepticism about the claims of revealed religion and were born of advances in scientific knowledge, as well as from humanistic reflection and biblical criticism. They were supported by Baconian empiricism and the approaches to reasoning advocated by the likes of John Locke and John Stuart Mill. A striving for hypothesis-free neutrality became normal in all realms of nonreligious inquiry, including the discipline of history, which was just then acquiring the rudiments of its eventual full identity as an intellectual discipline. By the middle of the nineteenth century, it was generally understood that, through the application of critical thought and the pursuit of scholarship untrammeled by religious and other empirically unsustainable suppositions, as well as through the use of methods and tools of research and reasoning analogous to those of the natural and physical sciences, both the understanding of human life and humans' control over nature could be enlarged to mankind's benefit. Underlying these assumptions was widespread confidence in free inquiry and an unblushing conviction that what could be discovered and demonstrated through unlimited human, especially "scientific," thought, would prove demonstrably certain and valid everywhere because such kind of knowledge was taken to be independent of its social, cultural, and historical context. While such views took hold most deeply and widely in the West, rarely were they thought of as "Western" views. If they showed utility or gained acceptance in Paris, then they were assumed among a large proportion of historians to be useful and acceptable in Riyadh and Tokyo as well—that is, universally valid and universally applicable.

Caught up by the heady confidence in the progress of objective knowledge, the pursuit of historical understanding and advances in methods of historical research fell into line with the norms and methods of the other emerging disciplines of the humanities and social sciences—dependence on the use and evaluation of written documents, criticism by historian peers, and publication in openly available peer-reviewed books and journals.[2] For roughly a century and a half, these principles made possible a widespread conviction that historical truth—the past as it "actually," or "essentially," happened—could be approached even if not fully gained. By working together using the same agreed-on methods and by applying the same critical skills, historians could close in asymptotically, book by book and article by article, on what had occurred

2. History, it was agreed, could not be a science because its practitioners could not run experiments or try to repeat experimental results for confirmation or falsification. This fact did not, however, prevent history and other subjects of the humanities from bearing the French term *les sciences humaines*, the human sciences. But one should not be led astray by the plural noun. It means realms of knowledge—in this case, knowledge about human existence. History fits well within such "sciences" as a realm of knowledge.

in the past and why it had done so. That consensus was based as much on agreement that objective knowledge could eventually be gained as on a firm belief in the soundness of the methods historians used to gain it. Consequently, until the second half of the twentieth century the grounds on which historians worked seemed beyond serious challenge. Accordingly, these grounds became the foundation on which were erected the protocols by which all aspiring historians were trained. One became a historian in the years of this abiding confidence in eventual objectivity with deep faith that one was contributing to the gradual, collective creation of dependable knowledge about the past. This was, in Charles Beard's words, the "noble dream" that sustained every historian.

It did no harm that confidence in the possibility of arriving at "objective" historical knowledge was sustained by the emergence, in the same mid-nineteenth-century decades, of an analogous ideal in the natural and physical sciences. Science, including medicine, built up an increasingly large and impressive body of knowledge through inductive reasoning and deductive experimentation, all (unlike historical knowledge) gaining acceptance for being decisively demonstrated through repetition and practical application. Certainty about nature seemed within reach. As historians Lorraine Daston and Peter Galison write, scientists had committed themselves to Cartesian dualism—the conviction that the knowable natural world and the knowing scientists were distinct. They had come to believe in the possibility of the creation of knowledge "that bears no trace of the knower—knowledge unmarked by prejudice or skill, fantasy or judgment, wishing or striving," an aspiration that, as it did among historians, deeply affected the practices as well as the norms of research in scientific fields. By the early decades of the twentieth century, science had also gained the backing of philosophical thought. In reaction against Hegelian metaphysics, many philosophers, holding themselves out as "logical positivists" and influenced by thinkers as different as Bertrand Russell and Albert Einstein, gravitated toward an emphasis on formal logic, mathematical reasoning, and the clarification of language as basic to the advance of scientific knowledge.

But as Peter Novick makes clear in *That Noble Dream*, his masterly account of the history of the ideal of historical objectivity, the objectivity ideal never turned its adherents into members of a cult closed off from the rest of thinking people. Criticisms of the ideal, often harsh attacks on it, went back well into the very nineteenth-century decades in which confidence in science was building. Defending their flanks against the doubters who always existed, even those historians who most firmly set their course by the settings of objectivity usually kept themselves from uttering absolutist claims; they wished, they said, to try at least to approach objectivity even if they could not achieve it. By making the attempt they would keep the noble dream alive. Consequently, historians who took up their work in increasing numbers after 1900 came of professional age in an era of generally high confidence in the validity of their findings, in the soundness of their arguments, and therefore in the stability of their interpretive agreements.

That confidence was not to last. By the early part of the century, their dream and posture fell increasingly under pressure from the attacks of new schools of legal scholars, philosophers, and scientists against any reasoning in their fields that straitjacketed itself within rules and traditions and failed to allow for flexibility or any sort of relativism or presentism. Even if they were not directly affected by the formal thought and general disdain of metaphysics exhibited by such thinkers as Charles Sanders Peirce, William James, John Dewey, and Oliver Wendell Holmes, Jr., historians could not escape the general influence of such thought that was at work in larger, especially American, intellectual circles.[3] In addition, the philosophical school of formalistic logical positivism, with its emphasis on verifiable empirical knowledge, identified with Ernst Mach, Rudolf Carnap, and Ludwig Wittgenstein, eventually came under harsh attack from the likes William V. O. Quine, Karl Popper, and Thomas S. Kuhn, its tenets renounced even by some of its previously most fervent adherents. This twentieth-century-long "revolt against

3. The term "metaphysics" can have many meanings. In formal philosophy, it refers to the study of being and reality, a branch of philosophy whose origins date to no later than Aristotle. In more recent times, the term has also come to refer to broad theories of historical change and progress. Thus, while the logical positivists were rebelling against such formal metaphysical theories as that of G. W. F. Hegel (to name only a single figure), historians have tended to array themselves against those protometaphysicians, like Karl Marx, Oswald Spengler, and Arnold Toynbee, who have put forth grand explanations of the workings of human history and tried to arrange the messy facts of human existence into patterns and causal sequences.

formalism," of which Charles Beard's 1913 *An Economic Interpretation of the Constitution of the United States* was the first major historical example, at the very least served notice to historians, to the degree that they were aware of it, that a fixed adherence to the ideal of objectivity was unlikely ever to hold the field to itself. It also brought to the fore the realities that are the subjects of this book—that it was becoming increasingly difficult to maintain confidence in a single way of doing history and that differing interpretations of the past were now going to be more significant within historical studies than they had been before.

But it was above all the roughly parallel questions about unchanging, apodictic knowledge being raised in the sciences that suggested to increasing numbers of historians the weak foundations of their own reliance on objectivity. Most striking, after the burst of nineteenth-century confidence in the achievement of the unquestionably certain and stable conclusions of scientific inquiry, the goal of objectivity itself came increasingly to be seen in scientific circles as unattainable, the premises of objectivity being themselves unsupportable. Einstein's theory of relativity, as well as the emergence of non-Euclidian geometry and quantum mechanics, suggested that different logics and mathematical systems could be employed in seeking scientific knowledge. Subatomic particles did not behave like other observable phenomena; even observing them altered the record of their existence and thus distorted understanding of them. The nature of nature, it seemed, resisted consistent explanation; there could be different ways, not a single objective one, of understanding the realities of the world depending on how those realities were viewed.

Consequently, the belief in attainable objectivity was increasingly understood by scientists to be a code of values, a kind of belief system, rather than a demonstrably achievable goal. At the outset of its history, the norm of objectivity, write Daston and Galison, had led scientists to strive "for a self-denying passivity, which might be described as the will to will-lessness. The only way for the active self to attain the desired receptivity to nature was to turn its domineering will inward—to practice self-discipline, self-restraint, self-abnegation, self-annihilation, and a multitude of other techniques of self-imposed selflessness." But already by the early twentieth century, much of this was under attack from within science itself, a fact of which historians were not unaware.

Speculation about the "space-time continuum" and a "fourth dimension," Niels Bohr's theory of complementarity (that electrons could be particles or waves depending on how they were observed), and Werner Heisenberg's principle of indeterminacy forced guardians of objectivity, both scientists and otherwise, to reconsider their convictions. Subjectivity now came to be understood as the ineradicable, inherent obverse of objectivity, the latter now reduced to meaning "the aspects of scientific knowledge that survive translation, transmission, theory change, and differences among thinking beings due to physiology, psychology, history, culture, language, and . . . species." Trained judgment and reasoned argument, both allowing for controlled subjectivity—in Daston and Galison's words, "the self who knows"—were now seen as keys to scientific advance along with the necessary classic methods of the sciences—statistical, mechanical, mathematical, and experimental. Even so, while claims of objectivity could be seen as a masquerade of prejudice or of overconfidence in numbers and experimental results purportedly free of bias, it was also recognized that scientific argument and judgment could control for "individual differences in mental processes," so that the achievements of science were those of collective understanding rather than of anomic scientific selves.

Similar tensions within historical thought and history's kindred disciplines in the humanities and social sciences were making themselves felt at roughly the same time, sometimes but not always taking their cues from the natural and physical sciences. Anthropology, which like history had to face buffetings from new conceptual currents, is a case in point. In that discipline, led first by Franz Boas, Ruth Benedict, and Margaret Mead and later deeply influenced by the work of Clifford Geertz, practitioners came to emphasize cultural and cognitive relativism in a way that cast strong doubt on claims about a single human culture or universal ways of creating art and possessing knowledge. The variability of human thought, belief, perception, and behavior began to seem inescapable. Variability made the scientific principles of universalism, potential falsifiability, and replication appear untenable in the face of human experience, a line of attack on objectivity that would later yield the conviction that the very ideal of objectivity bore masculine, white, and Western freight that rendered it indefensible as a guiding norm. Such modern, relativistic corrosives were in fact eating away at long-held, formal convictions in most disciplines. Consequently, by the mid-twentieth century the way was open to full-scale assaults on the earlier confident faith in objectivity. If social, cultural, and intellectual systems could differ so widely, how could confidence in single, even consensual, interpretations of the historical past be sustained?

As it proved, it could not be. By the second half of the twentieth century, the nineteenth-century philosophical controversy over interpretation—what philosophers term hermeneutics—became a general matter of intense debate in all intellectual disciplines. The early-nineteenth-century German philosopher and theologian Friedrich Schleiermacher had laid the groundwork for this debate and prefigured Leopold von Ranke's confidence that the past as it intrinsically happened could be known. Schleiermacher argued that the intrinsic meaning of texts could be discovered even if their authors had not intended those meanings or were unaware of their embodiment in their work. Wilhelm Dilthey, another German philosopher, in distinguishing between the methodologies of the natural and human sciences, also believed that it was somehow possible to purge oneself of context to get at fundamental, universal truths. But it was another, more recent German philosopher, Hans-Georg Gadamer, who must be credited with helping convince a large body of thinkers to accept the existential, as well as contextual, limits to human understanding. It is a delusion, he argued, to think that one could discover the unadulterated, basic meaning and truth of most things. Thus, by the opening of the twenty-first century, historicism has passed from the acceptance of the need to take into account the context of everything to the now widely accepted, broader conviction that every attempt to understand the past is itself contextually relative. No majestic detachment about the past can be achieved. That is, we cannot, both as humans and as professional interpreters of human life and history, free ourselves from ourselves. Everything, therefore, is a dialogue between past and present, between historians and the pasts they study; nothing can be definitively settled. While never taking the field completely and despite strenuous attacks on it, this set of hermeneutical convictions is the context in which all historians operate today.

Furthermore, the societies and cultures in which historians

practice their craft have changed significantly in the past half century. Among thinkers and in the academic world, old hierarchies have broken down; white men and Westerners no longer monopolize their ranks. The internationalization of history work, which only adds to the questions historians ask and the approaches they adopt, increases the professional, ideological, and moral complexities of historical scholarship and thought. It is now recognized that Bohr's principle of complementarity can apply to normal thought and discourse as well as to particles and waves: the vantage point of observation makes a difference. The view that one can learn about the past by seeing it from the perspective of one's sex, tribe, ethnicity, and nation consequently has gained new strength and validity even though, ironically, the adoption of this very perspective was a charge first lodged against white males. Yet if focusing on matters of intense personal concern has greatly deepened our knowledge of the past, it has also had the paradoxical effect of narrowing it. Historians must now guard against surrendering one of their foundational assumptions—that historical knowledge advances as much through the extension of imagination to strange people of strange cultures in strange times as it does from study of matters close-up. When they successfully maintain that assumption, as many have, they can venture forth confident that the knowledge about the past they gain by asking questions that derive from their own situations is of a value equal to that of knowledge gained through attempts to be context-less and objective.

All of this is to say that the belief in the superior value of histories written with detachment and disinterestedness has proved over the course of two centuries to be more a useful fiction than an achievable goal. History, in Novick's words, has shown itself incapable of moving "toward a single, integrated edifice of historical truth." That reality—the ineradicable relativism of historical knowledge—was best captured in the title of historian Carl L. Becker's celebrated essay "Everyman His Own Historian." By that title (characteristically, for its era, unembarrassedly gendered), Becker meant to indicate that history is "an imaginative creation, a personal possession which each one of us, Mr. Everyman, fashions out of his individual experience, adapts to his practical or emotional needs, and adorns as well as may be to suit his aesthetic tastes." In writing of professional historians, he went on to say that "since history is not part of the external material world, but an imaginative reconstruction of vanished events, its form and substance are inseparable: in the realm of literary discourse, substance, being an idea, *is* form; and form, conveying the idea, *is* substance. It is thus not the undiscriminated fact, but the perceiving mind of the historian that speaks: the special meaning which the facts are made to convey emerges from the substance-form which the historian employs to recreate imaginatively a series of events not present to perception." Here, in 1931, Becker presented the relativistic approach to historical interpretation that by century's end had become the common stance of historians.

In Becker's spirit, the search for objective knowledge is now understood to be but one of many ways to advance humanistic and social scientific understanding rather than the only way to achieve a deeper understanding of the past. Objectivity is no longer taken to be synonymous with truth, certainty, and accuracy; as an epistemological reality, objectivity no longer commands the field. Consequently, many of the same historians who previously had absorbed the "noble dream" of objectivity from earlier historians now, in the spirit of Carl Becker, accept the sobering fact that in some fundamental way everyone can be, and probably is, his and her own historian, all the while subject, in professional historical circles at least, to venerable canons of verifiability, open evaluation, and the incorporation of new evidence into old frameworks (or, as the case may be, into entirely new frameworks). Like the sciences, the search for the historical past now proceeds as a general collective enterprise without evaluating individual historical works against the rigid standard of objectivity. That standard has instead been displaced by the fuzzier concept of plausibility—the quality of being reasonable, acceptable, credible, and within the bounds of the possible as well as conformable to existing evidence.

Much of this growing conviction that the very philosophical tenets of the objectivity ideal, tenets long underpinning thought from the seventeenth century on, can no longer be sustained—really a set of fresh theoretical claims about the nature of knowledge, language, and perception—has traveled under the term "postmodernism" (or, sometimes,

"poststructuralism" in contrast to earlier schools of "structural" linguistics and "structural" anthropology). The term "postmodern" seeks
to distinguish the phenomena to which it is applied from the assumptions
of earlier, "modern" principles of agreed-on methods, facticity, objectivity, progress, and demonstrable, presumably universal, certainty. Basic
to postmodernist thinking, wherever it has taken hold, is the conviction
that humans cannot have an unmediated access to reality; instead, what
they experience and know is socially "constructed," "invented," and
"imagined" through human perception, language, and culture. What
we think—indeed what we perceive and experience—does not exist
independent of the linguistic and cultural filters through which it must
pass before lodging in our minds and by which it is expressed. No certain knowledge exists, no language with inalienable meaning—in fact
no "I," no subject. According to the postulates of this "linguistic turn,"
all is "discourse" and politics, a never-ending contest over preferment
and power waged with words. Even the "authors" of words are "dead"
in the sense that writers' authority over the meaning of what they write
and the intentions they bring to their words can no longer be honored
or given precedence because, like everything else, these words possess
no fixed, stable meaning. All understanding is self-reflexive; rather than
inhering in the text, meaning derives from distinctive, individual encounters with a text's contents.

These tenets of postmodernist thought have challenged the foundational axioms of modern convictions—that reason, humanistic as well
as scientific, can free human existence from the bonds of religion and
custom and can unfetter freethinking individuals to advance impartial
knowledge and improve life on earth. They have called into question the
modern belief in progress, in the knowable reality "out there" beyond
ourselves, in the unimpeachable value of scientific inquiry, and in the
existence of a stable, autonomous, human self. They advance the proposition that no thought or conviction is without ideological or other
partiality—in effect challenging every certainty by which human society
has governed and understood itself for millennia. Many postmodernist
theorists are suspicious of all enduring meaning, including historical
meaning, and believe that all assertions about significance and thus all

interpretations are little more than cover for concealed argument cunningly buried. Since, in the thinking of postmodernists, all meaning is specific to each individual or community, the authority of any distinct interpretation of, say, a historical event or the documents recording it is thrown into question. If no single meaning attaches to any word or document, the historian's basic commitment to archival excavation can be dismissed as so much pretentiousness about the stability of significance, and every interpretation of the past can be seen as equal in validity and strength to every other one. This can mean, most radically, that the past cannot be known.

The conviction that history is principally the pursuit of knowledge based on empirical research has been called into question even from within the community of historians itself. In two immensely influential books, his 1973 work *Metahistory: The Historical Imagination in Nineteenth-Century Europe* and its 1987 successor *The Content of the Form: Narrative Discourse and Historical Representation,* historian Hayden V. White situated history within the realm of literature—an art rather than a science of empirical investigation—that owes its strength to its narrative qualities. Historians, not the past itself, White argued, create stories, ones that take form from the archetypal narrative genres of tragedy, comedy, romance, and satire. That is, content cannot be understood without attention to the form in which it is presented. Since history is always, at least in part, a narrative with a start and finish, the "emplotment" of history within one of those archetypal genres must be seen as making impossible the achievement of anything close to objectivity. In fact, history's meaning derives, White argued, not from its claims to facticity but from its narrative form and language.

As a result of this erosion in confidence in the possibility of achieving a single interpretive way of understanding any historical subject, a kind of stable pluralism of historical interpretation has emerged in its place. It is one in which many interpretative schemes and subjects that a half century ago were just making their initial appearance have now been firmly established. Yes, some interpretations have remained stable over time. But neither a permanent homeostasis in historical interpretation nor a belief in one any longer exists. Practiced historical views now fall ineluctably within the same dispensation as do physical objects

under Newton's first law of thermodynamics: they remain at rest only
until they are affected by an outside force.

∿

The philosophical and theoretical issues that relate to historians'
craft do not exhaust the challenges posed to the venerable dream of
objective history. The problem of historical objectivity has become
even more complicated in recent decades by advances in the scientific
understanding of human perception and memory and through new
knowledge about the human brain gained from the neurosciences,
cognitive psychology, and clinical medicine. Because these scientific
developments—rapid, penetrating, and numerous enough to constitute
a substantive addition to Peter Novick's otherwise definitive *That Noble
Dream*—have also raised questions about the evidentiary basis of historical interpretations, they bear on the matter of historical objectivity.

It is easy to conclude from popular reports of this increasingly large
body of scientific research that memory is a deeply compromised source
of historical understanding and that interpretations built on written and
spoken statements of recall must consequently themselves be assessed
with stronger suspicion than historians have normally brought to bear
on evidence. Much of what is reported to the public about memory
arises from growing fears in an aging population of memory loss and
various forms of dementia, as well as from press coverage of posttrau-
matic stress disorder, multiple personality claims, and the problems
associated with eyewitness reporting. As a result of the public's understandable interest in reportage its members find troubling, it becomes
easy to see memory as a problem and increasingly to doubt the veracity
and reliability of one of the basic elements of the historical record, the
close-up accounts and post-facto recollections of what happened. If
those accounts can be shown generally to be demonstrably unreliable
and seriously open to reasonable doubt, then can any store be placed in
interpretations of the past built on them? Is memory irrevocably tainted
for historical use? A brief review of current memory science suggests
otherwise.

Yes, much of the evidence on memory discourages faith in its reliability. As research has revealed, the brain stores the record of any event
in a still not fully understood biochemical and biophysical encoding of

an experience. While that coding, an "engram," can be reliably durable as a source of recall, its integrity is affected by a person's succeeding experiences. Fresh engrams encoded in the brain interfere with a person's ability to summon earlier memories uncorrupted by what has happened since their encoding. Even "flashbulb memories," intense recollections of where you were, say, when you learned of John F. Kennedy's assassination or the attack on the World Trade Center, gradually fade and change, even though they are more enduring than others because of their emotional, sometimes traumatic, impact. Moreover, the distortions of original memories are normal; memory consolidation and retrieval bring together from across the brain mental elements that may not be associated with the original experience. The brain's circuitry does not create and convey memories in any regular sequence or order.

Since different parts of the brain encode different aspects of experience, distortions, biases, and errors of memory frequently occur. Like historical events and interpretations of them, memories encounter context; they are encoded within old experiences inside an existing neural web, need other encoded memories for recall, and thus are never stored in a "clean" or linear form; they are collected in networks of associations, in oscillating elliptical loops, not in any stable, orderly fashion. Even though general aspects of the past that we recall are more accurate than specific elements of that past, corruption even of the most general recollection is an inevitable part of the reality of memory. And while accurate information is without doubt part of memory's content, neuroscientists and psychologists believe that memory has a point of view and is subjective to the degree that individuals possess particular brains and consequently recall events in particular, individual ways that are their own.

Furthermore, memory is affected by the purpose of the effort to recall something and by the associations in the brain of the experiences we try to summon, just as it is by the context in which our effort at recollection occurs. We recall the past only through the present, and what we recall depends strongly on why we do so. Memory is dependent not only on the cues that summon it; it also needs the "right" cues to come to consciousness. Consequently, since all memory appears to be relational, not all cues bring forth memories; recall is dependent on the neural links that exist within the brain. It is also thought that even long-term memory changes. Every time you recall the "same" thing, you recall it in a different way.

The encrustations of other memories and of one's earlier interpretation of related events can also stand in the way of seeing fresh events whole when they occur. In this sense, experience is filtered through what literary scholars call "interpretive communities" like nations and tribes, work and gender groups, and membership organizations. We perceive and recall what our ways of looking at things incline us to perceive and recall. Not that an encompassing, community-based way of seeing the world is determinative of perception or memory. Rather, what is determined and decided—that is, what is interpreted—is encoded and recalled within a context of norms, assumptions, and beliefs.

We also now know that memories fall into different categories, ones that psychologists have identified and given differing orders of importance. One category is working memory, recollection open to long-term retrieval and critical for complex tasks like reasoning, comprehending, and learning. Working memory differs from short-term memory, which, as the term implies, denotes small amounts of material retained for brief periods. Scientists also distinguish between explicit memory, which undergirds intentional retrieval, and implicit memory, which applies itself unconsciously through action and performance. Another pair of distinct kinds of memories separates autobiographical (episodic) memories—those that fit within a context of time and place and thus are easier than many other memories to summon—from data (semantic) memories, like dates and names, those less linked to personal experience and farther from intimate experience and thus more difficult to call to mind. Any historian using stated memories as sources about the past has to be aware of the varying strength of their clarity across lifetimes. For instance, people older than forty tend to recall autobiographical memories from their years between fifteen and thirty, a time of life that neuroscientists call the "reminiscence bump." And while people recall with decent accuracy the order of events (for example, that the invasion of France preceded Germany's final defeat in World War

II) and can place events in their contexts (for instance, that the Battle of the Bulge occurred sometime in the 1940s), they often fail at trying to recall precise dates, especially as those dates recede in time.

One's expectations, intentions, attitudes, and knowledge also affect memory. This reality gives sway to what neuroscientists term "priming," the inclination to retrieve the memory of events, as well as to overlook some of their features, in specific ways based on what a mind is inclined by intention to record and store. Memory also depends on what precedes retrieval: attentiveness is related to what is experienced. Errors of storage most frequently arise from some failure of attention, some lapse in recording what may have been experienced but not taken in. Much of what happens to each of us passes by without imprint and recollection, unnoticed and uncoded in our minds. A classic and now widely known demonstration of this fact is the 1999 experiment run by Christopher F. Chabris and Daniel Simons to test people's selective perception. Presenting to viewers a short film of a group of six people tossing a ball among themselves, the psychologists found that half the film's viewers, none of whom knew its subject or contents beforehand, never saw the woman clad in a gorilla suit who wandered among those tossing the ball because the viewers were not primed to see it.[4] From such studies of what psychologists term "inattentional blindness," a prudent historian will conclude that much of the past eludes us, not because evidence of it, like documents and artifacts, is lacking or corrupted, but because those who were present to record it did not in fact witness it fully.

Related problems arise with eyewitness evidence and face-recognition recall. Both are seen by historians, as they are by attorneys in court, as incomplete and potentially faulty, tainted by expectations, by postevent information, and by such individual attributes as race, ethnicity, gender, and age and more general factors such as ideology, interest, perceptiveness, and personality. Many can recall an exercise frequently employed by history teachers, who, early in a course, stage a classroom

4. I was once among roughly 250 unprimed people who were shown the film. At its conclusion, we were asked what we had seen. Only two viewers—not the fifty percent as measured by Chabris and Simons—had noticed the gorilla-suited intruder. I was not one of them.

event—say, a mock physical brawl or the sudden appearance of someone who runs noisily through the classroom. The students are then asked to record what they have seen and heard. Inevitably, the resulting reports reveal a wide variety of recollections, which confirms the selectivity of attention and recall and, from another perspective, the findings of the Chabris-Simons experiment.

All of this suggests that information and memory bear no one-to-one correspondence. Our brains' recollection of what we have experienced in the past is constructed and reconstructed from other memories and events, not presented to us as a complete, unchanging "given" from outside our minds engraved unchanging on them. An event is never independent of how it is experienced, believed, and interpreted. Our brains build their memories from distinct components, from fragments of experience, just as we build our lives and make history from what happens to happen to us—piece by piece, event by event. Thus no entire experience is encoded fully in our brains, in single parts of them, or as a single, permanent entirety. All memory is recombinant. It may be useful to think of the brain as a shelving system, with something like neural labels, whose contents are accessed through requests for retrieval, much as forklifts pluck goods from warehouse shelves on demand.

Yet despite the many complexities and defects of human memory, it turns out to be unwise to put too much emphasis on memory's limitations. Normal human memory is remarkably capacious, flexible, efficient, and robust—that is, reliably dependable. In the words of psychologist Daniel L. Schacter, a leading student of the subject, the defects of memory are "by-products of otherwise adaptive features of memory . . . that serve us well in many respects." That is to say, scientific understanding of memory does not require historians to be any more suspicious of historical evidence involving humans' reportage of what they experienced than they are of any other kind of evidence. A solid measure of distrust of evidentiary validity has always proved wise. Historians have had misgivings about evidence since the very dawn of historical inquiry; look at Herodotus's suspicion of much that he heard on his travels and then Thucydides' skepticism of much of Herodotus's narrative. Yet Valla's investigative triumph regarding the *Donation of Constantine* provided grounds for confidence, not doubt, that critical scrutiny of historical evidence can offset deficiencies in any historical source; it scarcely made the case for cynicism about history's entire intellectual enterprise. Historians have always had to acknowledge that the historical record is incomplete and possibly tainted—and not just because physical evidence of it, written records and artifacts especially, has deteriorated or been lost. They know that the preserved record of what has happened in the past is only part of what a filmed or audio record might have preserved had it, too, survived loss and deterioration; but even such a record would have been partial for having been taken or recorded from a particular vantage—from the right side or the left, from nearby or at a distance rather than from every angle—or, as the Chabris-Simons experiment reveals, from participants failing to see or hear, and thus to record, everything that occurred.

Fortunately, beginning with the birth of the formal discipline of history in the nineteenth century, historians have grown skilled at subjecting evidence to ever more demanding and effective scrutiny as critical methods to assess its validity have grown significantly in number and quality. Practitioners of oral history especially have devised methods to check interviewees' recollections against other known evidence, to aggregate interviews to determine what is most likely to have occurred when those who are asked to recall events speak and write about them, to reinterview people to discover how stable their memories are, and thus to consider the evidence they elicit from others as one among many kinds of material that allow historians to close in on what happened. All scholars of history are constantly on the alert for evidence that contradicts other evidence and that may require adjustments to, even the jettisoning of, previous portrayals of the past. Even if no final photograph-like capture of most portions of the past may be possible, historians work to attain something that can gain acceptance as the most plausible and accurate depiction of the past that is possible to achieve.

What recent knowledge of memory has added to historians' understanding of their craft is the need for intensified prudence in evaluating surviving written and other source material and thus in judging the relative merits of differing interpretations of any historical subject that uses it. Memory studies do not warrant a turn to wholesale relativism about the comparative strength of competing views of historical events.

The probably inevitable corruptions of memory do not necessitate the wholesale abandonment of all written and oral claims of participants in, or bystanders to, events, and neither scientists nor historians suggest that they do. For historians, the challenge is not that they cannot have confidence in what people report they know or have witnessed; the challenge is to skillfully assess the inevitable corruptions and misperceptions of what is summoned to memory and recorded and reported by those involved in the event. Even though participants miss some of what actually occurs, capturing something approaching the past as it both essentially and actually happened remains a justifiable goal of all historians. So while increasingly authoritative scientific findings about memory strengthen the case against interpretive certainty, in many respects the now known vagaries of perception and memory can be seen as complicating but in no fundamental way undermining acceptance of what can be learned about the past or of the recalled experience of individual lives. No more than the tenets of so much postmodern theory do they negate the usefulness of evidence in arriving at plausible accounts of the past and consensual agreements about what happened earlier and why it did so.

∾

After reading about these many obstacles to interpretive certainty and objectivity, one may be forgiven for wondering whether historical thought finds itself in the early twenty-first century standing on undefendable, unstable theoretical ground. Clio, history's legendary muse, can now seem to be throwing up so many barriers to written history's venerable functions as a legitimate intellectual pursuit and moral art to suggest that historians should simply concede that the search for accurate knowledge of the past is, in Charles Beard's terms, an act of faith and little else. Yet though historians do not do so, nor do grounds exist for anyone else to do so, it remains to be asked how historians do in fact look on the messy world of historical interpretation. And how should everyone interested in the past look on it? With what expectations and confidence should they approach the inevitable controversies over the significance of what historians have written?

It should by this point be evident that there exists no white history —nothing like a *mariage blanc,* no rendering of the past that is pure, unadorned, classic, spare, unaffected by anything but unimpeachable fact, uninfluenced by the context and circumstance in which it is written, and author-free.[5] Instead, history's consummation exists in the meanings people give to it through interpretation. Without interpretation, historical accounts are mere chronicles. To practicing historians, this is beyond argument, and so integrated is this reality into historical studies today that scholars find nothing amiss in the existence of different interpretations of the same events. Revision, difference of view, and contest they accept as unavoidable. They also accept these scholarly realities as natural.

By natural, I mean that trying to make sense of the past is a kind of existential impulse, no doubt in some respects a need woven into human nature and impossible to stanch. At no point in known human history have people not sought to relate and explain their existence in historical terms, whether through myths, religions, or, in more recent times, secular historical works. So rather than being taken to be fixed and forever, history should be seen as the stories humans tell themselves to make sense of their specific worlds and times. We can never expect all these stories to be accurate or benign, nor can we be confident that the inaccurate and hurtful ones can be extirpated from the human record or kept from being told. Yet all historical stories can—and for historians must— be subject to analysis and critique and therefore to alteration. The challenge for historians is to respond to the human need for meaning in ways that are, first, congruent with the canons of research they honor while, second, remaining respectful of both the certainties and the problems of historical thought that have built up over centuries. Whatever modern and postmodern doubts about the objectivity ideal have arisen since the nineteenth century, it is impossible to imagine that the inborn human thirst for dependable historical understanding will suffer signifi-

5. In an influential 1968 essay, the French theorist Roland Barthes announced "the death of the author." By this he meant to declare the end of authors' purported repressive, imperial hold over readers and, by contrast, the arrival of readers' freedom to find in authors' words what they might discover there and what comported with their own selves. The assumptions on both sides of this equation—that authors previously had readers in their hard grasp and that readers had felt unbidden and unable to read what authors had written as they wished, could, and did—were always questionable. They remain so.

cantly among professional historians and members of the general public because of these uncertainties.

Thus, in fact, it has proved: historians continue to proceed more or less as always to seek plausible knowledge of the past as if mounting doubts about objectivity do not exist. They do so even after having accepted many of the most substantial reservations about objectivity, about the unlikelihood of learning everything about the past, and about the eventuality of achieving full agreement about it. Despite such obstacles, historians still hold to the conviction that they can and do make progress in closing the gap between historical ignorance and historical understanding. They also strongly resist the conclusion that, because all historical knowledge is partial, provisional, and uncertain, it is of no value. While they know that keeping ideology and culture out of their work is impossible, they still try to arrive at reasonably impartial knowledge of what happened and why it did so to the best of their ability. On this score, scientists can rest more easily than historians: they know that, even though some of their theories exclude or clash with others, they nevertheless yield replicable experimental results; they also know that, while the questions they ask can be determined by culture—say, new concerns about the environment and pressures to find cures for diseases—their findings are comparatively culture-free. Neither fossil fuel emissions nor viruses have nationalities or belong to particular cultures.

By contrast, evidence of the historical past requires the deeper involvement of culture- and time-bound human minds to be made sense of. To control such influences, historians have come to depend for interpretive progress on rules, conventions, and critical standards developed over more than two centuries. They have developed protocols of research and methods for validating evidence and verifying claims that render inadmissible unsourced claims about past events and that, over time, have withstood many of the charges of bias that are often lodged against them. There exists a general discipline-wide sense of what constitutes valid evidence, how it can be assayed for genuineness and accuracy, what is relevant in a historical argument, and who is to have authority over its evaluation. That is to say, even though their accepted methods and conventions cannot be scrubbed free of culture or politics, historians possess a general sense, one that enjoys nearly unanimous adherence throughout their professional community, about the standards that govern their work, standards that narrow the terrain on which historical dispute takes place and historical uncertainty remains.

The result is that, among professional historians, the pursuit of historical knowledge goes on confidently in ways that would be recognizable to historical practitioners in distant times. Historians still create narratives about the past. They continue to write biographies of past figures. They seek to understand the causes and consequences of past events. While, like everyone else, they often wonder counterfactually what might have happened had events not turned out as they did, they adhere mostly to analysis of how and why those events that did occur unrolled as they did. And they remain at the task of trying to draw from their labors and for their own times the meaning and significance of the past they unearth. It is altogether familiar terrain to historians that their knowledge is indeterminate and that there will be no end to their discoveries and to arguments about those discoveries' meaning. They accept the fact that as soon as something happens, it becomes the possession of its posterity, not of its actors. They have therefore learned to live comfortably with what the poet John Keats termed "negative capability"—a suspension of the search for a single truth or a single explanation of any phenomenon—and they somehow sustain the capacity, in Keats's words, "of being in uncertainties, mysteries, doubts" about life—in their professional case about life in the past. In that spirit, we should see the existence of vigorous debates about interpretations of the past, debates that have never been more numerous and complex than in our era, as pointing to the vitality, not the exhaustion, of the search for dependable historical knowledge. Interpretive orthodoxy is the diagnostic of intellectual rigor mortis. By contrast, interpretive differences reveal the robustness of historical thought. Accordingly, few historians succumb to the radical relativism of believing that all interpretations are of equal strength and coequally valid. While the argument over interpretations suggests that different people in different places at different times can find distinct meanings and distinct significance in particular events, for the historian a prudent relativism never gives way to the belief that meaning precedes or exists in scorn of evidence. Nevertheless, to paraphrase the historian C. Vann Woodward's witticism, historians have learned that if physicists can live with relativity, they can live with relativism.

Such prudent relativism in historical thought has never come close to being so unhinged and radical as to threaten historians' commitment to truth and accuracy. Revisionism, with its requirement that one remain open to variant interpretations of the past, does not require the abandonment of professional standards. It insists on its fidelity to the ideal of objectivity—or at least to what Joyce Appleby, Lynn Hunt, and Margaret Jacob term "qualified objectivity"—through confidence in what Hunt separately calls "practical realism." By that, these historians mean to emphasize their embrace of the central norms and practices of their intellectual world: first, reliance on historians' communities of knowledge and shared discourse, those communities setting mutually agreed-on standards for the analysis and evaluation of evidence; second, the democratic context of their intellectual discipline, in which interpretations and debates about them are genuinely open; and third, the acceptance of the possibility of revision of every established view of the past. Even if historians have serious differences with a specific interpretation of what happened earlier in time, they will accept its legitimacy as long as its author honors these norms.

Adherence to such standards does not, however, rule out disagreement, bar the existence of widely differing interpretations, or prevent alterations—sometimes radical ones—to what had earlier become orthodox views. Historians disagree with one another with considerable ease because they recognize one another as members of the same professional community—as people who pursue the same objective with the same general intentions and procedures. Like other professionals, they patrol the boundaries of their discipline and exclude those, like Holocaust deniers, whose claims to authority as serious historians are spurious and injurious to the shared effort to get things about the past right—or at least as close to being right as they can be gotten. Today's historians' interpretive community is a globe-spanning group of people dedicated to that end. Coprofessionals, its members recognize and share the standards of intention, method, argument, and presentation—the ways of thought—that have become naturalized among them and embedded in the very nature of who they are and what they seek to do. Those who do not honor and follow those standards are kept from their professional company, considered illegitimate practitioners, denied the title of professional historian, and arraigned for their departures from the community's norms, their works condemned or ignored.

And thus to conclude this book, it remains to ask with what confidence historians can be sure that, despite the obstacles that are epistemological, evidentiary, psychological, and neurological, they can gradually close in on an approximation of the past that answers its critics' protests while being granted the authority of accuracy and strength of argument by their peers. The answer, as inconclusive as it may be, lies at the heart of any discussion of revisionist history. And that answer must serve as the faith of a historian—a set of convictions different in the often tumultuous intellectual world of the twenty-first century than it was almost a century ago when Charles Beard reflected on them.

One should start with the basic human characteristics of curiosity and wonder. Although they may be the last to acknowledge and talk about it, historians are filled with both. Their incredulity, sometimes their exhilaration, about other times and their occasional despair at the way events have turned out usually lie near the root of their interest in the past. They ask themselves why people acted the way they did in the circumstances in which they found themselves. They are mystified by the realities of unknown places and long-past eras. They find unsatisfactory some explanation of a large-scale historical development. When they become professional historians, they address these proddings of wonder and curiosity with the practiced skills that historians have developed over two and a half millennia and have supplemented more recently as the media in which evidence can be accessed and historical work presented have expanded.

Their curiosity is what lies at the foundation of most historians' acceptance of diverse, sometimes clashing, versions of past events. They approach the past as strangers. They have learned not to close themselves off to surprise. They consider it to be natural to be brought up short by what they and others unearth about the past. Disputes goad them to seek additional knowledge and find ways to strengthen their own interpretive positions. Of course, some people read history for confirmation rather than new knowledge, just as some historians write it for the same reason. An adherent of the view that the South's defense of slavery was not the cause of the Civil War is not likely to gain pleasure or be open to the arguments of a work that provides clear evidence to the contrary. But most historians are accepting of the surprises that new knowledge of the past can confer and delight in being astonished and influenced by it. If the claim that one of history's chief intellectual functions is to lead its students and readers to understand the circumstances of other people in other times and other places is to have any meaning, it must mean that, in learning about the past, we open ourselves repeatedly to being startled by the unexpected, the unknown, the strange, even the horrifying. Exposing themselves to such experiences, historians know that the accumulation of new knowledge and the possibility of encountering new tangents on the past can then have the consequence of the recurring recalibration of people's stance in the world and their relationship to it. This is for some the joy of historical discovery, for others the source of deep anxiety. Diverse and changing interpretations of the past are likely to please those who delight in seeing things anew and being forced to rethink their former views. That same diversity of view is, by contrast, what can drive others to stubborn resistance. But most historians reject the grim satisfactions of certainty in favor of the joyful prospects of mystery and surprise. They hope that their readers will do so, too.

In accepting a professional world in which uncertainty, ambiguity, diversity, change, and surprise are their constant companions, historians learn that believing it possible to gain historical knowledge that is as certain and indisputable as mathematical knowledge is to commit a category error—to confuse one kind of knowledge with another with which it is ontologically and epistemologically incompatible. What is more, new information about the past requires adjustments in how previously held knowledge is viewed. Freshly discovered sources embodying new information—take, for instance, the uncovering of long-buried Mayan temples in Mexico or the discovery of the site of a Viking settlement at L'Anse aux Meadows on the northern tip of New-foundland—alter prior understanding. Advances in evaluating old evidence—say, the early-nineteenth-century deciphering of the Rosetta Stone—frequently destabilize previous understanding of the past, as do new methods of analysis, like oral history and the statistical analysis of existing data. Similarly, fresh thinking about human possibilities, different national, social, and cultural locations, the passing of old and the emergence of new generations, the passage of time that allows for a longer and broader view of life without parti pris commitments, and simply the variety of individual minds—Herodotus thinking culturally, Thucydides adopting a political viewpoint—make identical historical interpretations of the same events unlikely ever to be found. Even when historians studiously avoid using historical knowledge to shine light on present situations, the histories they write cannot avoid betraying inclinations of mind, approaches to the past, and the questions they ask of existing evidence that are distinct to them. So while the past may never change, our understanding of it always does. As an old Marxist joke has it, "The future's certain; it's only the past that's unpredictable." It is in the spirit of that jest to insist that the past is always in the future.

Furthermore, as I have tried to make clear throughout this book, to understand history one must understand the historians who write it. Those who deny the embodiment of historians' disposition, commitments, and convictions in everything they write—those who believe that there can be history devoid of the person who writes it—put themselves outside history itself. All historians are implicated in their own histories; none of them, no more than any other individuals, can escape being the product of his or her own circumstances. Consequently, the potential for revisions of every other previous history of a subject is inherent in the very act of thinking historically. It therefore falls to readers of history to be aware of the incompleteness and partiality, as well as the empirical foundations and strength of argument, of every history they encounter. While historians bear responsibility for presenting the past as well as they can, those who read it bear an analogous obligation to approach the past with an understanding that what they read is only a partial reconstruction of it. This necessary caution does not require of them radical doubt or outright rejection of historical findings and arguments because those findings and arguments lack full objectivity or are incomplete. It does, however, mean that each work of history must be taken on its own terms and understood in its own context as an only provisional rendering of the past.

It must also be borne in mind that neither the venerability nor the popularity of a historical interpretation has normative authority in the long history of historical thought. It is fidelity to the past that possesses such authority. At the root of historians' labors is the conviction that, even though the present can benefit from their knowledge, their greatest responsibility, ethical as well as intellectual, is to the past and its inhabitants, a responsibility that must be understood as referring to historians' inherent civic role—the "office of historian"—as custodians of the integrity of the past. To unearth past reality and to present that reality as accurately as can be achieved given current knowledge is their guiding purpose.

In a sense, however, historians' responsibilities—to try to capture the past as it was and to answer to the needs and interests of their own time—face in opposite directions. The latter responsibility is typically the one that brings them criticism from both their coprofessionals and members of the public. And understandably so, in that it calls on scholars to find the voices and employ the styles that make the past immediate and comprehensible to a population of readers altogether different from most of those depicted in works of written history. Yet not making that effort is a denial of the claims the living have on the past just as the past has claims on the living. Only by writing for their own times and in response to questions of their day can historians make the past comprehensible to those who wish to learn of it. For that reason, what to one person and one age is orthodoxy to another is revision, and vice versa.

Behind criticisms of new versions of the past—that, say, the history of emotions is a trivial subject compared with the history of wars; or that a work of history is faulty for responding to some contemporary problem, like race relations, rather than possessing a time-honored concern with monarchies and presidencies; or that a book is too feminist or too sympathetic to gay people, or that it fails to follow a conservative or liberal approach to a subject—usually lies the antipresentist fallacy that written history should not answer to the present. But the alternative belief, that history should be written only in terms of the present—"whig history"—is little better. Yet as compelling as criticism of whig history has proved to be, however salutary a warning against the worst traits of presentism such criticism offers, it can no longer in fact stand as an authoritative guide to the now understood realities of the possibility of achieving the ends of objectivity through the avoidance of historians' immersion in their own worlds. Criticism of "whig history" fails in the sense that it ignores the realities of historicism—the fact that there exists no stable observational point from which the past can be viewed. Even if works of history successfully avoid presentism and a commitment to the idea of historical progress in favor of the analysis of complication and change in the past, they are ineluctably bound to the present and to the makeup of the historians who write them. If the theories and methods of the natural and physical sciences can now be considered to be reflective of the eras of their development and application, how can we imagine that historical understanding, far less dependent on theoretical guidance and experimental experience, can be less so? Historians are always in danger of finding in the past what was not there, but to try to exile the present from their efforts to understand history is to close off a major portal into comprehension, an opening that sensitivity to new ways of thinking provides. It is not the evidence that historians encounter alone that matters; it is what that evidence suggests to them. The challenge is not to rid historical thought of the historian's self; it is to apply that self to evidence from the past in such a way that it enriches understanding of what happened earlier in time.

Works of history have always been written in many keys. Some historians—Thucydides, Sallust, Julius Caesar, Guicciardini, Jaurès, and Schlesinger come to mind—participate in the events of which they write, and their histories gain by their authors' immersion in events. Other historians—of which today's academic historians are examples—are more observers than participants, their works of scholarship gaining from scholarly distance and a relatively dispassionate approach to their historical subjects. Similarly, one line of history derives from rhetoric, seeks to discover and teach the "lessons of history," and sees itself as "philosophy teaching by examples." Its aim is persuasion. It tries, as the twelfth-century German court historian Otto of Freising wrote, "to extol the famous deeds of famous men in order to incite the hearts of mankind to virtue, but to veil in silence the dark deeds of the base or, if they are drawn into the light, by the telling to place them on record to terrify the minds of those same mortals." In this view, if history may not offer lessons, at least it offers a record of possibilities. Another line of history derives from "science" and seeks to be objective and analytical, its aim being to demonstrate what occurred and to leave moral lessons to others. Some historians, to adopt Charles Darwin's terms, are lumpers, others splitters. In more formal expression, some, although few these days, are Cartesians—people interested in propounding and trying to test and confirm theories of historical development and to provide unified, universal explanations of historical phenomena. Others, encompassing most historians today, are Baconians—those inclined to hew to known facts, to emphasize the riot of life's details, and to unearth the wondrous diversity and particularity of existence. If Cartesian history has gained little strength and scholarly acceptance in the past two centuries and if advances in theorizing historical thought and method have produced little momentum, there is scant reason to think that over the long run either Cartesian or Baconian history will permanently triumph over the other in historical scholarship and writing. Each complements the other, and neither approach is likely to exist free of the balancing influence of its opposite.

Whatever their inclinations, today's historians accept the fact that their own search for greater understanding involves them in a never-ending argument with their predecessors as well as their contemporaries. They take it as natural that argument, traveling on the back of scholarly research, always holds the promise of revealing something new and advancing historical understanding. They know that the past is like a giant lens, changing what it reveals with every alteration in the perspective from which something is viewed through it. They are confident that, in the face of even the most savage opposition and the strongest efforts to stifle free thought, nothing can stop their search for understanding the human past or the application of their imagination to create new knowledge.

Celebrating diversity, historians view their intellectual world as a vast ecosystem of knowledge. They consider this reality the bedrock of the lively play of their intellectual world and the principal way in which knowledge and understanding increase. It is the interplay of distinct minds and dispositions applying themselves to distinct historical problems that advances knowledge through books and articles, now films, art, novels, and plays. Arguments about the past, the never-ending search for dependable knowledge, are a basic feature of academic freedom freely exercised, of democratic disputation, and of the maintenance of the common good.

Historical understanding originates in need—that of the individual historian to understand the past, that of an audience to discover its members' own origins, that of a culture to reimagine its future. No history can gain traction unless it responds to something. The function of historians is to haul the past into the present for the present's benefit, yet in such a way that the integrity of the past is preserved in all its pastness. How do we tell a story, historians ask themselves, so that it makes sense to us as well as remains true to the past? Their reinterpretations of history must be seen as one of the ways humans have of bringing into some equilibration the past and present. Employing evidence that the past has left to us, historians re-create as best they can the events of earlier times and then try to explain how those unfolded as they once did using every mode of understanding that their own present holds out to them. Yet it makes no sense to create historical accounts that are indigestible to the present. The greatest historians have always made the distant past immediate to their own days. When these historians look back, as Edward Gibbon did, to answer questions critical to his era—in Gibbon's case, how empires, like the British Empire, can fall as well as rise—their present-mindedness illuminates much more of the past than it shrouds.

The faith of most historians is grounded in the conviction that the practice of history is a democratic art available to everyone in an open society. History is that kind of art because all of us, in thinking about and living our lives, perform the work of history and refashion our understanding of it every day. As Carl Becker long ago reminded us, all people are their own historians. If professional historians are true to their calling, they make the most of the variety of historical thought that Becker summoned. They embrace and do not run from their roles as interpreters, for their own times, of the past. They gain their greatest satisfactions from helping others find meaning in their lives through imaginative engagements with other people, cultures, societies, and times that will never be their own. The result of their efforts is always the same: fresh, diverse, distinctive interpretations of the past that leave the past different than it used to be while setting it on course to a new, unpredictable future. That is the twinned promise and reality of revisionist history.

For Further Reading, Chapter 6

Every discussion of the ideal of historical objectivity must commence with Peter Novick's indispensable *That Noble Dream: The "Objectivity Question" and the American Historical Profession* (Chicago: University of Chicago Press, 1988), a classic of modern historiography. Focusing on history as practiced and debated in the United States, it reveals, among other things, how fragile the foundational conviction of so much modern historical thought always has been. An older work that embodies confidence in the gradual approach to dependable, plausible, and objective history is Morton White, *Social Thought in America: The Revolt Against Formalism* (New York: Viking, 1949), especially chapter 14 and its critique of the historicism of Charles Beard. A later work on the history of the concept of objectivity in the sciences—a work with major and so-far overlooked implications for understanding the history of the ideal of objectivity in historiography—is Lorraine Daston and Peter Galison, *Objectivity* (New York: Zone, 2007). A useful collection of essays on the objectivity issue in a variety of intellectual disciplines is Allan Megill, ed., *Rethinking Objectivity* (Durham, NC: Duke University Press, 1994). A work of especially sobering reflection is David Lowenthal, *The Past Is a Foreign Country* (Cambridge: Cambridge University Press, 1985). Its contents, reaching back to ancient times and, incorporating evidence from many cultures, provide powerful arguments against the possibility that a contextless, universally agreed-on account of any part of the past can exist. Insight into the resistance that some historians have mounted against attacks on the ideal of objectivity can be found in Gertrude Himmelfarb, *The New History and the Old: Critical Essays and Reappraisals,* rev. ed. (Cambridge: Harvard University Press, 2004). On the vexed question of counterfactual history, two books incorporate the latest arguments and positions: Jeremy M. Black, *Other Pasts, Different Presents, Alternative Futures* (Bloomington: Indiana University Press,

2015), in favor, and Richard J. Evans, *Altered Pasts: Counterfactuals in History* (Waltham, MA: Brandeis University Press, 2013), opposed. For evidence of how even left-oriented attacks on conventional "objective" approaches to the past can themselves fall under assault from the Left, see Michael Kazin, "Howard Zinn's History Lessons," *Dissent,* Spring 2004, pp. 81–85, and Sam Wineburg, "Undue Certainty: Where Howard Zinn's *A People's History* Falls Short," *American Educator,* Winter 2012–2013, pp. 27–34.

All consideration of collective memory must start with Benedict Anderson, *Imagined Communities: Reflections on the Origins and Spread of Nationalism,* rev. and expanded ed. (London: Verso, 2006). Four other related works among many are John E. Bodnar, *Remaking America: Public Memory, Commemoration, and Patriotism in the Twentieth Century* (Princeton: Princeton University Press, 1992); John R. Gillis, ed., *Commemorations: The Politics of National Identity* (Princeton: Princeton University Press, 1994); Jay Winter, *Sites of Memory, Sites of Mourning: The Great War in European Cultural History* (New York: Cambridge University Press, 1995); and Sanford Levinson, *Written in Stone: Public Monuments in Changing Societies* (Durham, NC: Duke University Press, 2018).

While the current state of thought about the philosophy and language of historical knowledge is mired in controversy, it is possible to learn the general lineaments of contemporary views and disputes in this vast, complex, and history-laden subject from Roy Harris, *The Linguistics of History* (Edinburgh: Edinburgh University Press, 2004). Three books, differing in intention from Harris's, provide other entrée into some of the elements of modern and postmodern historical thinking and scholarship briefly covered here. They are Joyce Appleby, Lynn Hunt, and Margaret Jacob, *Telling the Truth About History* (New York: Norton, 1994); Sarah Maza, *Thinking About History* (Chicago: University of Chicago Press, 2017); and Lynn Hunt, *History: Why It Matters* (Medford, MA: Polity, 2018). A more specialized and demanding study is William S. Sewall, Jr., *Logics of History: Social Theory and Social Transformation* (Chicago: University of Chicago Press, 2005). A related work of robust confidence in the value of combining adherence to the idea of objectivity with skepticism about the finality of any historical interpretation is the collection of essays of Thomas L. Haskell, *Objectivity Is Not Neutrality: Explanatory Schemes in History* (Baltimore: Johns Hopkins University Press, 2000). A sharp protest against historians' lack of interest in theoretical matters, as well as a criticism of its cost, is the short *Theses on Theory and History,* whose title evokes Karl Marx's *Theses on Feuerbach,* by Ethan Kleinberg, Joan Wallach Scott, and Gary Wilder. It can be found at theoryrevolt.com. C. Vann Woodward's witticism about historians and relativism can be found in "The Future of the Past," *The Future of the Past* (New York: Oxford University Press, 1989), 3–28. Charles Beard's statement of professional convictions is contained in his "Written History as an Act of Faith," *American Historical Review* 39 (1934), 219–231.

Daniel L. Schacter, *Searching for Memory: The Brain, the Mind, and the Past* (New York: Basic, 1996), is an authoritative, discursive introduction to current understanding of the principal dimensions of memory. In a later work, *The Seven Sins of Memory: How the Mind Forgets and Remembers* (Boston: Houghton Mifflin, 2001), Schacter emphasizes the evolutionary, adaptive origins of memory's distortions. A textbook that possesses the clarity that all good books of its kind should embody is Alan Baddeley et al., *Memory,* 2nd ed. (London: Psychology Press, 2015). Less accessible than Schacter's books, it is nevertheless more comprehensive and exhaustive, as well as more current, in its coverage. Christopher Chabris and Daniel Simons's celebrated video can be found at http://theinvisiblegorilla.com/gorilla_experiment.html. See also Chabris and Simons, *The Invisible Gorilla: And Other Ways Our Intuitions Deceive Us* (New York: Crown, 2010).

Index